# Discovering Black Vermont

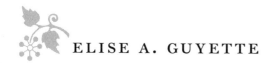

ELISE A. GUYETTE

# Discovering Black Vermont

*African American Farmers in Hinesburgh, 1790–1890*

University of Vermont Press
*Burlington, Vermont*

Published by University Press of New England
Hanover and London

University of Vermont Press
Published by University Press of New England
One Court Street, Lebanon NH 03766
www.upne.com
© 2010 University of Vermont and State Agricultural College
All rights reserved
Manufactured in the United States of America
Designed by Katherine B. Kimball
Typeset in Monticello by Passumpsic Publishing

University Press of New England is a member of the Green Press Initiative.
The paper used in this book meets their minimum requirement for recycled paper.

For permission to reproduce any of the material in this book, contact Permissions,
University Press of New England, One Court Street, Lebanon NH 03766;
or visit www.upne.com

*Library of Congress Cataloging-in-Publication Data*

Guyette, Elise A.
    Discovering black Vermont : African American farmers in
Hinesburgh, 1790–1890 / Elise A. Guyette. — 1st ed.
    p. cm.
Includes bibliographical references and index.
ISBN 978-1-58465-760-6 (pbk. : alk. paper)
1. African Americans — Vermont — Hinesburg (Town) — History.
2. African Americans — Vermont — Hinesburg (Town) — Biography.
3. African American farmers — Vermont — Hinesburg (Town) —
History. 4. African American farmers — Vermont — Hinesburg (Town) —
Biography. 5. Hinesburg (Vt. : Town) — History. 6. Hinesburg (Vt. :
Town) — Biography. I. Title.
F59.H56G89 2010
305.896'073074317 — dc22                                    2009038965

5 4 3 2 1

A teacher's guide for this book is available free for download at www.upne.com.

*To Mom and Papa (I wish you were here to read this)*

*To David, Kathleen, and Sarah, who remind me daily what is important*

*To the spirits of the Hill*

# Contents

# Illustrations

# Preface

More than a dozen years ago, I discovered that a black family, the Williamses, had moved to South Burlington, Vermont, in 1865 and farmed land not far from where I lived. Having studied the Vermont census reports from 1790 to 1870, I knew that it was unusual for a family of color to own farmland in Vermont at that time. Only 4 percent of black farmers owned land, as compared to 32 percent for the total population. Most people in Vermont of African descent were servants or laborers on other people's farms in the nineteenth century. For this reason, I was drawn to do further research on the mysterious Williams family and their post–Civil War experiences in Vermont. I wondered from where they had come, why they had chosen South Burlington, and how their white neighbors had received them after the bloodiest war in our nation's history.

What I found, initially, was a wonderful feel-good story about Edward Williams, who was born in Baltimore, Maryland; may have risked travel to Vermont on the Underground Railroad; and had made good in this staunchly antislavery state. His wife, Harriet, was a mystery, since I did not know her maiden name at the time. Their daughter, Rachel, married Aaron Freeman from nearby Charlotte, a Civil War veteran who had fought in the Massachusetts Fifty-fourth Infantry Regiment to end the slavery that had perhaps constrained the lives of his in-laws. It was a fantastic story, beginning with Edward Williams liberating himself from a Southern slave society, continuing with his life as a landowner in the North, and capped with the romantic ending of his son-in-law's fighting and surviving in the war to end slavery.

I could have stopped there. The Williams-Freeman story fit so perfectly into the stories that we Vermonters tell about ourselves — of being the first state to outlaw slavery in 1777, of heroism on the Underground Railroad and safe houses in every town, and of courageous soldiers in the war to end slavery. This story, however, added the little-known element of daring black soldiers also representing Vermont in that epic struggle. It fit neatly into the inspiring narrative of freed people gradually moving toward greater and greater freedom as America fulfilled its promise of liberty and justice for all.

However, I wanted to know one more thing: Where did the Williams family get the money to buy their land? If I hadn't asked that question, I would have missed the more complicated narrative. This story is of black Americans' prolonged struggle against oppression, of hard-won gains, constant resistance to subjugation, and thrilling progress that ultimately left them with the sand shifting under their feet and pulling them backward, but nevertheless persevering.

What I discovered by looking back into the Williamses' lives was a hill in Hinesburgh, Vermont, partly cleared and settled in the 1790s by free blacks from southern New England. It was into this group of families that Edward was welcomed after his trek from Baltimore. In this place he found an extended family of several generations descended from the original black pioneers, Violet and Shubael Clark. They were Harriet's parents, and it was from them that he received his first plot of Vermont land and learned to live in a free society.

The Clarks and another pioneering family, the Peterses, their children and grandchildren, their in-laws, and friends lived, farmed, loved, and died in this remote place in northern Vermont. Here, they learned to negotiate new ways of living for themselves and their descendants as members of a new class of people — free blacks. Although there were free people of color earlier in the eighteenth century, free blacks *as a class* had been unheard of in New England before the American Revolution.

Many of the family members are still there, buried in an abandoned cemetery that has suffered neglect and vandalism. Only one or two lichen-covered fieldstones peek through the grass. Old maples stand guard near the collapsed stone wall, marking its boundaries, and a century of leaves blankets the remains of these black settlers. This story resurrects them in prose and returns them to their rightful places among Vermont's early pioneers.

Some years ago, I attended a lecture at Middlebury College about a black professor in Liberia, Martin Freeman, who was originally from Rutland, Vermont. After the talk, I told the lecturer of my relentless pursuit of the story of this community and how its people were never far from my mind. "I just can't stop thinking about them, I don't know why," I said. He looked at me closely and without missing a beat said, "Well, they chose you." I hope I have done them justice.

# Discovering Black Vermont

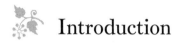 Introduction

Local legends transmuted certain men into founding personages, certain women into phantasmagorical creatures, and black Americans into non-entities.
—Anne Elizabeth Yentsch, "Legends, Houses, Families and Myths"

At some point the silence became an unbearable violence.
—Toni Morrison, *Playing in the Dark*

We drove slowly up the wooded dirt road, scattered with crumbling stone walls and arthritic apple trees barely visible through the underbrush, to what used to be called "the old Negro burying ground." As I studied the landscape, I became increasingly excited about exploring the remnants of an older world that coexists with our contemporary one. This isolated Vermont Hill[1] had once been home to many families of color, and on this autumn day fellow historian Jerry Fox guided me to the ground where they were buried, no longer recognizable as a cemetery. As we parked on the edge of their resting place, I saw maples, birches, and firs growing haphazardly, their roots embracing these long-forgotten farmers. It amazed me that so many people knew about the old cemetery, but no one knew the history of the African American community that had once surrounded it.

As I stood among the shadows and studied a few limestone shards, my mind began to weave through time and space. First I questioned the people of the past: Who were you exactly? When and why did you come to northern Vermont? What were your lives like in Hinesburgh? Then my thoughts turned to the present: Why had no one discovered this community's story? Why had its tale been erased from memory, with hardly a mention in local folklore? Why the great silence about these people?

Then I returned to my own past, where I had felt the sting of my people's exclusion from written histories. Rutland, Vermont, a working-class town at the foot of the Green Mountains, encompassed a rich stew of immigrant and religious groups when I was growing up. Our Irish-American mother and French-Canadian-Lebanese father raised my four siblings and me as Catholics. In the 1950s and 1960s, Catholics in Rutland lived in three separate sections of town: Irish on the hill, Italians in the gut, and French Canadians, including my family, in between — each with its own church and school. For a short time, we rented a house near the city's only synagogue, which my religion prohibited me from entering at the time. I was both surrounded and infused by diversity.

And yet, when I was in fourth grade, my teacher distributed a Vermont history text that turned out to be filled with only white European/American men. I kept wondering when we would come to "my" people and others like those I saw around me. I wondered why there were no women in the book. What was the rest of the population doing while the Yankee men made history?

As my school years went by, I found similar gaps in all of my history books. By the time I was thirteen, I had begun to feel ashamed of my heritage, since apparently my ancestors never did anything of significance. My people had been erased by other people's ideas of importance. Consequently, as an adult, I made it my mission to uncover histories of women and men that have been hidden by traditional definitions of historical importance.

Here, on this Hill, I found another community that had not made the cut, had not been chosen to be in the books. But traces of their lives remained. I had learned from area hikers and hunters that barn foundations, stone walls, and cellar holes were hidden in the landscape. Henry Louis Gates Jr. calls such artifacts "history-in-waiting, history in suspended animation," waiting to tell their story.[2] The silence of historical discourse on black communities in Vermont had long ago poured "rhetorical acid" on the fingerprints of these pioneers.[3] But it could not destroy the things their hands had built or the records they had left behind in the town vault. These lingered, awaiting a researcher to bring them to life.

What accounts for the muteness of these people of color in Vermont? One answer stems from the fact that there was intermarriage between blacks and whites on the Hill, and in the highly racialized climate of early America, any trace of black blood would necessarily make one black, at least in the eyes of whites. Such a heritage could turn one into a "permanent stranger" whose very existence could be ignored.[4] According to David Roediger, the color of one's skin became more important than gender, social class, or religion in assigning roles in the developing nation.[5] Roles assigned to people of color were usually service and laboring positions that offered little chance to advance. As a result, some African-descended people who could assert a white identity, and all that it implied, often hid their lineage from the following generations until all recollections of their ancestry had vanished. Guarding this family secret became a necessity in order to sustain economic, social, and political advantages.

Many people across America still carry this secret, as do some descendants of the people who settled on the Hill in Hinesburgh, who are scattered throughout northwestern Vermont, New York, Massachusetts, and other parts of the country. Some of the progeny of the Hill pioneers guard the secret knowingly, refusing to admit it to their children or grandchildren, telling them their skin shade comes from Indian or Italian ancestors — anything but African ones. Others, however, carry the secret unwittingly, never having been told of their ancestors' courage while confronting life as farmers on the northern frontier. One descendent whose ancestry had been hidden explained this familial silence to me, "See, they came from the time period where black people were seen as second-class people, and they were treated poorly and tormented by other children, and those hurt feelings don't go away and never will."[6] These torments and ensuing silences have contributed to the story of this Hill in Vermont remaining hidden.

## The Invention of Blackness and Whiteness

The idea that African Americans were second-class citizens can be traced to a widespread fallacy generated in early America. This fallacy was the idea that blackness and whiteness carried different quantifiable and inheritable characteristics. Before the American Revolution, people understood that all human blood, regardless of skin color, was exactly the same. White Americans considered non-Europeans inferior only culturally — their traditions were the problem, which could be "corrected" by assimilation into Christian, European culture. After the Revolution, however, as people of color began to lay equal claim to Enlightenment ideas of the right to life, liberty, and property,[7] a new ideology began to take shape, which proclaimed that "blacks and whites had unlike blood, indicating different origins [and] different qualities."[8] *Blackness*, synonymous with forced servitude, gradually came to mean un-free, subservient, dependent, weak, savage, unintelligent, not worthy of citizenship, history-less.[9] The perception of *whiteness* slowly developed in reaction to blackness and as its polar opposites: white men were viewed as free, civilized, virile, autonomous, powerful, worthy of citizenship, makers of history.[10] The idea of inalienable rights for whites became ineradicably linked in the minds of whites with the belief that immutable and inferior blood flowed through the veins of people of color.[11]

Because many white Americans believed these racial stereotypes, our founding fathers had an ideological basis for their political decision to leave people of color out of the body politic. Since enslaved blacks had no constitutional protections, were indeed not whole human beings for purposes of representation and taxation, they therefore were not Americans and, by extension, not Vermonters.[12] The real Vermonters, legends tell us, who conquered the wilderness and built the state's democratic institutions were white. The presence of any African Americans, or native Abenakis, for that matter, who were not included in this definition of "Vermonter," was not worthy of much mention in eighteenth- and nineteenth-century writings.[13] The invention of whiteness supplied the foundation for budding white identities as northerners, as pioneers, and as Vermonters. Many African-descended people seized this powerful white identity as soon as circumstance allowed in order to protect themselves and their children from the growing racial stereotypes connected with blackness.

## The Myth of a Slave-Free, White North

The spreading whiteness in northern Vermont allowed the state to often be identified as the whitest state in the union, leading to a second fallacy that contributes to the silence surrounding this Vermont community of blacks: the mythology that Vermont is now and has always been not only slave free but also almost completely white. People are usually surprised when I tell them I'm writing about black history in Vermont. "That'll be short!" they say, laughing. Historians focus their attention where there is plenty of documentation, and believing there is none on African Americans, they bypass Vermont.[14]

However, my previous research had shown that although the state as a whole was only .2 or .3 percent black from 1790 to 1870, the averages obscure the pockets of relatively high percentages of people of color in certain towns.[15] For example, in 1790 Vergennes was 7 percent black and Ferrisburgh 2.5 percent; in 1800 Braintree was almost 3.8 percent black, and in 1810 Windsor was 3.6 percent people of color. By 1820 Burlington was 3.4 percent free people of color and Hinesburgh almost 2 percent.[16] These small communities have seldom been investigated, but the numbers are tantalizing clues to an unwritten history.[17]

This historical myth of a white, slave-free Vermont grew out of the desire to save white, Anglo-Saxon, Protestant culture and identity in the face of large migrations to the North before and after the Civil War.[18] The myth had been present long before the war, and some writers fought against it,[19] but it hardened into absolute truth as new Canadian and European immigrants flowed into the area in larger numbers than any Yankee could remember. Between 1870 and 1920 Vermont's foreign-born population had swelled to 14 percent, only slightly lower than the national average of 15 percent.[20] In addition, some of the newly freed people in the South began migrations north after the Civil War. In the 1910s and 1920s, Vermont's African Americans represented .5 percent of the population, the highest in history until that time. The old immigrants of British stock began to fear their traditional institutions would be torn apart by the newly arriving migrants and their unfamiliar ideas and customs. As a result, white Yankees in Vermont "increasingly articulated a self-consciously and assertively Yankee cultural identity," with "Yankee superiority a consistent theme."[21] Historian Kevin Thornton claims that the struggle over who was a "real" Vermonter became the "primary issue defining the politics of the second half of the nineteenth century."[22] Some white Yankees embarked on "an exercise in selective remembering," writing romantic memoirs cleansed of embarrassing truths, with no mention of American Indians or enslaved people.[23] Others started history museums and preserved houses of famous Anglo-Saxon men to safeguard the history of their social class.[24] All other histories and identities were forgotten as Vermonters ignored their slaveholding past and created models of heroic Americans worthy of emulation by immigrants. Over time, amnesia set in, and traces of forced servitude in the North were lost from historical memory.[25]

The truth is quite different. During the fervor of the Revolutionary War, the New England states began painful and gradual emancipations of those whom they had enslaved. In some states, blacks could be enslaved until their age of majority, usually eighteen for women and twenty-one for men, as in Vermont. In other New England states, like Connecticut, those born after March 1, 1784, could be held in servitude until the age of twenty-five. Those born prior to that date were enslaved for life. Few people of color found anything to cheer in gradual emancipation, and after the Revolution, enslaved people were still struggling to excise the venom of slavery from their lives. In 1788, enslaved people of New Haven, Connecticut, presented a petition to the General Assembly still using Revolutionary rhetoric:

> all our wishes ar that your Honours wou[ld] grant us a Liberration wee are all Deturmand we Can to[il] As Long as thir is Labor we woul wish no more to be in Sl[avery] to Sin Seene Christ is maid us free and nald our tanants to the Cross and Bought our Liberty.[26]

Their principles were very clear: All people have rights, including liberty, which have been bought by Christ's suffering. New England blacks insisted on freedom from slavery, insisted on the same liberty for which they had fought and suffered alongside white soldiers. Their Revolution was not yet over.

Since it was a tradition to call slaves "servants," it is difficult to tell if servants found in the census reports in Vermont were free or spent much of their lives in forced servitude. For most of Vermont's early history, larger percentages of blacks lived in white households than headed their own. For instance, in 1790, whites headed 83 percent of Vermont households that contained any black people.[27] That leaves only 17 percent of households containing people of color being headed by a free black man or woman. For all the years of this study, whites controlled between 50 percent and 83 percent of households that included blacks. In 1820, when age information is supplied for the first time for people of color, we discover that black servants were generally fourteen years old or over, but one-third were children thirteen years old or under. Two-thirds of these young servants were girls. In 1830, one-fifth of Vermont's black servants were nine years old or under, two-thirds of them girls. These youngsters generally lived as the only black person in the household, leaving them isolated and lonely.[28]

Whether these servants were enslaved, indentured, or salaried is difficult to ascertain, but we do know that some of them were enslaved and legally subject to the gradual emancipation clause of Vermont's Constitution. However, even gradual freedom for their slaves was too rapid for some slave owners, who resisted the 1777 mandate to free their slaves at their age of majority and instead sold them out of state. The Vermont legislature made the practice illegal in 1786, and slaveholders tried to overturn the law but were defeated in 1791.[29] Clearly, some inhabitants of Vermont were enslaved, and elite whites tried to protect their privileged position as slaveholders, but these dramas are no longer a part of our historical memories.

It was an easy jump from amnesia about slavery in Vermont to the idea of no black presence at all. The "proof" was in the Constitution, which outlawed slavery (at least for adults). People overlooked the process of gradual emancipation to conclude that since Vermonters couldn't possibly have enslaved people, there was no reason for a black presence on the northern frontier. The result of such faulty reasoning was an almost complete amnesia toward people of color, except for a few notables and, of course, Civil War soldiers and runaways on the Underground Railroad.[30] Folklore about the Underground Railroad that I heard as a girl growing up in Vermont centered on heroic whites, while the blacks remained nameless and faceless in their own escape story. This erasure of people of color was bloodless violence, but violence nevertheless. Only now at the turn of this century have some historians turned their attention to the possibility of black community history in Vermont.[31]

Joanne Melish argues that the "re-visioning [of New England history] as a triumphant narrative of free, white labor" made it easy to ignore the stories of free people of color.[32] Our northern forebears, with their selective backward gaze, rejected the world as it was lived and replaced it with the world as they wished it had been.[33] In the resulting version of American history, blacks were relegated to the South, as the white North began its bold experiment in democracy. Evidence of a black presence has often been explained away as related to the Underground Railroad, as it was on this Vermont Hill.[34]

The silence about the Hill's residents allowed only their shadows—not clearly defined human beings—to exist. This history returns these families in sharp definition to the Vermont landscape, depicting how they lived, loved, and worked for decades in the fourteenth state to join

the union. In writing this narrative, I have attempted to make the surprising idea of a black community in the Green Mountains seem familiar and to offer historical people, as fully drawn as possible, for readers
to get to know. In doing so, I challenge Vermont's identity as a white
segment of the new nation and question familiar notions about race
and identity. There are other hills and villages in rural New England
and elsewhere in the North where relatively large percentages of blacks
lived in the nineteenth century.[35] All of these people did not move away.
Some of them stayed and, through intermarriage and time, many passed
over into whiteness. Their progeny are still present, often hidden behind
a white veil of family secrets.[36]

## Historical Themes

An important historical theme in this narrative is the nature of a rural
nineteenth-century agricultural community. We know so little about the
history of rural black people that it is difficult for historians to make
generalizations about them. This project adds to the few studies we do
have.[37] The families on this Vermont Hill lend truth to David Danbom's
claim that although the family was "the most important visible institution in rural America, the neighborhood was the preeminent invisible
one."[38] In these families we find not only the self-reliance and industry of
Jefferson's yeoman farmer,[39] but also cooperation and interdependence
among the men and women in their biracial farming neighborhood.
The earliest people to the Hill, in the 1790s, were from Connecticut and
Massachusetts: Samuel and Prince Peters; Hannah Lensemen, Prince's
wife; Violet and Shubael Clark; and several toddling children. Assum-
ing their white neighbors would stereotype them with all the qualities that *blackness* implied at the time, they apparently craved isolation
at first, but that did not continue for long. As newly forming white
beliefs about the inferiority of blacks bumped up against the hard realities of rural life on the Hill, the needs of the neighborhood often, but not
always, took precedence over the prevailing ideology of the country. On
this Hill, black and white neighbors would come to work together, pray
together, and even loan each other farm animals when the need arose.
This may have been easier in the 1790s and early 1800s before scientific
racism took a firm hold of white minds. Until later in the nineteenth
century, the fulfillment of the needs of family and neighbors was some-

times more important than ideology, competition, and markets.⁴⁰ This seemed true on the Hill as well, regardless of race, as blacks and whites learned to trust and respect each other.

The popular conception that slavery had weakened the integrity of the black family as an institution is brought into question by the lives of the Hill community. This community mirrored Ira Berlin's "Revolutionary generation" that found a space to settle far away from the site of their enslavement and established households under their own control.⁴¹ A mother and father headed every family on this Hill, eventually with grandchildren and great-grandchildren living nearby. There was no higher goal among the newly freed than maintaining the integrity of their families, and only death or war separated them. For some, those family ties remain unbroken into the twenty-first century, as witnessed by some descendants of this community still proudly bearing their ancestors' names.⁴² Knowledge of the struggles, achievements, and failures of the people on this Hill add richness to American family history and are an important part of the larger history of our society.

Their story also sheds light on our country's military history. During the Revolutionary era, there was a rebellion within the larger one that we seldom encounter in either Vermont or American history texts, one involving African Americans. Thousands of blacks, including Prince Peters from the Hill, joined the fight for freedom—not only from the British monarchy, but also from slavery and the ideology of the institution that "presses down upon free people of color (like) deadly poison."⁴³ Many believed that as long as slavery existed, the conviction that blacks were fit only for servitude would be toxic to the aspirations of all people of color—free or enslaved.

The hopes of African Americans soared as Enlightenment ideas of a God-given right to liberty spread throughout the colonies. In 1779, nineteen enslaved men in New Hampshire presented a petition to the legislature using the Revolutionary rhetoric of inalienable rights. They wrote, "The God of nature" gave them life and freedom, and that freedom "is an inherent right of the human species, not to be surrendered but by consent."⁴⁴ When speaking of freedom during the Revolutionary era, many blacks enfolded the abolition of slavery within the larger ideal of natural human rights. This group included Vermonter Lemuel Haynes, who used enlightenment rhetoric to describe liberty as a gift from God in his poem, "The Battle of Lexington." Haynes, the son of a white mother and an African father, was brought up as an indentured servant in Massachusetts and was among the Vermont Green Mountain Boys who captured Fort Ticonderoga in May 1775.[45] In 1788, he came to Vermont to lead a Congregational parish in Rutland for thirty years. This is part of his poem about the war:

> For liberty each Freeman strives
> As it's a Gift of God
> And for it, willing yield their Lives
> And Seal it with their Blood.
>
> Twice happy they who thus resign
> Into the peacefull Grave
> Much better those in Death consign
> Than a Surviving Slave[46]

Better to die in battle than remain enslaved. As a free man, he was using the word "slave" with a double meaning—alluding to America being a slave of Great Britain, as well as to the institution of human slavery that many blacks fought to end with their service in the war. "The moral logic and natural right of linking two ideas—freedom for whites and freedom for blacks—was in the air" and seen as a gift of God.[47] But while blacks nestled the abolition of slavery within the patriotic ideal of freedom from Britain, many whites felt that only they had received the gift.

At least two black men from the area of the Hill fought in the American Revolution—probably not as much for freedom from Britain as for the principle of inalienable rights for all, regardless of race, and for the destruction of the institution of slavery. One black patriot was Prince Peters, of Northampton, Massachusetts, who settled on the Hill during the second division of the lands in 1798. He was a young farmer, five feet four inches tall and about sixteen years old at his enlistment.[48] Because he enlisted in 1780, we do not know if he was enslaved—at that date, both enslaved and free blacks were enlisting.[49] From his 1818 pension we know that he saw action starting in 1780 in Captain Pierce's Massachusetts line, Eighth Company, Third Massachusetts Regiment.[50] He served for three years and was honorably discharged after his service. If he had been enslaved, this service would have freed him.[51]

In addition to Prince Peters, Charles Bowles, a free man from New Hampshire and a Revolutionary soldier turned preacher, later moved to the adjoining town of Huntington and held Free Will Baptist revivals on the Hill.[52] He served in several regiments from New Hampshire and Massachusetts from 1776 to 1779 and was honorably discharged.[53] His biographer tells us, "Those who served so nobly sacrificed their time and strength in the common cause were obliged to return to their homes unrewarded," because while tyranny under the British may have been abolished, slavery and prejudice against blackness was still the lot of most African Americans in the country.[54] This "left the necessity for a second revolution," claimed historian William C. Nell, one "no less sublime than that of regenerating public sentiment in favor of universal brotherhood."[55] Many years later, several grandsons of the Hill's pioneering generation fought in that "second revolution," the Civil War, to gain freedom for African Americans. And one family continued the struggle in the South during the Reconstruction years.

### The Effects of Prejudice in the Nineteenth Century

Prejudice and discrimination against people of color is another theme woven throughout this story. I was conscious of the possibility that racism or prejudice may have been the foundation for conflicts between the people of the Hill and the wider white community. But I was also aware that poor treatment could have other bases: valley people discriminating against hill people (there really was such a dichotomy in Vermont, with the mountains as the spine of the state); businessmen prejudiced against hardscrabble farmers; the formally educated looking down their noses at the unschooled segments of society. I needed to be conscious of race and social class at the same time and not automatically assume one factor trumped the other.

Nevertheless, I constantly asked myself how the prevailing racial ideology might have worked upon the minds of the white neighbors of the Clarks and Peterses and thus affected their lives on the Hill. This is a "zone of contact" story—a story of a small neighborhood in Vermont that can illuminate the dynamics of race relations that existed when free blacks were a small minority surrounded by overwhelming numbers of whites.[56] Writings by both blacks and whites in the nineteenth century introduced me to their possible experiences. Black or white, American or foreign, they all examined this indefinable, irrational thing called prejudice and how it affected both blacks and whites in different ways.

The French writer and early sociologist Gustave de Beaumont, the traveling companion of *Democracy in America* author Alexis de Tocqueville, wrote a fictionalized account of race prejudice in the North during the 1830s. The most extraordinary thing about America, Beaumont wrote, "is the violence of the prejudice which separates the race of slaves from that of free men."[57] Whether blacks are free or enslaved, prejudice "deepens the abyss which separates the two races and pursues them in every phase of social and political life."[58]

Beaumont first became interested in the plight of black people in Pennsylvania, whose Constitution is sometimes compared to Vermont's in elements such as a unicameral legislature, a council of censors, and rights that extend to both blacks and whites.[59] In Philadelphia, he noticed, "According to the Constitution they are the equals of whites and have the same political rights. But laws don't change customs. One is accustomed here to see in a Negro a slave, and as such one continues to treat him."[60]

It is possible that Beaumont and Tocqueville visited Vermont during their 1831–1832 travels, which included a steamship journey aboard the *Phoenix* along the shores of Lake Champlain on the western border of Vermont. Although they never mentioned Vermont in particular, they often wrote about Northern states. In a short section on race in *Democracy in America*, Tocqueville seemed to be speaking specifically of northern New England: "Race prejudice seems stronger in those states that have abolished slavery than in those where it still exists; and nowhere is it more intolerant than in those states where slavery was never known."[61]

Many nineteenth-century writers concentrated on the effects prejudice had on the minds of whites. Edward S. Adby, an English traveler to the Americas during 1833–1834, maintained that prejudice was an "infirmity" that degraded the minds of white Americans.[62] Many black writers of the time agreed wholeheartedly. In his popular 1841 textbook, James W. C. Pennington, who had escaped slavery in Maryland, claimed that prejudice was not mere aversion but a hatred that "establishes in the whites a character for injustice."[63] To justify their hypocritical democratic system that assured equality for all, he claimed, they created inferiority theories, which gave themselves "the right to oppress, and to hate and abuse their fellow men!"[64]

In his 1837 pamphlet, a black Connecticut minister, Hosea Easton, condemned prejudice in the North and denounced the hypocrisy of the

American system, which guaranteed equal rights only to whites. "Were I capable of dipping my pen in the deepest dye of crime, and of understanding the science of the bottomless pit, I should then fail in presenting to the intelligence of mortals on earth, the true nature of American deception."[65]

These men were writing broadly about racism in New England — but did their comments apply to the Hill? What were the similarities and differences between the broader currents of prejudice and racism elsewhere in New England and those found on the Hill? Did these people have to deal daily with hypocrisy, injustice, and hatred in the hills of Vermont? Adby gave me hope it might have been otherwise in a rural state. He observed that Northern blacks employed by farmers "sometimes even sit down to the same table with the whites. . . . [This] shews that their services are more wanted in the country than in the towns."[66] In general he found farmers to be "better informed and less narrow-minded than the inhabitants of the cities."[67] In an examination of occupations in the 1860 Vermont census, in spite of the mostly service jobs open to blacks, I discovered an almost equal percentage of blacks and whites employed as farm laborers.[68] Records also indicate that the people on the Hill were accepted into the farming neighborhood and the Baptist Church by their white neighbors. These rural farmers seemingly had attitudes different from village and city people.

This story about Vermont conjures up another theme of the larger world beyond the time and place of this community: identity formation. Although Vermont is often called the whitest state in the union, it is much more of a racial blend than many people admit. In general, we need to see whiteness as the complex combination of colors that science reveals — reflecting all the colors of the visible light spectrum. More of the histories and stories we tell our children need to reflect the mix of peoples and ideas that led to what we are today. If we could make this leap away from a color blindness that masks the complexities of our history, we could begin to change the way we think about social constructions of race and of Northern identity.[69] Historian Paul Searls contends, "In trying to better understand the ways the designation 'Vermonter' has been interpreted, reinterpreted, manipulated, and contested, we can better learn how identity is constructed not just here, but elsewhere."[70] This is a universal human story, not simply one of the Vermont frontier.

I had hoped that I would find documents to shed light on how these black farmers identified themselves as well as the quality of life for the women, men, and children on the Hill. In the best of all worlds, I would have found diaries and letters and other primary sources from their point of view. Unfortunately, I found very few documents written in their words. In order to recreate the story of their lives from their perspective, therefore, I used what little I found: military pension records, a few letters from Civil War soldiers, and two wills from the Civil War era. I did find many official documents involving these families that helped me interpret their lives: census and land records, court records, probate documents, inventories, and grand lists.[71] However, most such documents are not from the point of view of the Hill people, but from an official perspective—for example, town clerks recording land sales and federal authorities deciding if men deserved military pensions.

Because of the paucity of personal documents, especially in the earliest years of community building, I often relied on the testimony of other Vermonters not from the Hill—both black and white—who left copious records in their own words. Their experiences helped me, first of all, to examine the early settlers' conflicts with nature and apply their experiences to the Hill people. Second, for human conflicts, I relied on the writings of people of color from Vermont and elsewhere in New England. In this way, I was able to put together a plausible picture of this early farming community and depict probable dimensions of their lives through others' experiences. For the later decades, I could draw more and more on public documents and their own words.

These sources of data are labor intensive to find, read, and interpret, but they are often the only sources available to expand our national and state narratives to include marginalized people. This is an alternative history, one that establishes the presence and persistence of people of color in Vermont. My data sources, however, represent only fragments of their decades on the Hill. As Sigurdur Magnusson observed, "Historians always have to work with fragments and lacunae, with revelations and secrets. We may crave coherence and synthesis, but because much remains indecipherable we do not get it."[72]

As I fitted the fragments together, a picture of a small community of at least eight black families and additional black laborers eventually emerged, linked to a larger network of blacks throughout central and northwestern Vermont. This is one of the most important aspects of this story—the revelation that such a place as this Hill existed. The public records allowed me to add depth to my understanding of these families' lives as the century wore on. Although they lived in a remote rural area, they were not isolated from the farming neighborhood, the wider town of Hinesburgh, or the state and national issues of their times. They lived as pioneers, farmers, and local activists while bearing children, joining churches, engaging with their neighbors, and raising families on the frontier. They, especially the women, joined rural networks of both blacks and whites, and the men voted in town and state elections and fought in our country's wars. This is not only black history—it is a classic Vermont story and a piece of the larger story of our nation. Through the perspectives of these people on the Hill, we can examine not only Vermont's history, but also that of our nation as we trace their experiences in the years following the Revolutionary War through the Civil War.

## CHAPTER ONE

Founding Mothers and Fathers
of the Hill, 1790s–1800s

It's a blessing to own land.
—John F. Ficara, *Black Farmers in America*

HINESBURGH, located in the southern part of the county, in lat. 44° 19',
and long. [7]3° 57', was granted by New Hampshire, June 24, 1762, to
David FERRIS, Abel HINE and sixty three others, mostly resident in
New Milford, Conn., the said HINE acting for many years as proprietors' clerk, hence the name "Hinesburgh." In outline the town is very
regular, its boundary lines being each six miles in length, forming a
perfect square, and enclosing a tract whose area is just thirty-six square
miles, or 23,040 acres. —*Child's Gazeteer of Chittenden County*, 1882

*Finding Their Place*

Shubael Clark paused his horse at the bottom of the Hill and studied
the 2,000-foot rise that was darkened by a canopy of old-growth beech
and maple trees, many six feet around, that prevented the sunshine from
reaching the forest floor.[1] Mushrooms and mosses grew profusely in the
moisture that never leaves woodlands like this. He had ridden north
from Monkton to Hinesburgh on a well-used path; the mud was a foot
deep in places, causing his horse to sink with each step. But that had
been easy compared to the tedious climb he now began up this Hill to
his acreage at the top. The ground was often hidden by knots of soft,
mossy logs, heaps of rotting vegetation, and tangled undergrowth. The
soil had never been cultivated and lay beneath a rich layer of humus,
so the trees extended their massive roots horizontally. The largest trees
were sometimes felled by the wind or by their own weight, tearing up

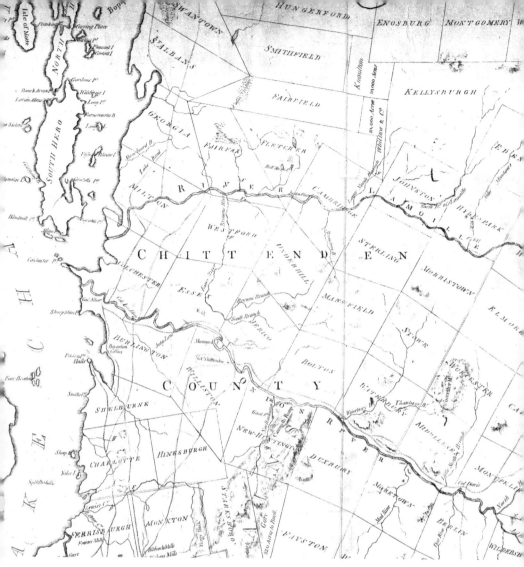

FIGURE I.I 1789 Blodget map of Chittenden County, Vermont. Hinesburgh is the square township on the southern border of the county. Monkton is on its southern border with two roads coming north into Hinesburgh.

an extensive network of roots and making it impossible for a wagon to get through. The old-growth forest of the Hill was gloomy and the smell of its swampy beaver dams disagreeable.[2]

In June 1795, Violet and Shubael Clark had chosen the top of this Hill in Hinesburgh on the border with New Huntington as home for themselves and their two toddling children. They bought 100 acres from Nathan Douglas of Monkton for ninety pounds.[3] Not until three

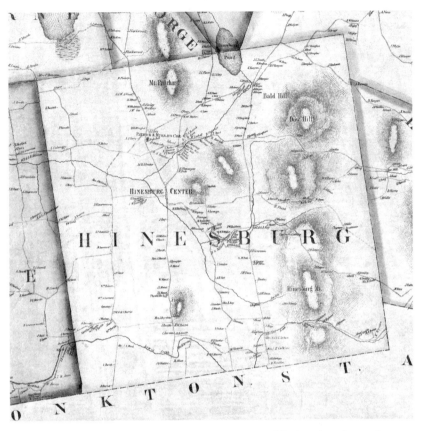

FIGURE I.2  1857 Wallings map of Hinesburg, Vermont. Monkton is on its southern border; Huntington on the east; Charlotte to the west. These are all towns that are important to the story of the Hill.

years later would a road be surveyed and laid out to their land.[4] The earliest settlers had chosen the more fertile farmlands on the western side of Hinesburgh. By 1795, that land had all been claimed. But there were still lands in the east that rose rapidly "in large and broken ridges to a height of 1,200 to 2,000 feet, mostly covered with a strong, arable soil," an ideal space for a family of color to assert their personal identities away from the surveillance of whites.[5]

Shubael had surely trekked here many times from his land in nearby Monkton, since it was the husband's task to clear the house lot and build the cabin before bringing the family (see figure 1.1 for the roads from Monkton into Hinesburgh). We know they had a horse in 1799 because

Shubael was taxed for one, along with three cows.[6] He may have had one earlier to help him move the massive logs after he felled trees to clear the house lot, but oxen would have been much more useful. The cabin he built would have been one room with a dirt or split-log floor and a fireplace with a mud-and-stick chimney. He could have rolled the logs into place by himself for the lower portion of the cabin, but would have needed help with the upper part. A neighbor from Monkton might have helped with this task.

When all was prepared, even if they had a cart in which to move the family's belongings, getting it to the top of this Hill would have been grueling, since they would have to widen the path by clearing under-brush, trees, rotting logs, and larger stones. They must have packed on their backs most of what they needed to survive. It was said that if you couldn't carry 100 pounds on your back for ten miles, you weren't fit for settling the Vermont frontier. Over the next seventy years, they proved they were survivors.

One might wonder why the Clarks chose the top of the Hill, on the border between Hinesburgh and Huntington, when more accessible lots were still available elsewhere. They left no words describing their motives, but one can imagine Shubael scouting the area to find good farmland. Being smart about where husbandry would succeed, he would have noticed that the top of the Hill faced southwest, with the sun hit-ting the hilltop two hours earlier than in the valley and lasting about two hours longer in the evening. Once the thick canopy was cleared, the growing days would be longer than lower on the Hill. Bending down to dig up a handful of soil to let it run through his fingers, he would have been satisfied that the "sandy or gravelly loam" was rich enough for wheat and potatoes.[7] This Hill was also an excellent habitat for game. The abundant seeds of the trees fed squirrels, deer, porcupine, bear, rabbit, and woodchucks. Many of the mushrooms, mosses, and other vegetation were edible as well. Here was a cornucopia of survival sta-ples for those hardy enough to harvest them. It would sustain the family until the first harvests.

Three years later, another family of color chose this Hill as their home. In January 1798, Samuel Peters, with ties to Connecticut and Massa-chusetts, bought his first plot of land at the bottom of the Hill.[8] He soon shared land and other resources with Revolutionary War veteran, Prince Peters, his wife Hannah Lensemen,[9] and their son, a toddler.[10] By then, Hinesburgh was an up-and-coming town with a sawmill, a gristmill,

FIGURE I.3  1857 Wallings map of the Hill, detail. The road (just north of Hinesburg
Mt.) runs from Hinesburgh in the northwest to Huntington in the southeast. The names
"J. Peters" and "C. Waters" are on the western end of the road at the bottom of the Hill.
This was where Samuel, Prince, and Hannah first lived. "Mrs. V. Clark," Violet, is on
top of the Hill on the eastern end just before the road continues into Huntington, where
the Clarks also owned land. The McEwen farm and a small cemetery are west of Hinesburg Mountain.

and a carding mill, which "though a rude affair, was considered at that
time a model of mechanical genius."[11] That same year, the town surveyed a road over the Hill into the adjacent town of Huntington.

Samuel and Prince Peters lived close together, sometimes in the same
house, so they were likely brothers. The men might have had heard about
the Hill in Hinesburgh from the Clarks—possibly Violet Clark was a
Peters or a Lensemen. Although I have no record of that, I have learned
there are few coincidences on this Hill. When I first began this research,
I looked for military relationships among the men to explain why seemingly unrelated black families like the Clarks and Peters would move to
this isolated Hill in Vermont. As my research progressed, though, in
other circumstances I usually found that the relationship was through
the women, whose married names made it difficult to ascertain relationships. It would be perfectly reasonable to believe that they had a prior

relationship, and evidence that it might have been kinship is that the families never intermarried.[12]

There is no evidence that the Peterses had lived elsewhere in Vermont before settling on the Hill, but they certainly may have. Addison County, just south of Hinesburgh, was the site of many black families and people of color living within white households in the 1790s. (See table 1.1 for information about the nearby towns of Ferrisburgh and Vergennes.) The federal census revealed that the Bostwick families, founders of Hinesburgh, were slave owners in New Milford, Connecticut, and that Edmund Bostwick had three black people living within his Hinesburgh household in 1800. One man of color lived in the Hinesburgh home of Nathan Leavenworth, also originally from Connecticut. Therefore, there were people of color already living nearby, either as free people or in white households, by the time of settlement on the Hill. It is possible the Peterses had been part of one of those households.[13] Only the heads of the house, however, were named in the early census reports, and enumerators missed many families, especially if they were not seen as worthy of much notice.[14]

Samuel bought his first plot of land in January 1798, and the Peterses may have started coming to the Hill during the winter to build. This was a good season to travel because the waterways were frozen and deep snows covered stumps and rocks, allowing easier transport. For example, Mr. and Mrs. Jehiel Johns, the first white settlers in nearby Huntington, migrated in the winter from southern Vermont. They used waterways for most of the trip, traveling on Otter Creek to the ice of Lake Champlain, then north to Burlington and up the Winooski River to Richmond Flats. From there Jehiel used his ax to clear the rest of the way.[15] A sled pulled by oxen would have made the trip easier, but the snows were four feet deep, making it a problem for animals to navigate and browse for food. Samuel and Prince Peters more likely used snowshoes to bring supplies to build the cabin, and when it was prepared for the family, perhaps Prince and Hannah's small son walked the new path trodden down by his parents or was carried on someone's back.[16] The trip would not have been quite as tedious as the Clarks', since the Peterses' land was closer to a town road and not at the crest of the Hill.

Settling any area of northern New England, regardless of the season, was not for the fainthearted. A Connecticut minister who made a preaching tour of Vermont during the spring of 1789 complained that he found himself in "mud belly deep to my horse and I thought I should have perished."[17] Even a seasoned traveler, President Timothy Dwight of Yale, marveled at the way settlers on the northern New England frontier adjusted to hardships of travel "over the worst roads, where both horses and men, accustomed to smoother ways, merely tremble, and creep."[18]

> Over roads, encumbered with rocks, mire, and the stumps and roots of trees, they ride upon a full trot; and are apprehensive of no danger. Even the women of these settlements, and those of every age, share largely in this spirit. I have often met them on horseback; and been surprised to see them pass fearlessly over those dangers of the way, which my companions and myself watched with caution and solicitude.[19]

TABLE I.I
*Largest African American Communities in Vermont*

| Town | African Americans | percentage of population | Town | African Americans | percentage of population |
|------|------|------|------|------|------|
| 1790 | | | 1820 | | |
| Bennington | 20 | .8 | Burlington | 71 | 3.4 |
| Vergennes | 14 | 7.0 | Rutland | 53 | 2.2 |
| Thetford | 14 | 1.6 | Windsor | 39 | 1.3 |
| Brattleboro | 14 | .9 | Swanton | 25 | 1.5 |
| Guilford | 13 | .5 | Hinesburgh | 25 | 1.8 |
| Ferrisburgh | 12 | 2.5 | | | |
| | | | 1830 | | |
| 1800 | | | St. Albans | 54 | 2.3 |
| Vergennes | 27 | 5.2 | Burlington | 53 | 1.5 |
| Windsor | 27 | 1.2 | Bennington | 43 | 1.3 |
| Rutland | 25 | 1.2 | Woodstock | 36 | 1.2 |
| Bennington | 25 | 1.1 | Windsor | 30 | .9 |
| Braintree | 20 | 3.8 | Hinesburgh | 25 | 1.5 |
| 1810 | | | 1840 | | |
| Ferrisburgh | 48 | 2.9 | Rutland | 67 | 2.5 |
| Burlington | 45 | 2.7 | Bennington | 47 | 1.4 |
| Rutland | 42 | 1.8 | Woodstock | 45 | 1.4 |
| Windsor | 32 | 3.6 | St. Albans | 40 | 1.5 |
| Hinesburgh | 32 | 2.5 | Burlington | 38 | .9 |
| Sheldon | 32 | 3.6 | Hinesburgh | 19 | 1.1[a] |

Surely the Peterses and Clarks met the dangers of the frontier as fearlessly as those witnessed by Dwight. They had come to this Hill in northern Vermont to begin life anew as part of the recently freed Revolutionary generation and to live in liberty as part of a new class of people: free blacks.[20]

## Status Prior to Settlement on the Hill

While we know much about the Vermont lives of the Hill's residents, unanswered questions remain about the lands of their births and their

TABLE I.I *(continued)*

| Town | African Americans | percentage of population | Town | African Americans | percentage of population |
|---|---|---|---|---|---|
| 1850 | | | 1860 | | |
| St. Albans | 67 | 1.9 | Rutland | 93 | 1.2 |
| Burlington | 62 | 1.0 | Woodstock | 53 | 1.7 |
| Woodstock | 58 | 1.9 | Bennington | 49 | 1.1 |
| Bennington | 54 | 1.4 | Burlington | 46 | .6 |
| Rutland | 37 | 1.0 | Hinesburgh | 30 | 1.8 |
| Hinesburgh | 27 | 1.4 | Castleton | 30 | 1.0 |
| | | | 1870[b] | | |
| | | | St. Albans | 86 | 1.2 |
| | | | Burlington | 77 | .5 |
| | | | Bennington | 75 | 1.3 |
| | | | Rutland | 69 | .7 |
| | | | Castleton | 58 | 1.8 |

SOURCE: Elise A. Guyette, "Black Lives and White Racism in Vermont 1760–1870," MA thesis, University of Vermont, 1992, 72 and 85–86. Also, the 1850–1870 tables can be found in Guyette, "The Working Lives of African Vermonters in Census and Literature, 1790–1870." *Vermont History* 61, no. 2 (1993): 70. Some figures were updated in 2009.

[a]Seven Langleys were counted in the Huntington census with Calvin Wells, perhaps working on his farm when the census taker came, but they were certainly living on the Hill. If added to the Hinesburgh figure, the percentage would be 1.5.

[b]Hinesburgh had twenty residents of color in 1870. With the increase in the black communities in Vermont cities that year, this small number no longer qualified as one of the largest in the state. The twenty people included thirteen Peterses, Edwardses, and Waterses who remained on the Hill. The remaining people were six agricultural laborers and one domestic servant who were all living in white households.

❧ *Founders of the Hill*

CLARKS buy land at the top of the Hill, 1795:
  Shubael (b. ca. 1760, perhaps Connecticut, d. 1835, Hinesburgh)
  Violet (b. 1775 in Connecticut or Massachusetts, d. 1863,
    Hinesburgh)
  Nine children born in Vermont: Lewis, Almira, Sybil, Phoebe,
    Hiram, Harriet, Charles, Caroline, and Minerva

PETERSES buy land at the bottom of the Hill, 1798:
  Samuel Peters (d. Hinesburgh by 1840) — unknown relationship to
    rest of household
  Prince Peters (b. 1759, perhaps Massachusetts, d. 1832 Hinesburgh)
  Hannah Lensemen, Prince's first wife (d. by 1818, Hinesburgh)
  Four children born in Vermont: Samuel 2nd, Josephus, Sarah,
    Electa
  Eliza Peters, Prince's second wife (d. by 1840)

status earlier in their lives. It is possible their histories go back to another continent. According to William Piersen, most New England blacks during the eighteenth century were born in Africa.[21] So it is possible that the earliest inhabitants of the Hill had started life across the ocean in a western or central African village and had been forced to the Americas on the terrifying Middle Passage. If these earliest black men and women of the Hill had originated in an African country, it is likely they continued African traditions in America. Their move to an isolated Hill in Vermont may have been an attempt to find a space where they could conserve what they remembered about their culture, purposefully maintaining their identity in the larger Yankee community.[22]

Just prior to their migration to Vermont, however, they were New Englanders. Prince Peters's military record reveals he fought for the town of Northampton, Massachusetts, during the Revolution. The land records of Monkton, Vermont, on the southern border of Hinesburgh, reveal that Shubael Clark came there from New Milford, Connecticut.[23] This was the usual pattern for migrants to Vermont. Migrants came from all over New England, but the majority of the Vermont land settled during the eighteenth century belonged to people from Connecticut, whose traditions would serve them in Vermont. In fact, when Vermont was declared an independent republic in 1777, its name was "New Connecticut." Prince Peters was most likely not enslaved, due to his coming from Massachusetts and his service in the Revolution. It is possible, however, that the Clarks had been enslaved and brought to Vermont by white migrants, since by the time of the Revolution the slave population in Connecticut was greater than in any other New England colony. Connecticut was also the last New England state to gradually outlaw slavery in 1784. The total black population in Connecticut, free and enslaved, exceeded that of all the other New England colonies combined, so they also could have been free.[24] Unfortunately, the records do not reveal their status one way or the other.

In 1791, before moving up to the Hill, Shubael had bought 100 acres for one pound from an original Monkton proprietor, David Ferris, a land speculator from New Milford and also a proprietor of Hinesburgh. The cheap price for the land might indicate a prior relationship or reward for Revolutionary service.[25] Monkton was also the home of the Bostwicks from New Milford, who were original proprietors of both Monkton and Hinesburgh. Few proprietors migrated to the frontier to settle. They were generally speculators, comfortable with their lives in lower New England, who resold the land to others who braved the dangers of the Vermont frontier. The Bostwicks, however, settled in the new state. They were also slaveholders, as were one in every four families in Connecticut at the time.[26] If the Clarks had been enslaved or indentured — and we have no conclusive evidence one way or the other — they could have migrated to Vermont within the household of a proprietor or other white settler from the New Milford area. We know that by the 1790 census, the majority of blacks in Vermont were listed as "other persons" living in white households, perhaps living out their years of gradual emancipation or living as indentured servants.[27] According to census reports, many black children, as young as seven, came to Vermont as servants in white households in the earliest days. Unfortunately, we do not know their names, since only the heads of households were named at that time.

We know that Prince Peters served in a Massachusetts regiment during the Revolutionary War.[28] If he had been enslaved, that service would have freed him.[29] He might have heard about the cheap farmland in Vermont while deciding what to do with his hard-won freedom, as had happened with Jeffrey Brace, a man of color from Connecticut who fought in the Revolution and subsequently migrated to northern

Vermont. Brace's experiences may provide a clue as to why the people on the Hill chose Vermont. Brace had been kidnapped from Africa in the 1740s and was still enslaved for the five years during which he fought for liberty in the Revolution. Afterward he headed toward Vermont as a free man. In his memoirs he wrote:

> After we were disbanded, I returned to my old master at Woodbury, with whom I lived one year; my services in the American war, having emancipated me from further slavery, and from being bartered or sold. My master consented that I might go where I pleased and seek my fortune. Hearing flattering accounts of the new state of Vermont; I left Woodbury, and traveled as far as the town of Lenox, in Massachusetts, where for the first time I made a bargain as a freeman for labor; I let myself to a Mr. Elisha Orsborn for one month, at the price of five dollars.[30]

The Peterses and Clarks may have heard similar flattering accounts and made their way north on their own into the fourteenth state. Regardless of their status and geography before the 1790s, these black settlers came to the Hill as free people during the time when Vermont was the fastest-growing state in the union. The "magnetic allure of the land [and its] promise of boundless opportunity" for those tough enough to stick it out were pulling many settlers, black and white, to the new state.[31] In "landownership lay independence."[32] It must have been a powerful attraction to people of color from southern New England—to own a plot of ground, to till it in freedom, and to receive all the blessings that came with controlling land.

After the Revolution, as white settlers from lower New England pushed north into the Green Mountains, proud of winning their freedom from the British monarchy, black settlers traveled from and to the same geographical locations. However, the landscape of their minds was distinctly different—they knew that slavery was still a part of the fabric of the nation, and they felt its effects in their lives in insidious ways. The Revolution "became a metaphor for the disappointment, betrayal and contradictions" that African Americans suffered during the following decades.[33]

Although landownership became a reality for Shubael and Violet in 1791, their stay in Monkton did not last long—something pushed the Clarks out of that town by 1795. Since Vermont was not immune to the racism of the larger society, trouble with neighbors may have caused the move. Two other families of color, the Braces and the Princes, who migrated to Vermont in the eighteenth century, left behind writings and court documents detailing their problems with neighbors.[34] They both had had white neighbors who disliked living near a black family and who tried to force them to move by regularly pulling down their fences, destroying their crops, burning their hay ricks, killing their animals, and spreading slanderous lies about them. In the case of the Brace family, it worked, and the family moved many times trying to avoid angry whites before finally settling in the northern Champlain Valley of Vermont.

For the Clarks, there may been have more of a pull toward the remoteness of the Hill than a push out of Monkton. Perhaps they moved to be better able to continue African traditions. Historian William Piersen found that many New England blacks used African farming methods and tools, resisting European methods of butchering, cooking, planting, and harvesting.[35] For whatever reason the Clarks migrated, they must have found the isolation of this Hinesburgh Hill to their liking, because it was the last move of their lives.

*Settlement*

Shubael and Violet first appeared in the federal census of Hinesburgh in 1800 as married with three children. Violet was born in either Connecticut or Massachusetts in 1775, before any emancipation laws.[36] Therefore, if she had been enslaved, she was brought to Vermont in a white household before her age of majority. In 1793, she reached her eighteenth birthday and should have been emancipated according to the laws of the state. As we know, this did not always happen, but it may have worked in her case if she had an enlightened master, or if she or Shubael knew the law and pressed for her freedom.

The Clarks initially bought a 100-acre lot in 1795, and in 1796 they added to their acreage by buying land on an adjacent lot from Asa Moon, a white neighbor.[37] Clark bought and sold land in another part of town, but by the end of the decade, the Clarks were consolidated on the top of the Hill near a white family named Yaw. The Clark and Yaw families would develop a long-standing relationship in the decades to come.

At the bottom of the Hill, the Peters family appeared in the 1799 grand list of Hinesburgh for the first time. In 1798, Samuel Peters had bought lot 83 from Rufus Crossman for $500.[38] This lot becomes a central piece in the story of the Peterses over the next 100 years, being bought and sold and bought again by various members of the family. It obviously held great importance for the family. One year after Samuel bought the lot, Crossman appeared before the town clerk and acknowledged the sale to be "his free act."[39] He likely did this because Peters was having difficulties with his land title. Shortly after Crossman's appearance, Dr. Bostwick (the tax collector at the time) confiscated the land for nonpayment of taxes of one cent per acre, but in June of 1799, Samuel bought it back for $1.17.[40] Apparently, he had lost it for unpaid taxes, but bought it back at auction.

Samuel ended the decade farming on lot 83 at the bottom of the hill. By 1804, according to the grand list for Hinesburgh, Prince Peters's family was living in the same household as Samuel. That same year, Samuel bought all of Burlington resident John Wray's interest in lot 83, owning it free and clear.[41] The white Wray[42] and Peters families eventually developed a long-standing relationship lasting many decades. As with the Clarks, the Peterses had found a permanent home. More than lot numbers to them, this Hill became their farm and home for decades, the site of births and deaths, joys and sorrows, and their final resting place to this day.

It was not easy, however, turning this old-growth forest into a successful farm and raising large families. The Clarks and Peterses had many mammoth trees to clear or girdle[43] before planting could begin. A case in point comes from Horace Greeley, later to become a nationally known journalist, who described helping his father clear acreage on the Vermont frontier:

> When we first attacked [the forest], the snow was just going, and the water and slush were knee-deep. . . . [We started by] cutting trees; chopping up great trunks into manageable lengths, drawing them together, rolling up and burning great heaps of logs; saving out here and there a log that would do to saw; digging out rotten pines from the soil . . . so that they might dry sufficiently to burn; piling and burning brush and rotten or worthless sticks, and carting home such wood as served for fuel.[44]

Settlers did not clear the land only for fuel, crops, and grazing animals. An illustration of this comes from the writings of an early white settler to Vermont, Elias Smith, who describes another purpose. As

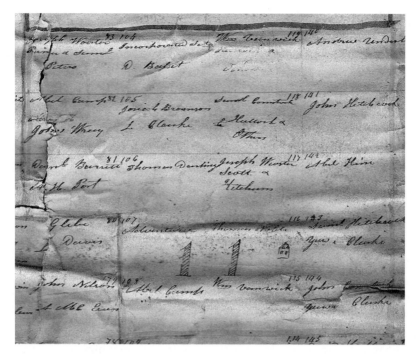

FIGURE I.4   Early, undated map of District 11, the Hill district, in Hinesburgh.

soon as the snow melted, he wrote, "We began to clear off the timber, and make ready for planting and sowing. The first place we cleared, my father fixed upon as a burying place . . . and when he died, he was buried in the same ground he and I cleared first on his farm."[45] Since there was a family cemetery on Clark land at the top of the Hill and probably one at the bottom, one can imagine Shubael Clark and Samuel and Prince Peters clearing ground for their eventual resting places — death was likely never far from people's minds, especially among blacks, whose life expectancy at that time was about thirty-four years.[46] Creating the cemetery, still evident at the top of the Hill, may have been one of Shubael's first tasks.

Other farm duties focused on harvesting from the wilds until the first crops were ready. In 1789, Nathan Perkins, an early white settler of nearby Williston, described the rich environment of lands halfway up the Green Mountains as being "well intersected with streams full of small fish; plenty of moose to hunt and eat and get their tallow . . . plenty of bears and wolves." The women he finds particularly interesting: "Tough are they, brawny their limbs—their young girls unpolished—and will work as well as mules. Woods make people love one another & kind & obliging and good-natured. They set much more by one another than in the old settlements."[47] Had he visited Hannah Peters and Violet Clark, he likely would have found them tough and unpolished as well, ready to take on the struggle to survive in their new world.

Everyone in the Peters and Clark households would have labored unceasingly to ensure survival. On the preindustrial farm, husband and wife formed an economic unit, mutually dependent on each other, and as the children became old enough, they, too, would join the household labor force.[48] In the Peters household there were two adult males to share the workload. Shubael, Samuel, and Prince's sphere was normally the field and the workshop. Violet and Hannah's sphere was generally the house and yard, including the garden and small animals, in addition to caring for the children. Everyone, however, worked wherever and whenever there was work to be done. The men might spin and weave in the evenings; the women might work in the fields when needed.[49] Neighbors helped each other when the need arose, raising barns, maintaining roads, and even loaning one another cows and sheep. Early settlers sometimes reported that when a cow died, a neighbor loaned them one until they could afford to buy another. We can safely assume that the Clarks, Peterses, and their neighbors mirrored this preindustrial farm model in the early years. We find animal loans occurring later when one of the families on the Hill borrows a few of a white neighbor's cows and sheep for their "use and to profit thereby which is customary amongst farmers."[50]

However tough and difficult their early days on the Hill may have been, the Clarks and Peterses were not on the bottom of the economic scale; that place was held by nonpropertied servants, tenant farmers, laborers, transients, and those enslaved. The other end of the scale was a small group of elite, large landowners and speculators who controlled the land supply and owned the gristmills, saw mills, and inns. The people of the Hill were neither of these. They were members of the largest group of early Vermonters: modest landowners.[51] In 1799, Samuel owed taxes on fifteen improved acres, and "Shewbill" owed taxes on two improved acres, two cows, and one horse.[52] Most of these modest landowners had come with little capital; settled for marginal lands; and made deals to pay back mortgages with grains, cattle, or cloth.

Shubael Clark made such a deal in 1809 when he added to his acre-

age in Hinesburgh by buying an adjacent 100-acre lot in New Huntington from a Richmond man and agreed to pay him back over the next
three years in cattle or wheat.[53] Newly cleared Vermont lands produced
twenty to thirty bushels of wheat per acre, and settlers often used the
first crops to pay off early debts from buying land and seeds. Shubael
Clark was able to do just that, paying off his debt in three years. The
new plot in Huntington expanded his acreage considerably, but the family cultivated few of those acres; as was the rural tradition, they used
the rest for grazing their animals and woodlots for fuel. People traveling through the forests knew they were approaching a farmhouse when
they found cows grazing among the trees.

By the 1810s, both of the founding families of the Hill had grown and
were prospering. Their increasing numbers helped make Hinesburgh
2.5 percent black, according to the federal census report. However, the
enumerators did not list family names that year, as they did for whites;
they listed only one line item: thirty-two "other persons" in town. This
shorthand method of enumeration clearly shows that blacks were not
considered important as individuals or families, only as a class of laborers to be managed.[54] However, these people are an important part of
Vermont's pioneering heritage. And now some of those thirty-two people, those living on the Hill, can be revealed: Hannah and Prince Peters
had four children, Josephus, Samuel 2nd, Electa, and Sarah.[55] Shubael
and Violet Clark had five children at that time: Lewis, Almira, Sybil,
Hiram, and Harriet.[56]

By 1808, changes are apparent in the Clark and Peters households.
Both families had added to their livestock. The Clark farm had four
cows, two oxen, and three horses grazing on twelve improved acres,
proving they had been very busy clearing the virgin forest.[57] Lewis,
fourteen years old by then, would have been helping by this time, but
Shubael likely did much of the earliest work alone (or possibly with
the help of the Peterses). The Peters farm at the bottom of the Hill had
seven cows and two oxen on their ten improved acres.[58] Shubael and
Prince likely rented their oxen and horses to others with none, as farmers in nearby Cornwall did.[59] Hannah, Violet, and the children certainly
could have been earning cash or credit to pay taxes or buy staples by
making and selling butter to their neighbors. These data about their
lives put the Clarks and Peterses squarely in the middle-class bracket
of farmers who owned at least ten acres and double the stock of poorer
farmers, who owned only one or two cows or horses.[60]

These families exhibited the qualities of other people of color in New England. The men and women seemed to be "virtuous and hardworking farmer(s), sober and honest, combining small mixed farming with a jack-of-all-trades search for economic security."[61] On this Hill, they had found a secure space and a middle-class lifestyle by early in the nineteenth century.

### Civic Life in Hinesburgh

Whereas none of the men was paying poll taxes in 1799, all three were by 1808, a significant year for people of color in the United States. On January 1, the ban on the importation of slaves into the United States went into effect. Blacks all over the Northern states gathered in prayer meetings to celebrate the anticipated freedom that would follow for all those enslaved. This was a moment of heightened hopes for people of color, many of whom believed the end of the slave trade signaled the final deliverance from slavery.[62] These expectations carried with them a soaring optimism and an anticipation of equality and may have led the men from the Hill to claim the precious right of suffrage. If one of their goals in moving to Vermont had been to become civically engaged as free people, they had reached that goal by the year the legal slave trade ended. On town meeting day, therefore, there would have been some black faces among the Hinesburgh voters.

Because of networks of exchange within rural communities, it was hardly necessary to go into town. So town meeting day was one of the few times people left the farm neighborhood. If they were white, they no doubt looked forward to socializing in town. However, because of the racialized world and the prejudicial behavior of many whites toward people of color, we cannot automatically assume the people of the Hill were welcomed into town life in early Vermont. The Clarks and Peterses must have approached whites in town warily, not knowing how they or their children would be treated. This was an extra stress for black families.[63]

Today when there are public discussions of race and conflict in the United States, deliberations often turn to the behavior of people of color as the issue, not the behavior of whites. However, the "white problem" has been a theme of black discourse for hundreds of years.[64] Many people of color have claimed that the behavior of whites toward blacks was abnormal human conduct. By the 1790s, whites in New England circulated jokes and "outlandish cartoons to ridicule free blacks and demonstrate their social inferiority."[65] Black thinkers of the time often asserted that white behavior toward blacks was "decisively shaped by the exercise of power . . . the experience of dominating . . . the need to dispossess, subjugate."[66] One way to discover white Vermonters' attitudes toward blacks in the eighteenth century is to examine the legislation of the time.

Laws successfully passed, those that failed, and those that were ignored provide valuable insights into the mores and conduct of some of the inhabitants whom the Clarks and Peterses would have met in town. In 1777, Vermont (then an independent republic) outlawed adult slavery. In 1786, the legislature passed a law making it illegal to sell enslaved people out of state at their age of majority. Obviously slaveholders had used that loophole to profit by selling their servants where slavery was still legal rather than lose them to freedom when they became adults. Five years later, some citizens, obviously angered by the new law, tried to repeal it. The proposed act stated: "Be it further enacted by the authority aforesaid that an Act Intitled an act to prevent the Sale & Transportation of Negroes and Molattoes out of this State passed Octbr 30 1786 be and hereby is repealed."[67] The repeal failed, but the Hinesburgh representative, Lemuel Bostwick, had supported it.

In 1791, after gradual emancipation had begun in all the New England states, the Vermont legislature attempted to pass an act that pertained to "transient, idle, impotent and poor Persons," specifically "Negroes."[68] Lemuel Bostwick also supported this, which read:

> Whereas Diverse Negroes Molattoes and persons held to Service in Other States & Kingdoms . . . frequently Escape from their Masters or owners and Run into this State and Doubts have arisen Whither they be not thereby discharged from Such Service or Labor — It is hereby Enacted by the General Assembly of the State of Vermont that the master of any Negroe Molattoe or of any person held to Service or labor in any of the United States . . . are hereby impowered favorably to take Such Negroe Molattoe or person thus held to Service as aforesaid and the Same to Convey to the place from Whence they Escaped.[69]

This was Vermont's first attempt at a fugitive slave law, and anyone caught hindering a master from retrieving the said person would have to pay the "Sum of Eight pounds Lawful Money." The bill was defeated fifty-nine to twenty-seven. However, Bostwick's support of the bill gives us insight into the beliefs of some of the powerful families of Hines-burgh and helps us imagine what the Peterses and Clarks faced in their earliest days in the town, contending with people who viewed them as inferior simply for their color.

Although these pioneers lived in a society where many saw them as inferior beings and sometimes as property, this narrative is not one of oppression. In post-Revolutionary America, they did as people had done for thousands of years—they uprooted themselves and migrated to find a space of their own to control. This is the story of the biracial community they created isolated from the town, where cross-racial col-laboration worked for a time. On this Hill they found a "blanket of pro-tection against the perils of freedom"—shielding them from a world that assumed they were not fully members of the human race.[70] They had staked out firm ground on which to establish new cultural traditions founded on freedom. The first generation of Peterses and Clarks charted a new world, both literally and figuratively. Their lives illustrate how people whose hopes for ending slavery in the Revolutionary era had been crushed nevertheless asserted their own identities in the cultural landscape of Vermont.

At the same time, other families of color, who would eventually join a network of people connected to the Hill, were putting down roots else-where in Vermont. In the Rutland-Pittsford area of central Vermont, Richard and Abigail Langley were also part of a small farming neigh-borhood of relatives. In 1794, their son, William Page Langley, was born, who later married Almira Clark of Hinesburgh and moved to the Hill.[71]

In 1810, a family of color in Massachusetts[72] had a baby boy named Charles Edwards. He would eventually make his way to Hinesburgh and into the heart of Sarah Peters, Prince and Hannah's first daughter. About the same time, a girl was born in the nearby Vermont town of Ferrisburgh; this was Pamelia Storms. Her parents, Primas and Pame-lia, had originally come to Vermont from New York with their owner, a man named Platt Rogers. Pamelia, a two-year-old in 1810, later married Lewis Langley on the Hill, the son of Almira Clark and William Lang-ley. In her will she referred to Lewis as "my dear husband."

Peaks and Valleys on the Hill Farms,
1810s–1820s

> People harvesting
> Work together unaware
> of racial problems
> — A Japanese immigrant in the early twentieth century
>   (quoted in Ronald T. Takaki, *Iron Cages*)

> Matilda Dorsey buys the "butter of Miss Clark" for 58 cents and the
> "Butter of Wm Langley" for 50 cents.
> — Nathaniel Dunham, in Hinesburgh, Vermont,
>   General Store Day Book

From statehood to 1810, Vermont was the fastest-growing state in the
union, increasing from a population of 85,000 in 1791 to about 218,000.
Most migrants were farmers, and many, like the Clarks and Peterses,
made permanent homes in the Green Mountains. However, as the once-
thick forest humus was burned, leached, and cropped off, the soil lost its
fertility, and farms became less productive. As a result, Vermont became
the slowest-growing state after 1810, as many farmers and entrepreneurs
migrated to more productive locales. At the same time, the black population in Vermont continued to grow until the 1820s, when it dropped
for the first time.[1] The people of the Hill community not only stuck
it out, but also increased their numbers by birth and marriage. They
seemed to have found a stable place to raise their children and safely
negotiate the racism of the wider society.

During the early decades of the nineteenth century, while the Clarks
and Peterses were clearing, settling, and increasing their families on the

Hill, societal racism and inferiority theories steadily increased. By the end of the 1820s, "biological theories positing the natural inferiority of persons of African descent would come to be embraced as time-honored truths by most white Americans."[2] However, African Americans did not quietly acquiesce to this new image foisted upon them; they fought it at every turn with well-established lines of argument emphasizing that all humans came from the same roots and were equal under God. By the late 1820s, however, color phobia had become so ubiquitous that even many antislavery whites believed the inferiority theories. After fighting the idea of blacks and whites being of different blood and different natures for so long, some blacks began to acquiesce to the idea of differences between the races — but they questioned whether it was the whites that might be the inferior race. David Walker raised the issue in his 1829 "Appeal to the Coloured Citizens of the World" when he wrote, "The whites have always been an unjust, unmerciful, avaricious and bloodthirsty set of beings, always seeking power and authority."[3]

In their fight against mounting racism, people of color in the North never stopped seeking and celebrating freedom and equality wherever they could find it, and they focused on events that proved they should be included in the "common civic identity" of the nation.[4] Although their 1808 hopes for abolition after the legal slave trade ended were dashed, they discovered a significant occasion elsewhere in the Western Hemisphere to commemorate: Toussaint L'Overture's Declaration of Independence for Haiti and the establishment of the world's first black republic. The Hill people may have celebrated this event in their own way, since we find two January baptisms into the Hinesburgh Baptist Church — not the best time for total immersions in Vermont — but a good time to celebrate freedom and acceptance into civic and religious life.

There were some, however, who preferred to abandon what they saw as a losing battle against racism and immigrated to Haiti and Upper Canada (present-day southern Ontario), preferring to stay in the hemisphere of their birth. One such migrant was Prince Saunders, originally an indentured servant born in Thetford, Vermont, about 1775. After gaining an education and teaching in Boston, he moved to Haiti at the end of the Haitian Revolution to help improve the state of education, health, and government in the republic. He became Haiti's first attorney general and was the author of the first Haitian criminal code. In 1816, he published the papers of the new republic, explaining that he felt the need to do this because of increasing inferiority theories. For a few individuals, he wrote, their

> habitual labor is the perversion, (and as far as they are able,) the absolute destruction of every object which has a tendency to show that the Blacks possess . . . that portion of natural intelligence which the Beneficent Father of all ordinarily imparts to his children; . . . such persons have endeavored to impress the public with the idea, that [our] official documents . . . are not written by Black Haytians themselves; but that they are either written by Europeans in this country, or by some who, *they say*, are employed for that purpose; . . . I upon my honour declare, . . . that all the public documents are written by . . . black men, or men of colour. . . . Let them dispute, if they please, the existence of our intellectual facilities, our little or no aptness for the arts and sciences, whilst we reply to those irresistible arguments, and prove to the impious, by facts and by examples, that the blacks, like the whites, are men, and like them are the works of a Divine Omnipotence![5]

While black intellectuals in the Americas were fighting inferiority theories with speeches and publications, the farm families on the Hill were cementing their place on the cultural landscape of rural Vermont as farmers, as civically engaged members of the wider community, and as members of the Hinesburgh Baptist Church. They were proving by example that they were men and women who were equally the "works of a Divine Omnipotence."

### The Clarks at the Top of the Hill

Violet and Shubael Clark had come to Vermont from southern New England. Like others from that area, they carried with them the Calvinist religious beliefs of the Congregational and Baptist churches. Although many in the pre-Revolutionary period resisted an established religion, a 1783 Vermont legislative order allowed town governments to tax residents for an official church and the support of its minister. As a result, established Vermont towns replicated the conservative religions of southern New England in the early days, even though non-Calvinists called it "ecclesiastical tyranny."[6]

One clue as to people's status was their church membership. The first and the official church in the center of the town of Hinesburgh was

Congregational, organized in 1789, to which the elites of the town belonged. None of the Clark or Peters families was a member. However, in 1810 the Vermont legislature dropped its 1783 order, which left the way open for other denominations, and Baptists in Hinesburgh organized their first church that year. Like the nearby Congregational church, this church was conservatively Calvinist. Its original articles of faith stated that all people are "in sin and an Enemy to the Reconciliation to God" and that God will call those chosen "out of an Estate of Sin Misery and Death, into a State of Salvation."[7]

Its earliest members were seven men and eleven women from Monkton, who brought a letter from their minister attesting that they were of good character and in good standing with the Monkton Baptist Church. The Clarks, also from Monkton, were not among these first members, but they joined soon after. Abby Hemenway's *Vermont Historical Gazetteer* described the Hinesburgh Baptist church this way: "Many of its early members were men of good ability, strong character, and earnest piety. Among these might be mentioned . . . Asa Moon, Philo Ray, Shubael Clark (colored)."[8]

The church records show that on September 2, 1815, "Shewbil Clark Came forward to this Chh [church] wishing to become a member with us, and after giving the reason of his hope to the Satisfaction of the Chh and being Baptized by Elder Green was rec'd into fellowship with us."[9] Four months later, "Vilot Clark came to the Church requesting to be a member [and] giving Satisfactory Evidence of her adoption into the Divine family, the Chh Recd her into fellowship."[10] "Evidence" of Violet's adoption would have been baptism by total immersion. Since this was January, she may have been baptized earlier in the fall, but a January immersion could have combined the celebrations of freedom for slaves in Haiti with freedom from sin as a newly reborn Baptist.

The Clark children, Harriet and Lewis, were baptized and accepted into the church during the spring of 1817, along with Lorany Yaw, a white woman who would become a friend of the Clarks and who offered a letter of recommendation from her church in Ira. Later, Sybil, Phoebe, and Charles Clark also joined. The Baptist Church had long reached out to people regardless of social class, and the Hinesburgh church obviously disregarded race as well, an enlightened stance for the time.[11]

There is some evidence that in the Hinesburgh Congregational church people of color had to sit in the balcony, but no one from the Hill ever belonged to that church. John Lewis, who wrote a biography of Charles

Bowles, the black Free Will Baptist minister in nearby Huntington, took churches to task for tolerating Negro pews and their "wicked intolerance" toward blacks.[12] Doctors of divinity of all the churches, he wrote, "argue the divine right of the American people to sustain [slavery, a] system of robbery, concubinage, bigamy, adultery and every violation of the moral decalogue against the African race."[13] Given this, it is no mystery why the Hill people avoided the Congregational church.

It is unusual, however, to find people of color among the congregants of a Calvinist church. William Piersen and others have claimed that Christianity was not emotionally or intellectually satisfying to blacks until the excitement of the Great Awakenings. At the same time, Piersen maintains that a tiny elite became assimilated Christians who believed in the promise that God would bring down the slaveholders and raise up the enslaved and deprived of the earth.[14] The Clarks' membership in the Baptist church in Hinesburgh may well signal the privileged status of people integrated into white society, as well as their belief (and the church's belief) in slavery as a sin against God.

Despite the racism of the wider society, there is no evidence that members of this Baptist church discriminated against its black brothers and sisters. All evidence is to the contrary. They were accepted into Christian fellowship apparently on an equal basis. Evidence of Shubael's being accepted, as well as his abilities and piety, is the fact that over his almost twenty years of membership, he was appointed to many committees to visit and investigate white people who had been reported for their poor behavior. In the spring of 1818, the church appointed Asa Moon and Shubael to visit two members to investigate their absence from meetings.

In the racialized world of the early nineteenth century, white people had a strong "desire not to be judged by those who were not white."[15] It was a time when people of color in this country were "forced to defend their claims to manhood, as well as their place in the human family," and yet Shubael Clark was sent on missions into white households to return them to the church.[16] In the town of Hinesburgh, the members of this Baptist church apparently had no problem sending a pious black man to judge wayward whites. Perhaps the black intellectuals of the time had convinced some white people of the truth of their counterstereotype: black people as a "redeemer race" who suffered for the redemption of America's sins, people with "gentle virtues" who were more moral and more pious than Anglo-Saxons.[17]

Later that summer, Shubael was on another committee with Brother Moon — this time to investigate a white woman concerning contradictory reports about her. Visits to her continued for one year as the committee asked for postponement after postponement to make further inquiries. Finally, Moon and Clark reported that it would be best to expel Sister Brand because she had been "railing against the chh, against particular members of the church . . . and has not seen fit to come to chh after being often and repeatedly requested."[18] The two men had tried their best over a long period of time.

Neither Shubael's work within the church nor the practice of democracy by the people on the Hill at the ballot box was "shadow politics" of the type carried out by urban blacks elsewhere in the North. Sociologists define shadow politics as "an alternate universe of political activity . . . in which powerless people act in place of and in conscious opposition to prevailing political practices. [This includes] the creation of parallel black political practices."[19] Voting records in Hinesburgh and Shubael's committee work show black men thoroughly integrated into the political and religious workings of church and town with no need for an alternate universe within which to exercise civic and religious rights.

In addition to Brothers Moon and Clark's church work, they also had a longstanding relationship through land. From 1795 until 1807, they bought and sold land at the top of the Hill from and to each other. Moon's name never appears on a map, and his first appearance in the census was in 1810. At that time, he seemed to be living closer to the Peterses near the bottom of the Hill. The facts of their relationship at church and their land exchanges beg the question: Were the families friends? There would be little question about friendly relations if they were all people of color or all white, but because of racial differences in a racialized society, we must examine the evidence more closely.

Hannah and Asa Moon had five daughters and two sons born in Hinesburgh from 1802 to 1815, some close in age to the Clark children.[20] Being on many of the same church committees, the men spent quite a bit of time together, likely socially as well. Moreover, the fact that Ruth Brown, a white member, eventually married Lewis Clark, Shubael and Violet's oldest son, is evidence of white-black sociable relations within the church. Hannah and Violet doubtless helped each other in this rural economy, which was traditional in farming communities.

Although Shubael's only apparent leadership post was within the church, Asa Moon also became a town selectman and school trustee by

1816.[21] Perhaps their children attended school together, but there are no extant early records for the school near the Clark land. The little school-house on the Huntington side of the Hill, however, was biracial, so we can assume that the one near the Clarks was too, since from later records we know the Clark children were literate. It seems that the Clarks had found not just a space to control, but also friends on the Hill through Violet and Shubael's membership in the church.

Shubael was a leader in the Baptist church and often mentioned in its records, but others from the Hill, in addition to Violet, belonged as well. Both Caroline and Calista Peters were baptized and voted into fellowship during the early 1820s. Their exact relationship to Samuel and Prince is unclear, but Caroline bought part of lot 83 from Samuel in 1830 and owned it for over thirty years, until her children sold it at her death. Calista later married and lived at the bottom of the Hill with her family. Another black couple who joined the church during this time is William and Almira Langley; Almira was the daughter of Shubael and Violet: William and "his partner Alma Langly [*sic*] presented their letters of commendation from Rutland" and were "received into our particular fellowship" in June 1825.[22]

As a youngster, William Langley had lived in Pittsford with his parents, Richard and Abigail, on the "Bebee lot," also known as the "Richard Langley farm."[23] William bought the farm in February 1816 from George Langley, likely an uncle. Called the "year with no summer," it was a devastating time for farmers, as cold weather and killing frosts plagued them during every month of the summer.

Exactly a year later, William mortgaged the farm—undoubtedly to buy seeds and feed for his cattle—they most certainly did not have much laid by from that horrible summer.[24] He apparently had better luck the next two years and fully discharged the mortgage, paying two notes of $75 apiece. By the time he finished paying the mortgage, he had met Almira Clark. Exactly how they were introduced to each other is unknown; however, from the marriage patterns of people from the Hill, it seems that there was a wide network through which people of color met each other.

The Langleys married on October 10, 1821, in Hinesburgh. The fall was a good time for marriages—the root vegetables still needed digging and apples needed to be dried or made into cider and sauce—but most of the harvest was likely in by then. The Justice of the Peace, Edmund Baldwin, officiated at the wedding, even though Almira's parents and siblings belonged to the Baptist church.[25] Baldwin was, however, a fellow Baptist and had been on committees with Shubael. He was likely happy to officiate at the marriage of Brother Shubael and Sister Violet's daughter.

The Langleys lived on the Rutland farm for the first two or three years of their marriage, and their first son, Lewis, was born there in 1823. Their second child, Henry Clark, was born in Huntington the next year, so Almira had moved back to the Hill by then.[26] There is evidence that they had built a house near Shubael and Violet's home on the Clark land.[27] Whether or not William was there permanently yet is not clear, because he did not sell the Rutland farm, "75 acres plus 49 rods," until January 1825.[28] Later that year, William and Almira joined the Baptist church of their parents.

Not until April of 1826 did William buy fifty mortgaged acres in Huntington on the southerly line of Hinesburgh. Milton G. Bostwick and Erastus Bostwick, two white founding fathers of Hinesburgh, witnessed the deal. William had to pay the note in four payments by October 1, 1829, in "good mercheantable meat cattle no bulls nor stags" or by January 1830 in grain.[29] He paid off the mortgage in full. By the time the Langleys were paying off the note, their third child, Newell Cyrus, was born. This time the birth was registered in Hinesburgh.

It must have been a profoundly gratifying experience for Shubael and Violet Clark to be surrounded by their children and grandchildren in the space they had created. Because Northern slave masters had usually needed only one or two servants or laborers and lacked quarters to house more, they discouraged enslaved women from marrying and usually sold pregnant women or sold their infants immediately after birth. Thus, grandparenthood was something few blacks ever knew in the North. Yet the Clarks, and others of the Revolutionary era, gloried in several generations of family life. This may have allowed them to continue fam-

---

❧ *Almira Clark and William Langley Family*

LANGLEYS in Hinesburgh and Huntington:
  Almira Clark (b. 1797, Hinesburgh, d. 1850, Hinesburgh) married
    William Langley (b. 1794, Rutland, d. 1876, Williston)
  Seven children born in Vermont, six on the Hill: Lewis, Henry,
    Newell, Jane, Jeremiah, Loudon, and perhaps Mitchell

FIGURE 2.1 Huntington District 8 schoolhouse. The building has been preserved near the bottom of the Hill on the Huntington side.

ily customs from West Africa if traditions had been passed down to them from other African-descended people.[30] In West Africa, grandparents could check parental authority over children — and children often appealed harsh treatment to them.[31] We can imagine the Langley boys crossing the road, crying to Violet and asking her to overrule a severe punishment from their parents. The benefits of such a close-knit family relationship may have been what held the family together long after white settlers abandoned their hill farms for the cities and towns.

Almira and William were surely grateful to have the boys to help them run the farm. Their first priority for their children, however, was their schooling. While urban blacks elsewhere in New England formed their own schools, children in Vermont went to biracial schools. Doing well in school was one way to prove to the world that the races were equal, not only in the eyes of God, but also in their natural abilities. From 1828 to 1832, the Langley boys were among the scholars attending the District 8 schoolhouse on the Huntington side of the Hill.[32] The thirty-six to thirty-eight students attending the small school along with the Langley boys were from families representing the entire social spectrum of Huntington at the time, from the small farmers to the richest in town. There are no records revealing how the students got along or

if the black students were discriminated against, but no one was block-
ing their way to a common school education. Later in the century we
see the outstanding results of this education in the Langley's youngest
son, Loudon.[33]

### The Peterses at the Bottom of the Hill

While the Clarks and Langleys were busy expanding their numbers at
the top of the Hill, the Peterses were having their ups and downs at the
foot of the Hill. Their experiences ranged from "bodily infirmities" for
Prince, to legal troubles for the elder Samuel, to service in the War of
1812 for Samuel 2nd.[34]

Jefferson's 1807–09 embargo prohibiting trade with British Canada
overshadowed the early part of the century. Most Vermonters evaded
the law, since Quebec was the major destination for Vermont exports.
Some saw disobeying the law as an act of good citizenship for the preservation of their families and the economy of Vermont.[35] Because of the
embargo, when war broke out in 1812 there was much sentiment against
it in the Champlain Valley, and few aided the war effort at the beginning. Most laboring men would rather earn eleven dollars per month
than risk their lives for the five dollars per month they received for
enlisting. Many merchants grew rich, however, smuggling goods to the
British in Canada or selling products to the 2,000–3,000 American soldiers stationed in Burlington who needed rations (meat and bread),
drink, and clothing. We do not know how the people of the Hill felt
about the war at the beginning, but they evidently did not participate in
many smuggling operations, since their economic status did not change
during that time.[36]

However, we do know young Samuel Peters's feelings by 1814.[37]
That fall, 11,000 British regulars and sixteen war vessels with ninety-
two guns began their southward movement on Lake Champlain toward
their target of New York City. With such a clear and present danger,
Vermonters put their differences aside and volunteered to fight the inva-
sion. One of those who enlisted was Samuel, who served in Captain
Stone's company in September 1814.[38] He and other "heroic Green
Mountain volunteers . . . set partisanship aside and fought together
against British Commander Sir George Prevost at the Battle" of Plattsburgh on the western side of Lake Champlain.[39]

In a chapter on the "Condition And Prospects Of Colored Americans" in his 1855 book *The Colored Patriots of the American Revolution,* William Cooper Nell wrote about the War of 1812 and claimed that the "victory upon Champlain has been well-known to have been achieved, in part, by the valor of colored men."[40] Master Commandant Perry, on Lake Erie, had complained directly to the secretary of the Navy that Commodore Chauncey on Lake Champlain had sent him "a motley set, blacks, soldiers, and boys" to defend the Great Lakes.[41] Commodore Chauncey answered his complaint in the following letter to Perry written from on board the *General Pike* off Burlington Bay in Vermont on July 13, 1813:

> SIR, — I regret that you are not pleased with the men sent you by Messrs. Champlin and Forrest; for, to my knowledge, a part of them are not surpassed by any seamen we have in the fleets; and I have yet to learn, that the color of the skin, or the cut and trimmings of the coat, can affect a man's qualifications or usefulness. I have nearly fifty blacks on board of this ship, and many of them are among my best men; and those people you call soldiers have been to sea from two to seventeen years, and I presume that you will find them as good and useful as any men on board of your vessel, — at least, if I can judge by comparison, for those which we have on board this ship are attentive and obedient and, as far as I can judge, many of them excellent seamen; at any rate, the men sent to Lake Erie have been selected with a view of sending a fair proportion of petty officers and seamen, and I presume upon examination, it will be found they are equal to those upon this lake.[42]

While it is not clear exactly what part Samuel played in the battles on the lake, he did participate in the war in Vermont's Champlain Valley, following in the military tradition started by his father in the Revolution. Military service had always been a chance for men of color to prove their courage and their manhood, and Samuel and others did not shrink from that opportunity in this war against Great Britain. We know he came back to the Hill after his service because Prince wrote in his Revolutionary pension application that he was supporting him in 1818.

After the war, Britain flooded the country with cheap goods to eliminate the competition from new factories that had popped up in the United States during the war. The effect on Vermont was devastating, with prices dropping and many new businesses closing. It seemed to

have had little effect on farmers in the northern part of the state, however, as the trade in farm goods between Vermont and Canada actually increased due to the thousands of British soldiers still stationed in
Canada who needed to be fed.[43] Unfortunately, the 1816 year with no
summer followed, reducing many families to eating only berries and
roots and sending disheartened farmers out of the state to find a better
climate. Nevertheless, the Hill people stayed—they had been through
tough times before and would make it through these with the support
of family. But Prince Peters needed help.

Prince had entered into an indenture, or formal contract, in 1810
with a white man who owned land near the Peterses' twenty improved
acres. Prince rented land near Samuel's house in which Prince and his
family were living. In 1817, Prince sold the rental deed back for ten
cents. He was struggling with his finances and his health, and in 1818
he applied for a pension for his Revolutionary War service.[44] In his pension records, filed when he was close to sixty, Prince states, "I follow
the occupation of farmer, but owing to old age and bodily infirmities, I
am unable to succeed."[45] White neighbors John Eldridge and Edmund
Baldwin, who had officiated at the marriage of the Langleys, testified
that Prince "by reason of many misfortunes, is reduced to a poor and
penniless Situation and actually stands in kneed of assistance from his
country. we further say that we firmly believe him to be an honest industrious and peaceable citizen and would not apply for relief if he did not
think himself Justly entitled to the Same."[46]

Honest . . . industrious . . . peaceable . . . important qualities among
the Calvinists of New England. If he had shown any sign of "disorder" in
the Yankee sense of the word, he would not have had this testimony from
his neighbors. The family had claimed the quiet, rural economy as its
own and had negotiated a measure of respect within the community.

The pension record also gives us a window into the Peterses' home
life. Prince said that he must support his four children: Samuel, twenty-
two; Cephus, seventeen; Electa, fourteen; and Sarah, seven. He never
mentions his wife, Hannah. It seems that one of his many misfortunes
had been losing her. How many had died before her? The spacing of the
children—sometimes with five to seven years between them—indicates
that they may have lost children in between; the normal spacing at this
time would have been every two years. The tragedy of losing children
was common among families in the nineteenth century. Some archaeological studies say that the rural houses of blacks were small with lim-

ited space for their large families.[47] The crowding caused unhealthy conditions in which infections could spread easily. However, these conditions were not confined to households of people of color. Raemsch and Bouchard found that the nineteenth century had "general ill health, pestilence, and high mortality" regardless of race.[48] Their analysis of the bones in a cemetery of a white family in rural New York showed poor nutrition and exposure to many infections through unsanitary conditions. Combined with cold and drafty houses and poor medical care, high infant mortality was to be expected.

The bones in the Raemsch and Bouchard study also showed many diseases such as periodontal disease, scarlet fever (from contaminated milk), diarrhea (from contaminated water), small pox, cholera, typhoid, diphtheria, and tuberculosis. All of this points to a high mortality rate in general among rural inhabitants, regardless of ethnicity. One of these diseases may have led to Hannah's death. Perhaps, as some have suggested, Hannah and her children lie in the "old Negro burying ground" at the top of the Hill on Clark land. But that was miles away up a steep hill;[49] more likely, the Peterses had a family plot on their own land at the bottom of the Hill, hidden away in a peaceful spot near their home on lot 83, which has not been highly developed to this day.

Prince also wrote in his pension application that he owned seven cows, one yearling steer, three sheep, one plowshare, one sow and six pigs, one small mule, one table, four chairs, one handsaw, one milk pail, and a few other items that are too difficult to decipher. The material items were few—he was not a rich man—but living in Samuel's house allowed the family to share what they needed. The family had plenty of milk, butter, and cheese, along with sheep's wool and flax growing nearby to make woolen and linen clothing. Hannah, if still living, would have been in charge of producing all the goods and selling some of them. The men would have slaughtered some of the pigs in early winter for the family's consumption during the cold months and sold the rest for a good price. Samuel 2nd and Josephus were fully grown by this time, so Prince and Samuel 1st had plenty of help with the field labor, which generated mostly feed for the animals. By 1818, the elder Samuel was being taxed for two cows, two oxen, and fifteen improved acres, so collectively they had enough land to till for the family's needs and oxen to rent to neighbors.[50]

With Hannah gone, one problem would have been the work needed in the vegetable gardens and in the house, which was to turn raw materials into food and clothing for the family. The two young girls, Electa and Sarah, probably could not do that alone. We know that Prince remarried a woman named Eliza, because she later received a widow's dower from his estate. Who she was exactly, where she came from, and when they married are all a mystery at this point. However, Prince would have married as soon as he could in order to maintain the balance of work in the fields and housework so important to survival in this rural economy. In the 1830 census, Eliza is enumerated in Prince's household as simply a black female between thirty-six and fifty-five. Marrying at her age indicates she might have been a widow or formerly enslaved and married later in life. Prince was getting on in years by the 1820s, and marriage must have brought a measure of security to both of them, with children nearby to care for them in their old age.

Soon after Prince delivered his application, he began receiving a pension of eight dollars per month, surely a great help to the Peterses. Then another blow hit the family. In February 1820, the Constable of Hinesburgh arrived at the Peterses' house to tell them he was attaching the "goods, Chattles or Estate of Samuel Peters of Hinesburgh by order of J. M. Eldridge, Atty for the Creditor."[51] No one was home, so he left a copy of the order and a list of the lands "at the last and usual place of abode of the said Samuel lying on the table."[52]

In the complaint, Moses Sash of West Hartford, Connecticut, said that Samuel owed him $1,000 for "meat, drink, washing, lodging, and necessary apparel by the sd. Moses for the mother of the sd. Samuel . . . yet the defendant though often requested both wholly neglected and refuses to pay." If Peters did not have the possessions to attach, the constable was to "take his body (if he may be found in your precinct) and him safely keep, so that you have him to appear before the county court of Chittenden on the last Monday of February."[53]

At the court hearing, Moses's lawyer contended that Samuel was "intending to deceive and defraud" him. The decision, rendered in June, went against Samuel. However, he was ordered to pay only $300 damages to Moses plus $23.02, which was the cost of the suit. This time, the deputy was ordered to "safely keep" him until he paid with his "goods chattels or land."[54] The Superior Court for Chittenden County had no record of Samuel being put in jail for nonpayment of the debt, so it's impossible to tell if Samuel spent any time in jail, but it was certainly a common occurrence in those days. He paid eventually, since he was home by 1824 and buying and selling land as before.

According to the U.S. pension records, Moses Sash had fought for Massachusetts in the Revolution as a private during the same years that Prince had: 1780 to 1783. He had enlisted at Cummington, a small town in the same county as Northampton, where Prince had enlisted, and fought in the Massachusetts Seventh Regiment. He applied for and received a pension in 1818. In August 1820, at age sixty-four, he appeared before the Court of Common Pleas in Hartford, Connecticut, to swear that he had no property, and since 1818 he had "not disposed of any property so as to diminish it."[55] He also swore that he did not have "any property or securities, contracts, or debts due to me," despite the fact that he had sued Samuel Peters in February 1820. He also stated that he was a day laborer but could "labor very little" and needed to support his wife and her mother, who was ninety-seven.[56] If this is the same Moses, it answers the question of why Samuel's mother was living in Hartford, Connecticut. Mrs. Sash was Samuel's sister.[57]

It leaves other questions unanswered, however: Was Samuel originally from Massachusetts as was Prince and Moses Sash? If Samuel and Prince were brothers, why didn't he sue both of them? Samuel 1st remains a mysterious character, since I have no early records for him, nor was he ever named in any census reports for Vermont. This suit against Samuel only deepens his inscrutability. However, one thing is certain — losing Hannah to death and perhaps Samuel to jail surely put a strain on the family, since someone had to take up the labor slack.

Samuel's trouble with the law and Prince's financial difficulties illustrate the widening gap between socioeconomic groups during the first half of the nineteenth century. Some farmers were getting richer and expanding, while others were selling out. Farmers who could afford it began a shift away from small family farms to larger ones with more room for grazing animals, especially sheep. In 1824, the United States had instituted a protective tariff on wool, making the raising of merino sheep a profitable enterprise. This was an opportunity of which both the Clarks and Peterses took advantage.

The merinos, brought to Vermont from Spain illegally during their revolution, were popular in Vermont because their cleft lips made it easy for them to browse in the stony soil. The Hinesburgh grand list illustrates the popularity of sheep, as listers count them for the first time in 1824. That year the Peterses seemed to be in better shape financially — the pension money must have helped. They bought the east part of lot 83 from a Middlebury man, who held the deed until they paid $183.57

in three promissory notes.[58] The Peterses apparently needed more land for their twenty-eight sheep grazing on the bottom of the hill. They also owned two oxen and three horses, which gave them the opportunity to rent the animals to neighbors who had none. All of this indicates they were hanging on to a lower-middle-class lifestyle.

In 1821, Lewis Clark, twenty-seven, began to show up in public records. This was about the age when young nineteenth-century men asserted their own identity.[59] He bought fifty mortgaged acres on the southerly line of Huntington and was to repay the note in three years with "mercheantable cattle" or "mercheantable grain," which he did.[60] He was still living at home, however, and so this land was surely used for the benefit of the extended family as a woodlot or to graze cows and sheep. By 1827, the Clarks had also joined the sheep culture with forty-five sheep on top of the Hill along with their nine cows and two horses on their forty improved acres. The family farm was now supporting eleven people, and the Clarks were doing fine with a small herd of merinos and plenty of grazing land.

The next year, the Clarks' neighbors, the Yaws, had joined the shift to sheep and owned twenty. By comparison, Erastus Bostwick, a well-known early white founder of the town, owned thirty sheep by 1829, and the various Wray families at the bottom of the Hill owned from thirty to eighty sheep. The black farmers on the hill were progressing with the changes in farming, raising wheat and merinos as some of their white neighbors did. They had shown they could successfully navigate the rural culture of this hillside and had built thriving farms that supported their expanding families.

### Economic Expansion and Black Voting Rights

These decades saw both the depression of the Vermont economy due to the War of 1812 and the rebound ushered in by the 1823 opening of the canal from Lake Champlain to New York City. The canal economy made the rest of the world a bit closer to the Hill, and we can see these connections in the 1827–1830 store accounts of Nathaniel Dunham in Hinesburgh. Using his book, one can paint a miniature of how life on the Hill was affected by the opening of U.S. trade with the Far East. The Peterses often bought Bohea tea, a black tea from China.[61] Prince sometimes bought camphor, which comes from a tree in Southeast Asia and was used in liniments to relieve the pain of rheumatism or injuries. At Prince's age, he likely had joint pains, which could be alleviated with a massage of camphor oil. These items sailed from Asia to New York City, then came by barge on the Hudson River, through the canal to Lake Champlain and into Burlington Bay. Eventually, they went into Dunham's wagon and then by horseback to the Clarks, the Peterses, and their neighbors.

The Dunham store account book not only illustrated global connections to the Hill, but also the local farm economy. We find the Clark and Langley women churning many extra pounds of butter on their farms and selling it to Dunham's store, not for cash, but for credit. In the spring of 1827, Shubael brought more than fifteen pounds of butter to Dunham's store for a credit of $1.88.[62] Shubael spent three cents on a little brandy before he returned home. In June, a white woman from town visited the store and bought the "Butter of Miss Clark," leaving a store credit of $1.62 for the Clark family.[63] She also bought the "Butter of Wm Langley" for 50 cents. Of course, Almira had churned the butter, likely with help from her mother. The labors of these women not only turned raw materials into useable items for the family—the typical job of women at this time—but also brought needed store credit and contributed to the local economy.

The account book also shows that Shubael's consumption of alcohol was not unusual on the Hill. As early as 1818, there was a still in a woodworking shop in Hinesburgh, for the commercial manufacture of liquor.[64] The Dunham accounts list gin, brandy, whiskey, wine, and rum, with brandy being the most popular. Even Elder Charles Bowles of the Free Will Baptist church stopped in for a quart of brandy now and then. Within four days of each other one May, Prince and Samuel Peters and Charles Bowles all came into Dunham's store to purchase alcohol. Prince bought a small amount of rum (along with salt and camphor); Bowles and Samuel bought a quart of brandy each; Bowles also bought salt and pins. Four months later, Prince bought more brandy and some tobacco, so they were not heavy drinkers of hard liquor, although like everyone else, they surely drank hard cider or maple ale every day.[65] Certainly alcoholism was not unknown, however; by 1828, Vermonters had established a Temperance Society to combat frequent drunkenness.

One occasion when the men might get together for a drink was on voting day. State elections were in September and town meetings in

February at this time. In the early years of the decade, interest in the new state's affairs was intense, and voter turnout throughout Vermont was high, 70–80 percent. Throughout these two decades, Samuel, Prince, and Josephus Peters; Shubael and Lewis Clark; and William Langley paid poll taxes and participated in their civic duty alongside their white neighbors by voting for representatives to the General Assembly and to Congress.[66] We can imagine Hannah Peters, Violet Clark, and Almira Langley bringing food to the town hall to share with the townspeople. The Clark men may have stopped at the Peters house at the bottom of the Hill to share a drink before continuing their journey home.

By the 1820s, voter turnout had fallen off to 30 percent at the most, because with the Federalist Party gone, only the Democratic Republicans were running for office. Presumably, one-party politics became boring. And yet we find the Peterses, Clarks, and William Langley all voting in both Vermont and town elections. Their sons, Samuel 2nd and Josephus Peters and Lewis Clark joined their fathers when they reached the age of majority. The Peters men and Shubael Clark also attended a special meeting on June 10, 1829, to vote for delegates for a convention meeting on June 26 called by the Council of Censors.[67] The racism of the wider country obviously did not keep them from exercising their voting rights. These were people who had fought to be able to participate in civic affairs as free men; they were not about to miss any opportunities.

Surely one of the topics of conversation among the men and women of the Hill, as well as politicians and activists elsewhere, was the issue of the spread of slavery. This was an important topic all over the state, and it certainly would have been on the men's minds as they rode into town in 1819 to vote for their representatives to state legislature. In reaction to the debate over whether or not to accept Missouri into the union as a slave state, the Vermont General Assembly of 1819–20 passed resolutions declaring slavery a moral and political evil. It also stated that the government had no right to introduce slavery into new territories. Nevertheless, the 1820 Missouri Compromise was passed, which made slavery illegal above the 36°30' north parallel except within the boundaries of Missouri. There was some comfort in that the U.S. territories would exclude slavery, but now more slave states could be added to the Union. Once again the hopes for ending the spread of slavery were dashed. It must have been a great disappointment to the people of the Hill.

Surely another disturbing development was the strengthening of the colonization movement, which proposed to send freed blacks to the Republic of Liberia in Africa. Many Northern whites favored the idea because they feared that blacks would inundate the Northern states. Both pro- and antislavery Vermonters started the first Colonization Society in the country in 1819. Many of Vermont's most prominent politicians, ministers (especially Congregational), and industrialists became actively involved in the society, which was the most successful and most active in New England.[68] Most blacks detested the idea, although some, including Vermonters, did immigrate to Liberia.[69] More typical were statements denouncing "all attempts to expatriate us from the land of our birth."[70]

## *Prejudice and Religion in Hinesburgh and Huntington*

Just how much the people of the Hill had to deal with prejudice and discrimination because of their color is not clear. Some of the evidence presented so far indicates that they had been accepted into the community as equals by their neighbors and fellow church members. That does not, of course, mean they were free from prejudice out of those settings. Another man of color, Charles Bowles, could shed light on this.

For twenty years, Bowles, a Free Will Baptist preacher, made Huntington, Vermont, his home, while he preached at revivals throughout the state. The early nineteenth century witnessed a burst of religious fervor known as the "Second Great Awakening."[71] Preachers exhorted people to increase their personal piety, rectify injustices, and relieve suffering. An outgrowth of this religiosity in the northeast was social activism, which spawned temperance, abolition, and suffrage movements. Charles Bowles was one of many minorities and women who were welcomed into the growing circle of revivalists who believed in the equality of all, regardless of race or gender. Although he did not live on the Hill, he lived and preached in close proximity, and his life provides a picture of the experiences of a man of color in northwestern Vermont during this time.

Originally a Calvinist Baptist in Wentworth, New Hampshire, Bowles switched to the Free Will denomination after his service in the Revolutionary War. Later he moved to Vermont with his wife, Mary, and three of their ten children. The 1810 order abolishing official town churches opened the way for multiple religions, making Vermont the first state in New England to separate church and state. As a result, many non-Calvinist religions, such as Methodists and Free Will Baptists, started to make inroads into the state. As other New England states followed suit, non-Calvinists rejoiced. "If the divine right of kings received a mighty overthrow on the plains of Lexington, Saratoga and Yorktown, the divine right of ecclesiastical tyranny and sanctified oppression received a mightier overthrow in the pulpits of New England," claimed Free Will Baptist John Lewis.[72] As missionaries began crisscrossing the state, competition among the many sects for the souls of Vermonters flourished. Bowles became a missionary for the Free Will Baptist Church, a competitor with the Calvinist Baptist church to which so many people from the Hill belonged.

In 1816, the family settled in Huntington, where Bowles "produced something of a stir in the way of making converts," notes a Huntington historian, apparently referring to his noisy revival meetings.[73] Although he had already been preaching for some time, he was ordained in Huntington. On November 26, 1817, public notice was given that "Brother Charles Bowles was this day set a part to the work of the Ministry by Ordination According to the New Testament and as such we recommend him to all people."[74] That same month, he organized the Free Will Baptist church in town. Henry Crocker, who wrote a history of Vermont Baptists, claimed that Bowles's "unblemished character and ability as a preacher won him confidence and gave him power" within the church.[75]

Bowles did not stay full-time in Huntington; instead, he became an itinerant preacher at revival meetings throughout the state and spent eighteen years traveling Vermont roads to convert people, start new churches, and visit wayward brothers and sisters. "His gift and manner of preaching was best adapted to an itinerant life," but he loved Huntington and made it his home base, buying land there in 1819.[76] In his journal, he talked about his "grove" in Huntington, where he went to get "his old gospel armor newly burnished, and prepared for heavenly warfare. . . . Away from manual and intellectual labor, his mind was free to soar aloft" in his grove, and he was able to "give himself anew to the great Redeemer."[77] At the same time, it was hard work maintaining the Huntington church. "No one but God knows the feelings in my heart in anxiety for the prosperity of that dear branch of God's Zion, and no one but God knows the groans and tears and prayers I offer for her spiritual interest."[78]

For eight of his nomadic years fighting for souls, he kept his journal. I never found a copy of it, so I had to rely on John Lewis, who wrote Bowles's biography in 1852. Apparently, Bowles met a lot of opposition in Hinesburgh and Huntington, both because of his beliefs and because he was a free man of color preaching to mostly whites. He often wrote about meeting with opposition from old-time Baptists and Methodists. He indicated that his revivals were "a shouting time of great power" and that some people were "tired with the noise of the meeting."[79] That tension was to be expected between the old and the new — between quiet, conservative Yankees and noisy gatherings that took place in usually peaceful meadows. It would be in keeping with Shubael's leadership in his church that he would have had words with Bowles about the clamor of the crowds and free-will issues.

With others there would be racial tensions as well. One account is from Hinesburgh, where Bowles often led "people down the banks of the beautiful lake in that town" to be baptized. Some men who disliked the fact he was preaching to whites decided to attack him after one revival meeting. They planned to tie him to a wooden horse and throw him into the lake. He was warned, however, and announced at the service that he knew of the plot and would not resist if men from the congregation could join him in the procession to the lake. He would sing and preach along the way and willingly let them tie him up when they got there. His courage broke the back of the mob, claimed Lewis.[80]

During an 1818 revival in Hinesburgh, a woman showed a strong dislike for Bowles and refused to listen to him and "severely censored others for going to hear the Nigger preach."[81] After this, he called on her, spoke to her about religion, and prayed for her as she angrily leaned against her window. Later that year in Huntington, he met more opposition. At Brother Pratt's house, "Satan presented himself" in the form of a "baser sort" of man who "disgraced the poor Indians" by appearing at the meeting dressed like them. They began to noisily disturb the meeting, "but such was the power of the gospel upon their guilty hearts, that they forebore to put into practice their hellish purposes."[82]

Bowles's biographer discusses color prejudice at length. Lewis asserts that Bowles often encountered "much cruel and bitter opposition" by Vermonters when entering a new place on account of his color. He says that there was deep-rooted prejudice against blacks, and even antislavery men did not like blacks preaching to whites. Others of a "baser sort" said they would not listen to a black person preach. "Little aristocrats" in all country villages imitate "city purse-proud nabobs" and turn up their noses at a black minister. One of these "cod-fish aristocrats" once invited Bowles to tea. They talked in the parlor until tea was served, then the man took Bowles into the kitchen to eat by himself. "Shame upon such nuisances of christianity; they are a stench in the nostrils of humanity to say nothing of religion."[83] If Bowles encountered such people in Hinesburgh and Huntington, we can safely assume that the people of the Hill had to contend with them as well. By 1830, "colorphobia" was so ubiquitous that even white antislavery people believed in the inferiority of blacks because of the "scientific racism" of the day.[84] It would have been hard for the people of the Hill to avoid such attitudes.

At the same time, Bowles made converts as well as friends in the towns. Interestingly, the people of color on the Hill were not among his converts, even though he preached near them many times. He wrote of attending monthly meetings at Brother Ross's house, where he baptized thirteen people, and he always visited there during his times in Huntington. We never learn Ross's first name, but the Ross family owned land in Huntington adjacent to the Clarks' land. In 1820, Bowles went to the "Hill neighborhood in Hinesburg and preached in the evening."[85] This could have been one of several hills, but perhaps one where he would meet other people of color.

At one time, he preached to a meeting of 300 at the schoolhouse where the Langley boys attended school, the District 8 schoolhouse on the Huntington side of the Hill. These revivals were generally camp meetings where people came for several days of preaching and uplift. The people from the top of Hill surely heard the noise of the meetings, but they were never swayed by the power of his revivals. Perhaps they were tempted but feared the stereotype of the disorderly black or were anxious of losing some of the respect they had built in town if they joined the new and noisy church. Also, being "old-time Baptists" was doubtless so much a part of them that they would not think of changing at this point in their lives, even to join a church started by a black neighbor. They had assimilated body and soul into another way of life.

Although Bowles talks about trials because of his color, "deep rooted prejudice being so rampant in the hearts and action of wicked men," he also says he made many converts and friends *because* of his color.[86] Lewis says he had a "natural sociability (and) warm Christian friendship (that) enabled him to enjoy the hospitality of every house where he stopped."[87] Bowles wrote about visiting friends in Hinesburgh who were making winter clothes for him, but his greatest pleasure was in returning to his home in Huntington. Friends there sometimes cut his grain for him and, of course, his grove was there. He says that Huntington was his "favorite spot (because) God had conquered it for him, putting down the host of opposition." He felt "as a father" toward all he baptized there, even those who had once been his enemies.[88] He goes so far as to say that Huntington was to him as Jerusalem was to the Jews. He evidently meant that Huntington was the site of his first church and the spiritual source for all the other churches he founded in the state. Friends and enemies—prejudice and open-mindedness—all were parts of nineteenth-century life in Vermont.

There is no doubt that along with Bowles, the Clarks, Langleys, and Peterses encountered people who welcomed them into their homes, as well as "cod-fish aristocrats" who eschewed them because of their color. It is also equally clear that they were doing more than simply surviving as a minority—they had created a safe space for themselves that they controlled, where they had found friends both black and white, and where relatives of three generations were living closely together in rural, middle-class style. This Hill in Hinesburgh was more than just a piece of ground; it had been baptized by their toil and likely held the dust of their children. To have such a place in America was something few liberated blacks could have achieved at the time. It would never be easy to leave such a place, and they had no intentions of doing so. No doubt owning land was an antidote to the poison of racism.


About 1813, far from the Hill in Vermont, a baby boy named Edward Williams was born in Maryland. We do not know if he was free or enslaved, but he eventually found his way to Hinesburgh and married Phoebe Clark. A few years earlier, Charles Waters had been born, also in Maryland. Charles later married Calista Peters and lived at the bottom of the Hill, but first these young boys probably endured years of what the Huntington Baptist church described as a system "fraught with ominous evils to humanity, and so derogatory to the Christian character."[89] If not enslaved themselves, they lived in the slave society of nineteenth-century Maryland with all the degradation that entailed.

Edward was about sixteen years old and Charles twenty-four in 1829, the year of David Walker's shocking "Appeal to the Coloured Citizens of the World." Walker lived in Boston at the time, and his writings showed what people of color had to endure. His "Appeal" turned out to be very popular throughout the country, as it went through several printings. It was even smuggled onto plantations in the South, where it was read at secret meetings in deep places away from white ears. Some enslaved people began to hide weapons in preparation for revolt. If Edward or Charles had attended a reading, they would have heard these words:

> My motive in writing . . . is, if possible, to awaken in the breasts of my afflicted, degraded and slumbering brethren, a spirit of inquiry and investigation respecting our miseries and wretchedness in this REPUBLICAN LAND OF LIBERTY!!!!!! The whites want slaves and want us for their slaves, but some of them will curse the day they ever saw us. As true as the sun ever shone in its meridian splendor, my colour will root some of them out of the very face of the earth. . . . [T]hey do not know, indeed, that there is an unconquerable disposition in the breast of the blacks, which, when it is fully awakened and put in motion, will be subdued, only with the destruction of the animal existence. . . . Get the blacks started, and if you do not have a gang of tigers and lions to deal with, I am a deceiver . . . if there is an *attempt* made by us, kill or be killed . . . there can be nothing in our hearts but death alone for them. . . . [We must] lay aside abject servility, and be determined to act like men . . . Oh! My coloured brethren, all over the world, when shall we arise from this death-like apathy? — And be men!![90]

In the very different setting of Charlotte, Vermont, in 1828, another baby was born, who as a man would fight in the Civil War. Aaron Freeman would eventually find his way to the Hill and into the heart of Rachel Williams, granddaughter of Shubael and Violet Clark. Aaron fought in the Massachusetts Fifty-fourth to end the slavery that had controlled his forebears and had surely circumscribed his own prospects in the North.

## CHAPTER THREE

# Life and Death on the Hill,
1830s–1840s

Ubuntu — I am because you are. — South African proverb

As the nineteenth century advanced, manufacturing in Hinesburgh flourished and life gradually became easier for those who could afford to buy
the expanded services and products of the industrial age. In 1832, Rufus
Patrick started an iron foundry to manufacture agricultural tools, making it unnecessary to travel the dozen miles south to Vergennes to purchase such implements. In the 1840s, Clark Whitehorn added another
carding factory to comb the raw wool of the abundant merino sheep
grazing in Vermont meadows. And a Mr. Hull built a new mill to turn
tons of locally grown potatoes into starch. Although the town was thriving, there is no record of any people of color working in the numerous
mills and factories of the county; those jobs were reserved for white
men, as people of color were generally funneled into service positions.[1]
Andrew Harris, a graduate of the University of Vermont who had been
denied acceptance to Middlebury College because of his color, described
this phenomenon in an 1839 speech in New York City at the Broadway
Tabernacle: "If he wishes to be useful as a professional man, a merchant or mechanic, he is prevented by the color of his skin, and driven
to those menial employments which tend to bring us more and more
into disrepute."[2]

By the 1830s racism was widespread, and people of color continued
to cry out against what they saw as nonsensical attacks on their humanity. Craniologists had entered the discussion and used comparative head
measurements of blacks and whites to "prove" their inferiority theories.[3] The American pro-slavery argument, therefore, had become fully

developed — complete with "scientific" data. The wave of Revolutionary-era egalitarianism that had washed over the Northern states had dried up completely and was replaced by a hardened landscape of intractable ideology of black inferiority and white dominance.

Black intellectuals, who loathed the exhausting need to defend their very humanity, developed arguments refuting ideas of inferiority based on skin color and head measurements, characterizing them as "born of absurdities."[4] They instead advanced the religious ideal of the unity of the human family, emphasizing Bible passages such as Acts 17:26: "God hath made of one blood all the nations of men."[5] There were others, however, who finally accepted that blacks and whites were different — that blacks were the better race, descended from a black Adam whom God had created "from the rich and black soil" of eastern Africa.[6] In the South, enslaved people used other methods, including violence, to struggle against pro-slavery advocates. In 1831, Nat Turner and others defying the slave system in Virginia killed 55 whites. In retaliation, the state executed 55 blacks, and mobs murdered 200 more people of color in revenge for the uprising.

Northern blacks also joined forces but in a less violent manner. September 1830 marked the emergence of the Colored National Convention movement, which continually advanced a political agenda of full citizenship rights for black men until its last national convention in 1864. For thirty-four years, the men and women at state and national meetings fought for equal rights for freedmen, debated colonization, resisted racist laws, supported temperance, and encouraged social and educational improvement.[7] These meetings were platforms for black intellectuals, and the black press reported on them, spreading their scholarly arguments far and wide, even as far away as the Hill in Vermont.[8]

Out of this black activism grew a stronger abolitionist movement, and by 1833 the American Anti-Slavery Society was formed. To many white Americans, however, the abolitionist movement was a foreign plot to destroy America by fomenting rebellions similar to Turner's. Such fears plagued the South in particular, but they also touched Vermont and other Northern states. Antislavery sentiment was accompanied by a stronger colonization movement that supported sending all freed blacks to colonize Liberia instead of staying in the land of their birth. In Vermont, membership in the colonizationist society was fashionable among the rich and powerful and was extremely active for over fifty years — longer than any other state society.[9]

In a speech before the Vermont Colonizationist Society in 1840, the popular speaker Rev. J. K. Converse, pastor of Burlington's Congregational Church, urged Vermonters to reject abolitionism, which promoted equality of the races, and try to move Southerners "by Christian truth and love, and persuasive argument" to free their slaves and send them to Liberia.[10] In an eerie foretelling of the future he said, "No human power can compel them (to abolish slavery), short of an army planting itself upon their soil and demanding liberty for the captives at the point of a bayonet."[11] In 1840, such a war was horrifyingly unthinkable to most whites, and if abolitionists' ideas might lead to that, many people felt they must be routed.

The Vermont Anti-Slavery Society was established in 1834, and by 1837 Vermont had ninety chapters and 8,000 members.[12] Antislavery, however, did not mean antiracism. Many Vermonters still supported only gradual emancipation or removal of freedmen and women to Liberia. Ideas of abolitionists, like the immediate cessation of slavery and the fair and equal treatment of all people, were too radical for many. At this time, many people in Vermont and elsewhere in the North associated abolitionists with insurgency and disorder. Numerous antislavery and pro-slavery advocates saw abolitionists as "rum-mad fanatics" and "sinister, reckless agitators."[13] In Vermont, mobs attacked abolitionist speakers in Newbury and Randolph. The trustees of churches in Windsor and Woodstock refused permission to abolitionists to speak in their churches. In Montpelier, forty town leaders protested the use of the State House by abolitionists and pelted a lecturer at the Old Brick Meeting House "with eggs and hooted (him) off the stage."[14] An early black historian and abolitionist, William C. Nell, dubbed the 1830s a "reign of terror" during which antislavery men and women were subjected to much abuse.[15]

Some of the abuse stemmed from fear that New England would be inundated with former slaves, becoming the Liberia of America. While white antislavery people often supported colonization, most people of color did not. Andrew Harris, a black graduate of the University of Vermont, felt that despite

> all the oppression and odium that is heaped upon us here, I for one would rather stand and endure it all, choosing rather to suffer affliction with my people, than to emigrate to a foreign shore, though I might there enjoy the pleasures of Egypt. And while I live, let my prayer be, that the same

soil which cherished my father may cherish me; and when I die, that the same dust may cover me that covered the ashes of my father.[16]

We know that the people of the Hill felt similar sentiments toward the soil of their home in Hinesburgh. During these decades, no one would emigrate, and the dust of the Hill would cover more of the older generation as they departed this world. We also know from the later letters of Loudon Langley that some of them were ardently antislavery and that the Langleys harbored people escaping slavery in the 1850s.[17] Providing shelter for runaways might have begun even earlier, since two men of color from Maryland were on the grand lists from the Hill district by 1842.

If the Langleys did help runaways this early, it might have been a particularly difficult time to have extra mouths to feed because Vermont was in the midst of a depression.[18] From 1837 to 1843, the depression pushed those on the margins of survival out of rural areas and into Burlington to work along the grimy Lake Champlain waterfront, in the expanding downtown area, or in the homes of the wealthy. Others moved west to New York, or even farther to Ohio country, as did Sybil Langley with her new husband, Jeremiah Loudin from Burlington.[19] However, it was not necessarily the farmers who were moving—it was the landless. Historian Christopher Harris claims that hill farmers "soldiered on" with horses and hay wagons, scythes and a few cows until the late nineteenth to early twentieth century.[20] Harris contends that hill farmers were actually doing quite well because of the nitrogen-rich soil due to sheep manure. By 1835, merino sheep mania had taken a firm hold of farmers who had the money to expand their landholdings for grazing sheep.

Most of the scholarship on people of color during this time is on urban blacks in the North. We know they identified closely with each other and formed their own churches, created black schools, and met together in self-improvement organizations. There has been little research, however, into black rural communities, partly because of the dearth of sources. The partial picture I have been able to piece together provides examples of successful farming on the Hill as well as both interracial collaboration and strife in an increasingly racialized America. During these decades there were cross-racial business dealings on the Hill, some harmonious, and some acrimonious that ended up in court. Blacks and whites attended church and school together and worked collaboratively on antislavery activities connected to the Baptist church and on the settling of estates. They also aided each other when in poor health. During the 1830s and '40s, the Peterses and Clarks persisted in the sheep culture, and their numbers continued to increase as the second generation married and had children, and other people of color migrated to the still-growing farming neighborhood.

## The Peterses

In the 1830s many inhabitants of Vermont hill farms and small towns continued their migrations from farm to city in search of work. However, in July 1830, Caroline Peters of Burlington bucked this trend and moved from the city of Burlington to the Hill, where she bought twenty acres on lot 83 from the elder Samuel Peters for $200.[21] Perhaps she was Samuel's daughter, although there is little evidence that he had children, since documentation on him is slim. However, in 1857 Hiram K. Scott, "attorney for the heirs of Samuel Peters," represented Caroline's children in a land transaction.[22] This inheritance supports a direct relationship between Caroline and Samuel, since all extant evidence shows children on the Hill, regardless of gender, received land at their parents' death. During the 1830s, Caroline joined the same Baptist church to which the Clarks belonged and seemed to be living on the Hill with extended family, seemingly to help care for her elderly relatives.

By 1830, the original pioneers to the Hill were aging, and when they passed on, those left behind would feel the loss intensely. That first generation had journeyed to an uncharted world, both literally and figuratively, and created their own maps of survival as free people. They contended with everything that white settlers had, plus the added pressures of knowing that neighbors might despise them for their skin color and treat them as inferiors. Despite it all, they survived and thrived. These pioneering men and women had shown strength of mind, determination, and courage in doing the backbreaking work of clearing the old-growth forest and planting a farming community in the free and safe space they had created on this Hill.

The first founding father of the Hill to die was Prince Peters in 1832; the second was Shubael Clark two years later. One of the founding mothers, Hannah Lensmen, had already died in the early 1800s and was buried somewhere on the Hill. They are all buried there still,

permanent inhabitants of Hinesburgh. By 1834, only Samuel Peters and
Violet Clark from the pioneering generation continued to live and work
on the Hill along with their growing families. Prince and Shubael were
mourned as leaders of the farming community, and their children and
grandchildren continued the rural traditions passed on to them by their
pioneering ancestors.

Prince Peters, who had endured good times and bad on their Hill
farm for almost forty years, died on a summer's day, June 30, 1832. He
was about seventy years old, and for fourteen years, to the day, he had
been receiving a pension of ninety-six dollars per year from his country for his military service in the Revolutionary War. His second wife,
Eliza; his four children; and the elder Samuel, whose relationship to
Prince remains a mystery, survived him. Surely tears flowed that summer day as they lowered his small frame into the earth near his first
wife, Hannah. Although there is no evidence that Prince belonged to
a church, Calista and Caroline Peters were members of the same Baptist church as the Clarks. Their Baptist minister may have officiated at
the burial.

In addition to the intense loss of his passing, the family must have
keenly felt the loss of his pension money. The settling of Prince's estate
shows that they were not rich in resources, and it shines a light into
their home and farm life and relations with neighbors. Soon after Prince
died, his widow, Eliza, wrote a note to the Probate Court in Burlington
asking that her white neighbor Calvin Wray be appointed the administrator of his estate.[23] Women did not choose administrators lightly —
she trusted him with her fate, since he would be the one to set aside her
widow's dower.[24] There were neighbors of color living nearby to whom
she could have turned, including Lewis Clark, who owned a lot adjacent
to her. Instead she turned to longtime neighbor, Calvin Wray, to admin-
ister her husband's estate. Her choice could be an illustration of cross-
racial kindness and the trust she had in him. It could also be a statement
about the power structures in town and evidence that she believed a
white man could navigate the legal world better. However, there is later
evidence that Hill people traveled through the legal system very well;
therefore, it seems that Wray was a trusted neighbor, and his diligence
in settling the estate showed she had chosen well.

The probate court appointed Wray administrator in March 1833, and
he started work immediately by publicizing a meeting in Mitchell Hins-
dale's office in Hinesburgh to adjust all claims against the estate and

hiring people to take inventory of Prince's possessions. After gathering evidence, Wray determined that the estate was insolvent and there must be an auction to pay Prince's debts. Some of the indebtedness was incurred during his final illness for doctor visits and medicines and after death for his casket and funeral expenses. One of Calvin Wray's sons had paid for Prince's medicines, reinforcing the picture of neighbors readily lending a hand when needed.[25]

Two months after Prince's death, his estate was auctioned off to pay his debts. It was solely a family and neighborhood event. Even though there were neighbors present who could have bid the prices up, Prince's relatives all bought items for less than they were worth. The elder Samuel bought the barn, two plows, one adze, one harness and a gun, spending over $17 for items inventoried at $34.50. Josephus bought his father's iron square, seven old "c.ks" [*sic*], a rake, his house and one-third of the cider mill, spending $12.54 for items inventoried at $40.75. Electa bought her father's spider pan, and Eliza bought a light stand from her home. Eliza had retained more important items, such as her loom and wheels as part of her dower, but apparently she needed the stand for her oil lamp. Josephus bought the remaining thirteen acres of land after Eliza received her third. She had been taken care of well by the administrator.

A close reading of the inventory uncovers a practice shared by both the Clarks and Peterses (document 3.1). Parcels of land and other items were always in individual names, due to the individualistic nature of the American legal system. However, the land, farm implements, and household items were used in common. Prince's name was on half of thirty-nine and one-quarter acres along with Samuel. However, he built his house and barn on Samuel's half of the lot, close to Samuel's home. They obviously saw it as common land and, as relatives, preferred to be near each other for support and sociability. Prince also owned half of the pair of oxen and one-third of the cider mill.[26] Samuel 1st, Prince, and his son Josephus owned the mill together. They had even shared one gun, used to hunt the ever-decreasing birds and deer in the area. A lumber sleigh in the barn, originally on the inventory as belonging to Prince, was later discovered to belong to Josephus. John Allen came forward, surely at the urging of Josephus, with a letter saying, "I sold the sleigh to Josephus Peters and it was from him that I received payment for the same."[27] The sleigh was undoubtedly used in common by all in the family, and Josephus ensured that it was not auctioned.

DOCUMENT 3.1

*Inventory of the Estate of Prince Peters, 1832*

---

REAL ESTATE

| | |
|---|---|
| One half of 39¼ acres of land | 196.00 |
| House standing on | 35.00 |
| Samuel Peters land | |
| 2 acres of land held by lease | 12 |
| from Jacob Snider for | |
| 999 years | |
| | 243 |
| Small barn standing on Samuel | |
| Peters land | 12 |
| | 255 |

PERSONAL ESTATE

| | |
|---|---|
| ½ a pair of oxen | 27.50 |
| 1 ? ball | 5.00 |
| 1 calf | 3.00 |
| 1 old Harness | 7.00 |
| 30 Dragteeth | 3.00 |
| 1 Lumber Sleigh | 15.00 |
| 2 old Ploughs | 3.00 |
| 3½ tons hay | 12.00 |
| 7 old casks | 2.00 |
| ½ gun | 2.00 |
| 1 axe | .75 |
| 1 broad axe | 1.50 |
| 3 lungers | .75 |
| 3 planes | .50 |
| 1 iron square | .75 |
| 2 Saws | .75 |
| 1 Adze | .50 |
| 1 Bedstead & covering | 7.00 |
| 2 Chains | 1.00 |
| 1 Chest | .50 |
| | 93.50 |

| | |
|---|---|
| Personal estate brot over | 93.50 |
| 1 Trunk | .50 |
| 1 Table | 1.00 |
| 1 Light Stand | .50 |
| 1 Loom | 5.00 |
| 3 ? | 1.50 |
| 1 Iron Kettle | 1.00 |
| 1 Tin Kettle | .75 |
| 1 Shi? | .50 |
| 2 Wheels | 2.00 |
| 2 Brass Ketchs | 6.00 |
| 1 Wash Tub | .50 |
| 11 Milk Pans | .92 |
| 1 Tin pail & callender | .50 |
| Sundry articles of table | 1.00 |
| furniture | |
| 1 Coat vest and pantaloons | 5.00 |
| 1 Pitchfork & rake | .34 |
| 1 Shovel & tongs | .75 |
| ⅓ of a Cider Mill | 3.00 |
| 5 Shocks wheat | 3.00 |
| flax in the ? for 45 lbs | 3.00 |
| 1 Crowbar 21st | 2.10 |
| 1 Pr Stulyards | .50 |
| Corn in the field | 2.00 |
| 1 Cant hook | .50 |
| 1 Hath | 1.00 |
| | 136.36 |
| | |
| ALL REAL ESTATE | 243.00 |
| | 379.36 |
| and Barn | 12.00 |
| | 391.36 |

---

SOURCE: Probate Court of Chittenden County, Vermont, Estate Probate File #844 for Prince Peters (Burlington, VT: Chittenden County Court).

The probate inventory was inadvertently useful in discovering cultural traditions in the family. Building their houses on the same plot of land, legally owned by Samuel, a practice also followed at the top of the Hill, imitates the African tradition of situating houses near each other and not on individual plots dictated by individual land ownership. This practice can be seen in both East Africa and West Africa.[28] Therefore, the tradition of situating one's house might have been carried over the ocean in the minds of kidnapped Africans, passed down through the generations, and manifested on this Hill in northern Vermont.[29]

After Prince's death, only Samuel and Josephus were assessed taxes for houses, never Eliza; she must have lived with Josephus, who bought his father's house and lands not owned by the widow. He was living there at the time of Prince's death, and he needed to retain the home for his growing family; he had married Charlot Bettis, another woman about whom we know little, and they had had their first of five boys, Henry.[30]

The Peterses' houses were worth between $25 and $35. The Shubael Clark house at the top of the hill was also worth $25. By comparison, Shubael and Violet's son, Lewis, had a newer house in the middle of the Hill worth $200. Houses owned by their white neighbors were worth a bit more: Calvin Wray's was worth $250 and John Norton's was worth $300. Augustus McEuen, on the other hand, a large-scale farmer and lawyer who often employed Josephus and his sons as laborers, had a house worth $1,000.[31] This one item on the inventory is an indicator of the increasing economic distance between the highest social class and others in the town.

The accounting of Prince's estate also illuminates the inner workings of an early nineteenth-century household, regardless of race. It is especially helpful in painting a picture of the work that women performed

---

❊ *Josephus and Charlot Peters Family*

Josephus Peters, b. 1802, Hinesburgh, d. 1869, Hinesburgh, married
  Charlot Bettis, b. 1804, d. 1850, Hinesburgh
  Five sons born in Hinesburgh: Henry, George, John, Joseph,
    Cornelius
  Amy Prince, second wife
  Sarah Jane Freeman, third wife
  Two children: Clara and unknown

in their daily lives. Along with the forty-five pounds of flax used to make linen, the loom and two wheels tell us that this house was a well-equipped manufactory. The sounds of the spinning wheel and the shuttle of the loom were often heard in this home. On nice days, Eliza, and Electa and Sarah, both in their early twenties, may have brought a wheel or two outside to spin wool or linen. Some of these goods were most likely sold at the store for credit or to neighbors who might have ordered items from the Peters women.

The fact that there was no stove on the inventory shows they were heating with and cooking in the fireplace, still a general practice at that time.[32] The spider pan was another clue to the use of the fireplace for cooking, since it was placed near the fire with hot coals underneath and, sometimes, on top.[33] The one light stand in the inventory was for an oil lamp that used some kind of animal fat. There was no ice chest on the inventory, so the Peterses may have had an outdoor icehouse and had ice delivered to their home or cut it out of a pond themselves. They certainly had an outdoor water source: a spring, well, or cistern.

It was not a life of ease, but they had what they needed in the safe space they had carved out of the frontier. The total of Prince and Eliza's worldly possessions came to $391.36. Their lot in life was meager, but this was not the total of their resources—they also had family and friends nearby and the liberty to control and share their assets as they pleased. It was the communal living arrangements of the family that had helped them thrive on the Hill and would continue to supply the next generations with a means of support.

After Prince's death, the other Peters men continued to prosper. In March 1833, Josephus bought land across the road from Prince and Samuel's original plot. This was their first incursion into another lot, and later it would be all that was left of their holdings, as Samuel sold much of his land two years later. Why they wanted to expand across the road is up to speculation. Possibly it had not been leached of all its nutrition and was still fertile ground for crops. With a growing family, Josephus and Charlot certainly needed more land. We know Charlot Bettis was a black woman from Essex, Vermont, but we know little else definite about her.[34] While on the Hill she bore five boys who survived to adulthood and, in all probability, more children who died young. Their progeny are spread throughout Vermont and beyond to this day.

According to the 1840 census, Charlot and Josephus's family continued to grow—by then they had four boys under ten, and the elder Samuel and Eliza were living with them as well. Surely Eliza had helped

Charlot with the birth of her children. During the decade, Charlot bore one more son, Cornelius, giving them five boys to raise and to help with the farming chores.[35] Charlot might have yearned for a girl to help her with the house and garden; however, Eliza and the younger boys would do that until they were old enough to join the men in the fields.

The Peterses' acreage stayed stable during the 1840s — there was no buying or selling of land recorded in the town records this decade. Presumably, the Peters family survived most of the decade as small farmers, growing hay to feed their livestock, likely selling surplus to larger farmers, using horses and the plows that Samuel bought at the auction, and using sheep manure as fertilizer. In 1841, Samuel and Josephus were together taxed for thirty improved acres, one house worth twenty-five dollars, three cows, three horses or mules, and twelve sheep.

Toward the end of the decade, Josephus may have started working for Augustus McEuen, a large-scale sheep farmer about a mile south of his homestead who owned 180 sheep.[36] Charlot, Eliza, and the younger boys would have been spinning and weaving, taking care of the cows, milking and churning butter, and undoubtedly selling surplus to a store for credit, as did the Langley and Clark women from the top of the Hill.

Although there are no death or burial records for Samuel or Eliza, they apparently died during the 1840s, since they were of the same generation as Prince Peters and Shubael Clark, and their names disappeared from public records during the decade. Samuel's name was missing from the grand list for the first time in 1844 after having lived on the Hill for forty-six years. This left the second generation of Josephus and Charlot as the elders of the extended family. Unfortunately, much of Samuel and Eliza's stories remain a mystery, but their roots were strong and deep into the soil of the Hill by the time of their deaths. They rest there in an unknown plot in the space they helped to shape on the Vermont frontier.[37]

## The Clarks

While the Peterses were grieving for the deaths of the pioneering generation at the bottom of the Hill, the Clark, Langley, and later the Williams families were farming their acreage at the top and even expanding to the middle. In 1831, Lewis Clark began buying and selling more land, expanding the amount of property in the hands of African Americans on the Hill. He bought all of lot 105 and half of 106 on the Hill, equaling 150 acres. This would place the Clarks among a select few of Hinesburgh. Historian Jeffrey Potash found that the adult sons of stable, elite farmers in adjacent Addison County reaped the benefits of their higher places in the hardening social stratification of the times by being able to afford land of their own. It became nearly impossible for new migrants to buy land and move into select circles. Judging from the patterns of land, house, and stock ownership of the Clarks, they were in the top 30 percent of all farmers, not the wealthiest 10 percent, but doing very well.[38]

Not only were they in a select economic stratum, but they also were fully engaged socially through the church and civically through their freeman status. In September of 1830, Shubael Clark, in his seventies, made the five-mile trip into Hinesburgh to cast his ballot at the freeman's meeting. Most likely, he took the horse-drawn wagon down the road into town, accompanied by Violet and some of the children. As the couple rode along, their thoughts may have returned to their early days on the Hill when the old-growth canopy was so dense that sunlight seldom reached the ground, and the road on which they traveled did not exist. Viewing the grazing animals, apple orchards, and fertile fields that supported their large family must have filled them with pride at what they had accomplished in the last forty years.[39]

The Clarks also continued their long and active membership in the Baptist church, Shubael continuing his work on committees to ensure the respectable behavior of it members. However, in April 1831, Lewis fell under the negative scrutiny of the Church. Someone reported that Brother Lewis J. Clark and Sister Ruth Brown "did unlawfully Lodge together which we think is contrary to the gospel. . . . [T]his information we obtained by the acknowledgement of the parties."[40] One can imagine the gossip and the moral outrage exhibited by their fellow churchgoers. The church members decided very quickly that Lewis and Ruth, not having "come forward and made a confession to the church . . . they have forfeited thire [*sic*] right of being in Fellowship with the Chh [church] untile they Shall Truly & voluntarily make that confession that the . . . offence demands."[41] No committee visited to cajole them into changing their behavior, as Shubael and his committees had done for others. The alacrity of the decision is most likely related to the fact that not only were Ruth and Lewis not married, but Ruth was white.[42]

Two years later, Shubael and Violet joined the newly formed Baptist church in Huntington—not Charles Bowles's Free Will Church, but a branch of the Hinesburgh Calvinist church, which had been organized in Huntington in 1828 with eight members. Did they leave the Hinesburgh church because of the trouble over Lewis and Ruth? As a leader in the church, Shubael conceivably argued with the church elders to change their ruling. Or did they simply like Elder Daniel Bennett and the members in Huntington better? Possibly it was simply the fact that it was closer to travel to Huntington down the other side of the Hill. However, such a move in the twilight of their lives points to problems with their old church.

Despite being ejected from fellowship in the church, Lewis and Ruth did quite well economically, improving their position as sheep farmers. By 1834, they had a house worth $200, sixty-five sheep, three cows, and three horses or mules. He and Ruth also had two daughters, Sybil and Caroline, and were likely married by this time, although there is no record of the wedding. At this point, they were a bit more prosperous than his parents, with a nicer house, since Shubael and Violet's was worth only $25.

Both Clark households were deeply into the sheep culture of Vermont. By 1840 there were 6 sheep for every person in the state. With 129 sheep between them, the Clarks were still prospering with sheep farming and must have been optimistic for their future on the Hill.

In 1834, however, the family endured the loss of Shubael, who died intestate (without a will). Shubael started coughing up black matter while clearing new land. He thought it was "charcoal-dust, which floats in the air in new burnt land when the dry timber is removed. . . . [However] he soon became so weak that he was obliged to repair to his bed. An intolerable gangrenous odor was evolved from the matter expectorated, and he lost strength and emaciated rapidly, . . . unable to turn himself in bed without assistance."[43] A doctor from Middlebury who visited him described Shubael as "a man of color, possessed of a good constitution, so much so that he informed me he had not lost a meal of victuals on account of poor health for the last forty years. This man was regular in his habits, used no intoxicating liquors, pious, prudent, and independent in his circumstances, and surrounded by a wife and numerous family of promising children." Shubael was in such pain that "he impatiently inquired how soon he would probably be released from his bodily suffering." The doctor diagnosed pulmonary gangrene and suggested the family "continue the tonics, quinine and bark, in combination with the root of sanguinaria, [and] use inhalations of . . . the fumes of boiling tar." After he had been in bed for seven weeks, Shubael was released from his suffering at the end of October 1834. Unlike the Peterses, we know exactly where all the Clarks are buried. A few townspeople still remember Shubael's large stone monument at the top of the Hill, since it was not destroyed until well into the twentieth century.[44] His sudden decline and death surely caused much sadness in his home and the wider community.

The remarks made by the officiating minister at his funeral would have listed Shubael's qualities: hard working, Christian, pious, father of nine children, and successful farmer. His sons Lewis, Hiram, and Charles, along with neighbors and fellow members of the Baptist church would have lowered him into the ground in his five-dollar casket. Illustrating his importance to the Hill community, Shubael had a headstone marking his grave larger than any other stone in the cemetery. The gravestone unfortunately did not survive the vandalism of later inhabitants of the town.

The Baptist church chose the year of Shubael's death to take up the case of Brother Lewis Clark and, by then, his wife Sister Ruth. "After mutual conversation on the subject the Chh feels that they acted prematurely in the case of their exclusion & feel desirous to acknowledge to them their mistake and appointed a committee to go and confess their wrongs to them." The committee, consisting of three white men, "confessed to these aggrieved individuals that the Chh had been hasty in their case and were sorry for it. After which they manifested that they were satisfied with the Chh as a body."[45] They must have felt sorry, partly, because of Shubael's death.

Eight months later, Lewis J. Clark stated his wishes to rejoin the church. "Having heretofore made a full and satisfactory confession of his wrong doings the Church then unanimously voted to restore him to its fellowship and he is again considered a member in good standing."[46] It took Ruth longer to get over the grievance—for five years she remained outside the church. In 1837, we find evidence of another possible motive for inviting them back into the church. That year the church proudly published the real estate owned by thirteen of its members. Lewis J. Clark was ninth in the list, with property totaling $1,171. He was sandwiched among wealthy whites: Rays, McEuens, and Baldwins. It is possible that his assets had made him a sought-after member of the religious community. He was certainly in good company and was once again an upstanding member of the church, with a white wife and four children.

When Shubael died in 1834, Lewis was appointed executor of the estate by the Probate Court. This was surely agreed to by the family, and, according to custom, Violet was entitled to eight months' support while the estate was being settled. Unfortunately, for some reason the estate was not finally settled for eight years. One begins to wonder about the relationship between Violet and Lewis. He was in no hurry to give her a dower, and she never lived with him, although he certainly could have afforded it at that time. Likely she preferred to stay in her own home, and Lewis knew the extended family would take care of her, since children still lived with her.

Eight years after Shubael's death, Lewis finally asked the court to appoint administrators to inventory his father's estate because it was insolvent. Lewis placed ads in local inns and stores and in the *Burlington Free Press* to alert people to a meeting at the Widow Clark's house to adjust claims against the estate. The inventory was speedily completed on April 19, 1842. As with the Peterses, the inventory was immensely informative about their daily lives and relationships in Hinesburgh (see document 3.2).

The inventory showed that the Clarks were an active farm family, better off than the Peterses, who worked together for the survival of the collective and shared items in common. Like the Peters' family, the Clarks followed the seasonal activities of Hill farmers, and the women performed the never-ending tasks of milking, butter making, washing clothes, and the like. The 175 sap buckets indicate that many of the giant maple trees had not been cleared but cultivated as a sugarbush. Collecting the sap for sugar was an early springtime family affair: tapping the trees, hauling the buckets with the help of oxen and a sleigh, and boiling the sap down into sugar. The hay items and wheat riddle tell us the men were busy planting wheat and hay in later spring. Extrapolating backward from an 1860 agricultural inventory, we can assume they also planted Irish potatoes, oats, and Indian corn. Because of the good business practice of allowing Norton's sheep to graze on the property and leave much-needed manure, they doubtless had good yields.[47]

The loom and three wheels indicate that the women were often busy spinning and weaving. Undoubtedly they would have sold extra linen or woolen cloth to neighbors for cash or to the store for credit. The one-half stove revealed that it was a shared appliance, evidently with son Charles, who was a shoemaker and lived with Violet, along with Hiram, another son. Hiram is never on the grand lists because Lewis had him declared insane during the settling of the estate. In his final accounting

DOCUMENT 3.2

*Inventory of the Estate of Shubael Clark, 1842*

| | | | |
|---|---|---|---|
| 175 Sap Buckets | 14.00 | 1 Loom* | 4.00 |
| (100 to Violet*) | | 1 Large Wheel (new)* | 1.75 |
| 1 Old Waggon | 4.00 | 1 Large Wheel (old)* | 1.00 |
| 1 4/4 Auger* | .06 | 1 Linen Wheel* | 1.25 |
| 1 5/4 Auger* | .25 | 1 Wheat Riddle (old)* | .17 |
| 1 Barn Hatchet | .25 | $\frac{1}{2}$ of a Cooking Stove* | 10.00 |
| 3 Sickles* | .45 | 7 Joints of Stove Pipe* | .88 |
| 1 Cheese Press* | .50 | 7 Chains (Old)* | 1.75 |
| 1 Plow* | 3.00 | 1 Porridge Pot* | .60 |
| 1 Chain* | .75 | 1 Bed Sted * | 1.00 |
| 1 Ring Chain* | .50 | 1 Small Kettle* | .25 |
| 1 Manure Fork* | .50 | 1 Large Wash Tub* | .75 |
| 1 Hay Knife* | .75 | 1 Small Wash Tub* | .50 |
| 1 Hay Fork* | .50 | 1 Churn* | .75 |
| 1 Hay Axe* | .50 | 1 Horse | 30.00 |
| 1 Cushion Saddle | 3.00 | 1 Cow* | 13.00 |
| 1 Harrow* | 2.00 | 49 Sheep[a] | 73.50 |
| 1 Wooden Clock & Case* | 4.00 | 2 Hogs[b] | 4.00 |
| 1 Ketchen Table* | .50 | | |
| 1 Tall Leaf Table* | 1.00 | Subtotal for personal estate = | $197.41 |
| 1 Light Stand* | .75 | | |
| 1 Bedstead, Bed & Beding* | 5.00 | ~100 acres home lot including, dwelling house & barn | $950.00 |
| 1 Bedstead, Bed & Beding* | 6.00 | ~25 acres on the north end of home lot | 237.50 |
| 1 Bedstead, Bed & Beding* | 4.00 | ~50 acres east of the home lot lying in Huntington | 475.00 |
| | | Subtotal for real estate = | $1662.50 |
| | | Total For Clark Estate | $1859.91 |

SOURCE: Probate Court of Chittenden County, Vermont, Estate Probate File #1093 for Shubael Clark (Burlington, VT: Chittenden County Court).

*Judge Charles Russell of the Chittenden County Probate Court ordered Lewis J. Clark to deliver these items to Violet as her widow's dower. Violet had complained to the court about not getting her "thirds." The order was dated February 22, 1843 — 10 months after the inventory was complete.

[a]Later said to be Norton's.

[b]Later said to have been slaughtered and consumed by the family.

for the estate, Lewis charged two dollars for paying the "Justices for making inquisitions as to Hiram Clark's insanity."[48] There is no note about how they decided the case, but later Hiram had a guardian to sign documents for him.

The inventory also indicates that the Clarks had a higher standard of living than the Peterses at the bottom of the Hill. Shubael's estate was worth more than four times that of Prince Peters, even though they were at the top of the Hill, where farming would have been a bit more difficult due to distance from town. However, the Clarks had much more land, 175 acres, and extra hours of sunshine on their southwest-facing property. The Clarks had a stove, a luxury the Peterses did not have, making cooking easier and supplying more efficient heat for the house on frigid days. Violet may well have been experimenting with a coal cook stove. By 1840, wood or coal cooking stoves were gradually being adopted by city and suburban folks and experimented with on farms. We know there was a coal pit on the Clark farm, and being an early user of new technology would be in keeping with their economic status among the local farmers.[49] These estate documents were invaluable in helping to piece together the early relationships and daily lives of the Hill people, who left no other records until mid-century. Violet's 1843 land dower shows she kept the house and shared it with her sons, along with half the barn and barnyard. The thirty acres she retained in her name spilled over the Hinesburgh line into Huntington. The dower document clearly states that her land and house were north of the road, helping us to locate the exact spot where their house stood.[50] Another estate record, an 1843 petition that Lewis presented to the probate court, was signed by all of Shubael's heirs.[51] These signatures were invaluable in discovering the names of two of Shubael and Violet's married daughters.

In 1844, just before the final settlement of the estate, Lewis and Ruth Clark transferred to the Huntington Baptist church, the same one to which Lewis's parents had switched. Charles Clark may have also joined the same church at this time.[52] That church was becoming more and more abolitionist in its public stances. Its members most likely held those views earlier, and those beliefs could have been the attraction that drew Violet and Shubael to the Huntington church. Conceivably, the influence of the Clarks can be seen in this message, which the church forwarded to the *Vermont Observer*, a local newspaper, for publication:

Preamble: American Slavery is based upon the right of man to hold property in man and whereas this right is a usurpation, and the exercise of it in cases a flagrant violation of the principles of natural justice and humanity and contrary to the spirit of the gospel, and in many cases a violation of the whole law of our divine Master. [Anyone professing to be a christian and member of the Baptist Church should] forever forsake a sin fraught with such ominous evils to humanity, and so derogatory to the christian character . . .

Resolved: [If we extend Christian fellowship] to those who openly live in a palpable violation of the divine law, we ourselves become in some measure partakers of their guilt, we as christians and members of a christian church cannot longer welcome to our communion table or to our pulpit, those who hold their fellow men [unreadable word] as property or advocate the right of doing so.

Resolved: While we acknowledge allegiance to the law of love, which forgets neither the oppressor nor the oppressed, we will labour by our prayers, by our actions, and by every other laudable means at our command to break every fetterband which holds as property him who was created in the image of his maker.[53]

The church was making public their rejection of anyone in their community who even advocated the right of others to enslave their fellow human beings. It was insufficient to simply not hold people in slavery; members must also use any means to work toward total abolition. This was an activist church that demanded action by its members, and soon we find evidence of Underground Railroad activity on top of the Hill.

At the same time, we find Lewis still struggling to wrap up the estate. He had written a number of letters to Judge Russell asking for a continuance, saying, "I havnot got returns from the west," apparently Ravenna, Ohio, where Sybil lived.[54] This is the earliest document I found written in the voice of someone from the top of the Hill:

To the honorable judg of the cort of probate as I havnot got returns from the west I theirfore am under the necesity of beging your indulgence for it for further continuence of the Settlement of Shubael Clarks Estate I think the leter must hav ben [unreadable word] I hav riten to them again in hopes to get Returns from them soon, as it is of som considrable imporance to me I therefor hope that you will be patient with me

Your humble servant

Hinesburgh March 8th 1844

Lewis J. Clark Administrator[55]

FIGURE 3.1  Lewis Clark's signature.

The letter shows an educated man, but without the flourish or punctuation of highly educated Victorian-era individuals.[56] I assumed that the Clarks had attended the District 11 school on the Hill and received a common school education there (see the school on figure 1.4). This letter seems to confirm that Lewis and probably his siblings made that schoolhouse a biracial one and that Lewis attended at least for a short time. His Langley cousins also attended a biracial school, but on the Huntington side of the Hill.[57]

Not until February 1845 did Lewis give his final account of the estate. In closing, he gave back $197.79 that was given to him in error, he said. That same year, he petitioned the court to divide the land he had held in common with the other heirs. He wanted to hold his land as "one undivided ninth part," instead of communally. That year, the other heirs sold him some of the land they had inherited from their father's estate "laying west of the land set to Lewis J. Clark," expanding his land holdings even farther and securing his place of honor as a landed gentleman in his new church.[58]

Lewis was becoming more of an individualistic farmer, in keeping with the changing mores of mid-nineteenth-century America, and eschewing the communal customs of his family and their rural society. He may have had increasing "assimilationist goals" that were becoming more and more important as the generation closest to Africa was dying, and the next generation took over.[59]

Two years later, Violet sold five acres of her dower land to Edward Williams, who had become a member of the extended Clark family by marriage to her daughter, Phoebe. Edward had been born in Maryland about 1813, likely into slavery, but he also might have been free, since Maryland had a larger free black community than other Southern states. The story of how he came to be on the Hill and married to one of Shubael and Violet's daughters by 1839 is unknown. Perhaps he escaped from a slave owner and found refuge on the Hill. Researcher Raymond Zirblis discovered that the Langley family on top of the Hill participated in the Underground Railroad in the 1850s, but they may have started the practice earlier.[60]

Evidence that points to Edward's enslavement in the South includes his making his mark on documents, rather than signing his name as the men on the Hill who grew up in Vermont did. Of course, even if he had been a free man in Maryland, chances are he would be illiterate. In 1850 and 1870, he told the census takers he was born in Maryland, but in 1860 he is listed as being born in Vermont. This falsehood could have been related to the 1850 Fugitive Slave Act, which caused fear among people of color who had fled slavery in the South (or even if they had not, since freed people were sometimes kidnapped and sold south). Many who had previously felt safe in Vermont fled to Canada lest they be found and returned to slavery. Some formerly enslaved people changed their name or lied to census takers, as apparently Edward Williams did. He might have felt it was too dangerous to admit to Southern origins, especially if he had freed himself from slavery by trekking to the North. The five acres he and Phoebe received from the Clarks were safely tucked away, far from the public road and secluded from prying eyes. All this points to his being a fugitive.

In 1836 Phoebe "related her Christian Experience" and asked to be a member of the Baptist congregation to which the rest of her family belonged.[61] The church voted to accept her, and on October 2 she was baptized by total immersion. In 1839, Phoebe gave birth to their first child, Rachel. The next year, Edward also related his Christian experience and was immediately baptized and accepted into the church. Elder Brown baptized Edward with full immersion, along with seven others, on a cold January day in northern Vermont. He had no doubt been through worse.

Edward and Phoebe started out with almost nothing at the end of the 1830s, and by 1845 they had two children and held some land in common with Phoebe's siblings, Charles and Harriet Clark. Two years later, Edward bought more land from his mother-in-law, Violet, and they were farming a fifty-acre farm worth $350. The couple had done well despite beginning their married life during a depression. With the help of the extended family and their traditional communal living arrangements, they managed to thrive on top of the Hill at a time when others in Vermont were failing at farming and moving into the cities or out west.

The Clark family had stayed on the Hill through thick and thin and

---

❧ *Phoebe Clark and Edward Williams Family*

WILLIAMS in Hinesburgh:

    Phoebe Clark (b. ca. 1820 Hinesburgh, d. ca. 1845, Hinesburgh)
       married Edward Williams (b. ca. 1813 in Maryland, d. 1877,
       South Burlington)
    Two children born in Hinesburgh: Rachel and George
    Edward later marries Phoebe's older sister, Harriet

---

created an extended family network in the space shaped by the toil of Shubael and Violet. By the end of the 1840s, Violet was surrounded by three households of her descendants: Phoebe and Edward Williams, Almira and William Langley, and Lewis and Ruth Clark. Violet, who was in her mid-seventies, also had thirteen grandchildren to help her in her old age. Most likely born into slavery, she must have been content surrounded by her own large family — something unreachable by those still enslaved. She most likely felt like Hannah Crafts, a formerly enslaved free woman living in New Jersey, who wrote, "There is a hush in my spirit in these days, a deep repose, a holy quietude. I found a life of freedom all my fancy had pictured it to be."[62]

Even though racism was widespread in the North, two families on the Hill illustrate that positive cross-racial relationships existed and even continued after they left Hinesburgh. There appears to be a thickening relationship between the Clarks and a white neighboring family, the Yaws, begun earlier in the century. Thomas and Lorany Yaw, originally from Ira, Vermont (and later Rhoda Yaw, Thomas's second wife), lived on land bordering the Clark farm for decades. Early maps note "Clark and Yaw" land. Lorany had been a member of the Hinesburgh Baptist church to which the Clarks originally belonged, and the Yaw children went to school with the Langley boys in Huntington. Certainly, the families had typical rural relationships. However, it might have been more than that.

After Shubael died, the Lewis Clark and Yaw families continued their relationship. In 1840, Lewis Clark sold to Thomas Yaw his 100 acres in the middle of the Hill. In exchange (it seems), Yaw sold Clark his 100 acres that were formerly owned by Shubael (see table 3.1) on the same day. Doubtless Lewis wanted to consolidate all his land together on the Hill — the part he inherited from his father and, now, this new section from Yaw. But why did Yaw make the switch? What did he have

TABLE 3.1
*Changes in Acreage on the Hill*

| Bottom of Hill | Middle of the Hill *near the bottom* | Middle of the Hill *near the top* | Top of the Hill | Huntington side of the Hill east of the Clarks |
|---|---|---|---|---|
| **1830s** | | | | |
| Samuel, Prince & Eliza Peters | Lewis & Ruth (Brown) Clark | Thomas & Rhoda (Wells) Yaw | Violet Clark & children hold land in common after Shubael's death | William & Almira (Clark) Langley |
| **1840s** | | | | |
| Samuel, Eliza, Josephus & wife, Charlot (Bettis) Peters | Thomas & Rhoda Yaw | Lewis & Ruth Clark | Violet, Lewis, & Ruth, and other Clark inheritors — Lewis buys much of the Clark land from them in 1845 | William & Almira (Clark) Langley |
| **1850s** | | | | |
| Josephus & second wife, Amy Prince Peters | Thomas & Rhoda Yaw — eventually go to Irasburgh | Lewis sells to Theodore Gibson; probably goes to Irasburgh | Violet Clark & sons, Charles & Hiram, still on the 37 acres of Violet's dower Edward & Phoebe (Clark) Williams | William Langley & sons |

to gain? The fact that both families may have migrated to the same town in northeastern Vermont within a few years of each other makes the transaction seem like a deal between friends.

In 1843, Lewis sold his 100 acres free of encumbrances for $500 and soon left Hinesburgh. In 1848 he is missing from the grand lists for the first time. Nothing in the public documents sheds any light on why the family moved. There is some evidence that Lewis and Ruth were living in Irasburgh in northeastern Vermont by 1850. Lewis J. and Ruth Clark were living there; however, Lewis was enumerated as living with the Lange family in the household next to Ruth and the children. None was designated as black. Neither were they designated as mulatto or white — the line was just blank, as it was for everyone. There were three daughters and one son, whose ages and genders exactly match the 1840 Hinesburgh census. It is possible that Lewis was simply working at the Lange farm the day the census taker came, so he was listed in that household, as was the custom.[63] By 1860, the Yaws were also living in Irasburgh; the move by both Clarks and Yaws to the same town strengthens the possibility that there was a strong bond between the families.[64]

We also find cross-racial relations continuing between two other Hinesburgh-Huntington residents after they migrated to New York: Charles Bowles, the Free Will Baptist preacher, and Carlton McEuen, brother of the wealthy white farmer for whom the Peterses worked as farm laborers. In 1835, Charles was elderly, going blind, and unable to keep up the pace of being an itinerant preacher in the Green Mountains. Elder Bowles was forced to sell his beloved grove in Huntington and move with his daughter to Rutland, Vermont, and eventually to Malone, New York, to be near his son.

In the winter of 1843, Bowles got erysipelas in the feet, a bacterial infection also known as St. Anthony's fire, which causes a deep red and swollen rash, along with fever, chills, and vomiting. Today it is easily cured with antibiotics, but in the nineteenth century it was a dreaded disease. His old friend from Hinesburgh, Carlton McEuen, was at Bowles's side as his health failed. The black members of the Hill community had not joined his Free Will Baptist church, but Carlton had become a devoted follower. When Charles got ill, Carlton was living in nearby Lawrenceville, New York, and came to his bedside.[65] He was obviously an old and faithful friend and was with Charles when he died on March 16, 1843. Carlton undoubtedly attended the funeral and burial of Bowles in Malone, far away from his beloved Huntington grove. Even in the midst of hard-edged racism, cross-racial friendships flourished.

## The Langleys

On the Langley side of the Hill in Huntington, we find more inter-racial relations, both cordial and rancorous. In April 1835, William Langley gave his deed for fifty acres in Huntington to John Norton as surety against borrowing some of his sheep. Norton was a member of the Hinesburgh Literary Society, and although no members of the Hill families ever belonged to any elite societies, they seemed to have decent relationships with people who did. According to the land records of Hinesburgh, Norton and William Langley had a deal that William could redeem the fifty-acre deed from Norton whenever he could afford to pay interest on the value of the loan, set at fifty dollars. Their relationship, since it crossed social classes, must have been based on rural tradition and neighborliness. At the same time, William still owned some land in Pittsford, where his father was living, and he mortgaged it in 1832 for twenty dollars. He also sold his rights to Shubael's estate to his cousin, Lewis Clark. The Langleys needed cash and animals and seemed to be just scraping by on the Hill.

In 1836, Almira Clark Langley delivered their sixth child, Loudon; their older boys were still in school. Generally, the Huntington School Records had only a total number of scholars for each family or school, with no student names recorded. However, in the 1840s, the records began to separate out the "William Langley Schollers" with names or numbers of children from the family.[66] This evidently had something to do with their attending a school out of the town. In the 1830s, they had been moved to a school in District 11. Since there was no District 11 in Huntington at the time, they must have gone to District 11 in Hinesburgh and into the schoolhouse near the Clark land. However there are no extant records for the Hinesburgh schools to confirm this.

The last time the Langleys were mentioned in the Huntington school records was in 1844, when there were still four children listed, including their daughter, Jane. Lewis Langley, twenty years old, and Henry, who was eighteen, did not attend anymore, but Loudon had entered the classroom by that time. Loudon turned out to be an excellent writer, and in the next decade, he gave testament not only to his activism on behalf of those enslaved, but also to the fine education that he and his siblings received at the Hill schools.

The Langleys, though still on the Huntington census in 1840, were mostly living and going to school on the Hinesburgh side of the Hill by the end of the decade. In the 1840 census report, eight free colored persons were written into Calvin Wells's white household of seven people. Just below Wells was William Langley's name, indicating another household, but the rest of the line was blank. It is probable that the enumerator wrote the numbers on the wrong line, or William and his older sons were likely working on the Wells farm the day the enumerator came around, so they were counted in the Wells household.[67] Their history on the Hill points to their needing extra money, so it is entirely possible that the family had become farm laborers for the Wellses, in addition to working their own farm.

There is evidence that the Langleys had their own small house on the Hinesburgh side of the Hill on Clark land. The land records mentioned that William Langley's house was near the cemetery, but they were never taxed for a house in either Huntington or in Hinesburgh, and their name never appeared on maps, unlike the Clarks. According to the 1857 Wallings map (figure 1.3) and Violet's dower, her house was north of the road, but there was another house just south of the road and near the cemetery at the time. This close-knit family had apparently built their houses close together on each other's land as Prince and Samuel Peters had done at the bottom of the Hill. The grand lists for the decade put the Langleys in District 11 in Hinesburgh, and they certainly had a house according to land records.

There is some evidence that their house is still standing on the Hill today. Imagine the porch and additions taken off this house (figure 3.2). There is an almost central chimney with a stone foundation behind the trellis, indicative of the period. The chimney indicates a fireplace in each of the two rooms on the first floor. The second floor loft for sleeping would be warmed by the heat rising from the fireplaces. They may have built a barn or used the Clark barn across the road. This house was also near the Langley land in Huntington and just east of the family cemetery. This was a perfect place for Almira, being close to her parents and siblings, especially with six children. It would also be helpful for William, being close to in-laws who would have helped each other with farm chores in a communal fashion, as did the Peterses.

FIGURE 3.2    Possible Langley house.

The Langleys seemed to have thrived in their small house, and sometime during the 1840s, William got together enough money to reclaim
the fifty-acre deed that he had given to John Norton in Huntington with
the stipulation he could buy it back for only the interest on the loan of
farm animals. It had been ten years since they had made the deal, and
Norton had died in the meantime. William expected his heirs to honor
the agreement; however, Norton's daughter, Amanda, refused to do so,
claiming she now owned his land. William knew she had no right to his
land and sued her, and it is from the court records that we get the story.

The Superior Court records for Chittenden County said that Langley was indebted to J. Norton for "divers cows and sheep which the said
Norton had before that time set out to said Orator (William Langley)
for his use and to profit thereby which is customary amongst farmers."[68]
The manure would have fertilized the land and the milk and wool would
have provided for the family. In addition, the Langleys could keep any
offspring born while the animals were in their care. Langley was to
return the original number of animals and a number of pounds of wool
at some point. However, Norton wanted some security, so William had
given him the deed to his fifty acres as a mortgage until he could dis-
charge the debt. Part of the deal was that William would continue in
possession of the land and Norton would never claim it as his own.

Norton filed the deed in Huntington, but he omitted written stipu-
lations that no land was transferred. William testified in court that no
money ever changed hands and that everyone understood the deed to

be only a mortgage to secure the indebtedness concerning the animals. Norton died intestate on January 1, 1842, before William could repay the debt, and Amanda Norton and Joseph Marsh became administrators for her father's estate. So it was to them that William applied to repay and cancel his debt with the estate. They resisted, saying they would not do it without an order from the Probate Court; so William filed an appeal with the Court on August 23, 1842.

The Probate Court ascertained that William was telling the truth and ordered Norton-Marsh to receive the goods and cash and cancel the debt. William owed forty-seven sheep and forty-seven pounds of wool by October 1, 1842, and $48.38 cash by October 10. He delivered the sheep and wool, but "by reason of poverty and the straightened circumstances of his family and the condition of the title to said land (he was) rendered unable to procure the cash" by October.[69] In September 1845, William applied to Amanda to accept the cash plus interest, which he had finally procured. She refused to accept it, saying that William now owed them the full worth of the land (between $400 and $500) or he would lose it to the Norton estate. William was incensed. No one from the estate had ever told him that they owned the land or were in anyway entitled to posses it. William complained to the Superior Court in Burlington.

The Superior Court went through the "usual process of subpoena . . . on said defendants," and Amanda eventually "confessed that said deed was a mortgage as alleged in said bill and that the only sum due thereon was the said sum" of $48.38.[70] The court decreed that William should have a year to pay the amount with interest of $11. One year later, William finally canceled his debt with the Norton estate.

It appeared that Amanda Norton and Marsh had knowingly tried to cheat William out of his property. This is the only instance that I uncovered of whites in either Hinesburgh or Huntington trying to take advantage of these families of color during these early years. Of course, it did not work, but Norton and Marsh apparently had hoped that William Langley would not understand his rights or be unable to sue them. He no doubt surprised them with his tenacity and knowledge of the court system. Racism may have had something to do with their mistakenly believing they could dupe him out of his land, but it had little to do with the outcome in Superior Court.

The outcome of this court case belies the traditional narrative of ubiquitous hatred and virulent racism directed toward people of color at this time. William Langley not only testified against white people in court, but also won his case against them. The judiciary had shown an even hand, with no racial favoritism. Yet there was more than judicial integrity at work in this community. The lasting friendships between the Yaws and Clarks and between Bowles and McEuen demonstrate that close relations between people of color and whites were possible, even in a time of hard-edged racism. These people who worked closely together in this rural neighborhood, whether in farming or religious activities, exhibited the real possibilities for cross-racial bonds despite the ideology of the wider nation.

Rowland and Rachel Robinson, white Quakers from a nearby Ferrisburgh farm, hired many formerly enslaved runaways from the South to help them with their transition to living as free people. They had been founding members of the Vermont Anti-slavery Society and, true to their beliefs, boycotted slave-produced sugar and cotton. They also hired free blacks from Vermont. One farm laborer in their employ was Aaron Freeman, who had been born free in Charlotte, Vermont. He was working at Rokeby in 1846 for five dollars a month, and by 1849 he was making twelve dollars per month. A letter from George Robinson, who did not share his parents' liberal bent, showed that Aaron might be looking for a wife.

In 1847, George was visiting Savannah, Georgia, and wrote home, "The Addison [County] folks seem to be going [to] their death or marrying. I hope they won't all get married. Tell Aaron I could get him a very nice wife here, either a little black, a good deal black, or as black as tar, as we have all the varieties."[71] It obviously never crossed his mind that Aaron would marry anyone other than a black woman, and the tone of his letter was likely not welcomed by the Robinsons or Aaron. Aaron later found his wife on the Hill in Hinesburgh: Rachel Williams, the daughter of Phoebe and Edward.

During this time, two baby girls were born who would also join the circle of the Hill families. Jane Maria Anthony was born about 1843 in Elizabethtown, New York, the daughter of Eliza "Lizzie" Thomas and Tony Anthony, who married and later moved to Burlington, Vermont, with Jane and their baby daughter, Annette. When they grew up, the Anthony women eventually wed men from the top of the Hill, cousins Loudon Langley and George Williams. It was not surprising that the Langleys and the Anthonys met and enjoyed each others' company, since both families were activists on the Underground Railroad. Their marriages to men from the Hill would take the girls, especially Jane, to other states and into unimagined adventures in the coming decades.

## CHAPTER FOUR

Prelude to War, 1850–1860

Let men so interested . . . lend their influence in favor of giving us "liberty and equal rights" in the land of our birth.
—Loudon S. Langley, letter to the editor
 of the *Green Mountain Freeman*, 1854

None but an American slaveholder could have discovered that a man born in a country was not a citizen of it.
—William Cooper Nell, *The Colored Patriots
 of the American Revolution*

From statehood to 1850, Vermonters had experienced political, geographical, religious and socioeconomic transformation. The old-growth forest had almost completely disappeared, and larger dairy farms were replacing mixed agricultural plots as milk products became important to the state's economy. Sizeable Greek revival homes graced the streets of larger towns, and sprawling farmhouses began to replace earlier modest settler cabins. Political parties had come and gone, religious revivals had burned over the state, and textile mills and factories dotted the landscape. Trains now chugged along new tracks from Boston to Burlington and telegraph wires would soon arrive.

Despite advancements in agriculture and industry, by mid-century Vermont was the slowest-growing state in the union. Many people took the advice of former Vermonter Horace Greeley in an 1851 *New York Tribune* article to "Go West!" A section of Rutland was nicknamed "Little Nebraska," because so many people left that neighborhood for the Nebraska Territory. Not only were people migrating to the wide-open spaces of the west, but sheep were too. The U.S. government had lifted its protective tariff on sheep in 1846, and the price of wool plunged, causing merino farmers to slaughter their herds and sell the meat or sell living rams to western farmers. Those who could afford the shift to dairy did so, but they needed capital to expand their farms, since cows needed considerably more grazing acreage than sheep to be profitable. Wealthier farmers bought out those who went broke during the slump in the merino market. With an increase in landless people due to failing farms and the economy moving toward depression in 1857, two out of every five people born in the state risked migration to the west or to larger cities of the north to find jobs in industry.[1]

At the same time, millions of immigrants were taking perilous trips across the ocean, many in steerage, with the Americas as their destination. By 1850, Vermont's population included 11 percent who had been born in foreign countries, the largest groups from Ireland and French Canada. Many women and blacks lost their industrial or labor jobs, as Yankee employers preferred to hire from the widening pool of white, male laborers. "The housing patterns for black Vermonters indicated they had been steadily rejecting roles as live-in domestics and laborers in white households, but again returned to those roles in mid-century as immigration numbers swelled. Presumably, in the increasing competition among Irish, French, and Africans, the latter lost."[2]

This was not unique to Vermont. Frederick Douglass lamented, "Every hour sees the black man elbowed out of employment by some newly arrived immigrant whose hunger and whose color are thought to give him better title."[3] Because of the passionate abolitionist activity in the North, activist Martin Delany had hoped that white antislavery men would raise blacks from their menial positions by hiring them into their businesses. The only way to elevation, claimed Delany, who had been ousted from Harvard because of complaints about his color, was through the hiring practices of white antislavery men. "There was no other ostensible object [of antislavery] in view. . . . But in all this we were doomed to disappointment, sad, sad disappointment."[4]

William Wells Brown, born enslaved in Kentucky in 1815 and considered the first African American playwright, took Americans to task because they welcomed millions of Europeans to their shores and into their businesses but kept native-born men and women in chains:

> If [Americans] would inspire the hearts of the struggling millions in
> Europe, they should not allow one human being to wear chains upon their
> own soil. If they would welcome the martyrs for freedom from the banks

of the Danube, the Tiber and the Seine, let them liberate their own slaves on the banks of the Mississippi and the Potomac. If they would welcome the Hungarian flying from the bloody talons of the Austrian eagle, they must wrest the three millions of slaves from the talons of their own. They cannot welcome the wanderer from the battle-fields of freedom in the old world, as long as the new world is the battle-field of slavery."[5]

By mid-century, much of the economic and social turbulence of Vermont's earlier years had subsided, "largely absorbed by the overriding issue of anti-slavery."[6] The U.S. Congress passed the Fugitive Slave Act in 1850, which provided for imprisonment and fines for people who aided those escaping slavery. In response, the Vermont General Assembly declared that any fugitive who reached the state would be declared free. Two years later, depictions of slavery in *Uncle Tom's Cabin* created more intense antislavery efforts in the country, while the 1854 Kansas-Nebraska Act fanned abolitionist fires by repealing the Missouri Compromise and permitting people of new territories to vote whether or not to allow slavery. Another severe setback for antislavery forces was the *Dred Scott v. Sandford* Supreme Court case of 1857, which declared that blacks were not citizens of the United States.

In 1858, the newly formed Republican Party chose Abraham Lincoln to run against Stephen Douglas, a native Vermonter, for a senate seat from Illinois.[7] In accepting the nomination, Lincoln gave his famous "house divided" speech, which declared that a nation could not survive half slave and half free; it must be all one or all the other. Even his friends and supporters considered the speech too radical for the American public. At the ensuing Lincoln-Douglas debates, Douglas democrats who were "militantly white" chanted "whitemen, whitemen!" over and over to ensure the candidates remained committed to white domination.[8] Douglas, who had grown to manhood in Brandon, Vermont, did nothing to stop the racist chants and accused Lincoln of being a race-mixer, an accusation, although untrue, that whipped up the militancy of his supporters even more. Douglas eventually won the senate seat.

Many blacks who had once disdained colonization gave up their dreams of freedom and equality in the United States and emigrated. By this time, Martin Delany, who had once believed in the equality of the races, was "practically a black supremacist" and felt that blacks could attain freedom and justice only through emigration.[9] He supported emigration to Canada and Central and South America, but not Liberia, since Liberia, "being the offspring of slavery—is in itself, sufficient to blast it in the estimation of every colored person in the United States."[10] His close friend from Vermont, Martin H. Freeman, did not share his revulsion of Liberia.

Martin Freeman was born in 1826 and grew up in Rutland, Vermont. He was tutored by his pastor at the Congregational church until he reached eighteen and subsequently attended Middlebury College, where he was salutatorian and voted by his class to give the commencement address, which he gave in Latin. From Middlebury, he moved to Pittsburgh, Pennsylvania, in 1850 to become the first black college professor in the United States at Allegheny Institute—later renamed Avery College. In Pittsburgh he became friends with Delany who had an enormous impact on him.

In this new environment, Freeman's thinking about race and emigration quickened. In Vermont, he had not experienced the real depths of American racism, which left him "totally unprepared to deal with the onslaught of unremitting slights and assaults that resulted from" his treatment due to race in Pittsburgh.[11] At the same time, the city was rife with educated, black activists whose worldviews were radically different from their parents'. The earlier generations had made great strides in opening doors for their children, but national legislation and Supreme Court decisions of the 1850s threatened all blacks with reduced rights and even loss of liberty.

After attending the 1854 National Emigration Convention in Cleveland, where he first heard Delany speak, he began to think about where people of color could succeed. He had became increasingly convinced that self-respect was what blacks needed most and that it could not be cultivated in urban centers, where blacks were met daily with harsh treatment. Perhaps thinking of his childhood in Rutland, he suggested that blacks move to the country to pursue agriculture or to small towns to pursue a craft. He advised, "be industrious and economical and you will secure a position in community for which you might strive in vain in the crowded city." He believed that only when blacks gained a full appreciation for themselves as human beings would "the race arise self-emancipated, self-elevated, and self-redeemed."[12]

By the early 1860s Freeman had decided to take his own advice and leave America for a small farm and a college professorship in Monrovia, Liberia. He explained one reason in a letter to the secretary of the Massachusetts Colonization Society: "We are anxious to leave this country.

. . . My little girl is imbibing ideas in regard to color, race, &c which I did hope she would never learn."[13]

By 1860, thousands of people of color had come to the same conclusion and emigrated. However, they took Delany's advice, which suggested that blacks become pioneers, like the Puritans, and migrate to Canada or Central or South America. He believed that, "God has . . . designed this great portion of the New World, for us, the colored races."[14] While the American Colonization Society sent more than 13,000 emigrants to Liberia, most emigrants stayed within the hemisphere of their birth: between 8,000 and 13,000 black Americans migrated to Haiti, and more than 30,000 chose Canada.[15]

### Coping with the Loss of Wives and Mothers

The Hill in Hinesburgh was relatively close to the Canadian border — a symbol of freedom for tens of thousands of people of color. Despite the fact that the 1850s began poorly for the Hill families, most did not view emigration to Canada or anywhere else as an answer to their difficulties. However, some of the long-standing residents were undergoing other changes in their lives. Josephus and Charlot Peters and their five boys, although included in the census for Hinesburgh in 1850, disappeared from the grand lists for four years. During that time his 100 acres dwindled to only 5 improved acres. We do not know what happened to the property during that time, but the loss may have had something to do with Charlot's illness and death and the accompanying expenses.

In January 1850, the family experienced the loss of wife and mother when Charlot died at forty-six years of age. At that time, the Peterses did not own lot 83 at the bottom of the Hill where the rest of the family was presumably buried, so Josephus, also forty-six, buried her in the cemetery near the wealthy McEuen farm in Hinesburgh, where he occasionally worked as a laborer. There were only a couple of stones there at the time, and many white citizens of early Hinesburgh now surround her.

Josephus was forced to take on the work of raising his five boys. However, there were soon two more boys to father, because Sarah Peters, his thirty-seven-year-old sister, moved in with them along with her two boys, one a new born baby. Surely Sarah was there to help care for her five motherless nephews, although she may have needed a home, since

FIGURE 4.1 Charlot Peters's
gravestone.

there is no sign of her husband, Charles Edwards, in the census or
grand lists for 1850.[16]

Josephus reappears in the town records as having paid his poll taxes
in 1851, but the family lands had dwindled to a few acres and buildings
according to the 1855 grand lists. The Peterses were never in the list
of *Writs and Executions* as having their land attached for nonpayment
of debts since the time Samuel was jailed, and I find no land records
of their having sold property. They may have sold much of their land
without filing the deeds at the Town Clerk's office, but they seemed to
have lost most of it by mid-century. Regardless, after Charlot's death,
Josephus and his sons survived on the Hill with the help of Sarah, by
continuing small-scale farming and laboring for a wealthier farmer
nearby.

The families at the top of the Hill were also in mourning for women
who had passed away. In September 1850, Almira Clark Langley, fifty-
three, died, leaving William and their children to carry on without her.
She had lived all her life on the Hill except for a brief time when she had

lived in Pittsford on William's farm. In addition to her husband, she left behind her children and her mother, Violet. Six of her children, aged from fourteen to twenty-six, were still living at home: Lewis, Jeremiah, Newell, Henry, Jane, and Loudon.[17] Since eighteen-year-old Jane was the only daughter, much work fell on her shoulders. She did, however, have a grandmother and her aunt Harriet nearby to help. Nevertheless, it was a difficult time for the family, not only because of Almira's death, but also because Almira's younger sister, Phoebe, had predeceased her.

Phoebe had been born and raised on the Hill and had never left— she was a real Vermont hill farmer until the day she died. Her husband, Edward Williams, migrated to the Hill from Maryland, and they had lived on Clark land for about ten years. In 1847, there was a Vermont flu epidemic; perhaps Phoebe died from the flu, leaving two young children to be cared for. With no death certificate, we cannot be sure of the cause of death or the exact year, but the cemetery at the top of the Hill was expanding, as Violet buried two daughters there within a short time. The members of the pioneering generation, including Prince, Samuel, and Eliza Peters and Shubael and Violet Clark, lived much longer lives than these women of the next generation. Charlot, Phoebe, and Almira unfortunately did not live long enough to experience one of the greatest benefits of northern freedom: holding their grandchildren in their arms.

In addition to mourning two of her daughters, Violet also witnessed the marriage of another. It was not unusual for a widower to marry his sister-in-law, and this was what happened on the Hill. By 1850, Harriet Clark had stepped into the void left by her sister, Phoebe, and married Edward Williams. Phoebe's children were not motherless for long. Harriet, in her fifties by this time, never bore children, but she devoted the rest of her life to raising her niece and nephew.

*Slavery and Colonization Issues*

In addition to their personal trials, the attention of some of the people on the Hill turned to the antislavery and colonization issues that were enflaming the country. For the families on the Hill, these were personal matters. Despite various occupations and social classes, all blacks in nineteenth-century America were expected to "work against the greatest disadvantage African Americans faced—the institution of slavery."[18]

It was the common problem that united all blacks in the Western Hemisphere, and those in Vermont were no exception in their hatred of slavery. Vermonter Andrew Harris, who had been denied acceptance to Middlebury College because of his color explained: Slavery "presses down upon the free people of color. Its deadly poison is disseminated from the torrid regions of the South to the frigid North. We feel it here."[19] Yet Harris, along with many other Vermont blacks, never supported colonization.

Another man who felt discrimination because of his color but would rather stay in the land of his birth was Almira and William Langley's youngest child, Loudon. It is unknown how much the Hill people immersed themselves in the issues of race and colonization in earlier decades. The experiences of the Hill people were so typically ones of Vermont pioneers that it seems as if they identified more as rural Vermont farmers than as African Americans. This may have been the case earlier in the century, but by the 1850s, Loudon Langley was showing that he identified closely with people of color all over the Americas, including those as far away as Cuba. We know he read black publications because he wrote letters to the editor of the *Anglo-African* magazine. He also read the *Green Mountain Freeman*, a Vermont abolitionist newspaper. In an 1855 letter to the paper, he revealed his passion for ending slavery in the Western Hemisphere and his hatred of colonization ideas. In the letter, which concerned Cuba, he indicated he would support revolt against those who held others enslaved: "I am no advocate of war, I mean an unjust war; and as bad as I hate war, I hate tyrants and tyranny worse. Yes, I go further, and I say, that every nation has a God-given right to rebel against any laws, unjust laws, that the tyrants may deem fit to make and enforce."[20]

In another letter he raised the question of freedman and women colonizing Liberia. "The writer should warn all people whose color is identified with his own, to resist, with more than usual energy, the extraordinary efforts now made by the Colonizationists."[21] Martin Freeman, of the same generation as Loudon, was reaching the opposite conclusion from his college post in Pittsburgh, Pennsylvania. In 1858, he wrote to Martin Delany, who had migrated to Canada saying, "I am more and more convinced that Africa is the country to which all colored men who wish to attain the full stature of manhood, and bring up their children to be men and not creeping things, should turn their steps."[22]

Letters from Burlington resident James Holly to the American Colonization Society indicated that other Vermonters of African descent did not feel as Loudon did. In 1850 we find brothers Joseph and James Holly living in Burlington with their sister and mother. In 1844, the family, originally from Washington, D.C., "removed northward to be releived [*sic*] of *some* of the disabilities free colored men labor under in the South."[23] Joseph and James were shoemakers, a trade they had learned from their father, and they had a shop in Burlington. The family has been documented as having harbored people escaping slavery during their time in the state.[24] They also staged debates over colonization: Joseph argued against it, and James argued for it.

According to a letter that James Holly wrote in 1850 to Mr. W. McClain of the American Colonization Society, he was studying the classics with the Rev. J. K. Converse of Burlington in order to escape American prejudice and move to Liberia. Converse was the same man who passionately argued against abolition and for colonization before the Vermont Colonization Society in 1840 and was the secretary of that organization by 1850. In his letter to McClain, James stated:

> If I prosecute a thorough Classical and Scientific education by devoting my spare hours to private study, and relying upon the incidental instruction of such private teachers as I may come across, my progress must necessarily be slow in arriving at a completion; but I hope to make a solid acquirement ultimately, and consecrate it to the service of Liberia.
>
> I wish it were in my power to devote myself entirely to Study . . . but I must be content with the decree of circumstances. Perhaps to fit and prepare myself through toil and privation for such a mission will furnish my life with a prouder event than if accomplished under easier circumstances. The *love of liberty* shall make me persevere.[25]

James was studying to be of service in Liberia, perhaps as a teacher or minister, for which the classics would have prepared him. In the same letter, he divulged how he spent some of his free time.

> I have succeeded in creating quite a spirit of inquiry in relation to Colonization amongst my associates here . . . by debating the following question with my brother, before several meetings, "Can the colored people of the US best elevate their condition by remaining in this country, or by emigrating to Liberia?" He supported the first proposition from earnest conviction, and in like manner I advocated the latter.[26]

Charles M. Clark, living with his mother, Violet, on the Hill, was also a shoemaker, and may have been one of James's "associates." It's possible he and others from the Hill attended one of the debates. They no doubt argued the issue among themselves. The following letter shows that it was certainly a passionate matter for Charles's cousin and neighbor, Loudon Langley, who wrote a letter to the editor of the *Green Mountain Freeman* in which he excoriated the idea of colonization:

> I shall bear down against them (the Colonization Society) without cere-
> mony. . . . Sir, my attachments for a good policy towards all those whose
> color is identified with my own, will forever make me the antagonist of
> that Society. . . . If the Society is actuated with such a love for my people,
> let men so interested, and every other, cease their efforts in behalf of that
> Society, (for their labor is in vain, so far as regards to the triumph of their
> policy,) and lend their influence in favor of giving us "liberty and equal
> rights" in the land of our birth. But they know very well that if colored
> people are equal with their "white fellow citizens" that their influence
> would be stronger for the immediate abolition of Slavery in the District of
> Columbia, (that is there tolerated, and with shame we may say it, before
> the very eyes of foreign ambassadors). . . .
>
> Mr. J. K. Converse, Secretary of the Society, in his report made in
> A.D. 1850, says that there were a few colored people in the vicinity of
> Burlington, whom he thought would go to the new Republic. Let me say
> to the Secretary that I am quite confident that no colored people in Burl-
> ington have gone or will ever go to Liberia. The majority of the emigrants
> from the United States are liberated slaves, who are compelled by the laws
> of free America to leave their native land; and even some of those, rather
> than go to that Republic, have been known to make their way north,
> under the pretense of going to Liberia after their arrival.
>
> The writer should warn all people whose color is identified with his
> own, to resist, with more than usual energy, the extraordinary efforts now
> made by the Colonizationists, inasmuch as they are founded on the most
> unjust prejudice against all the men of our race. What say you, Mr. Edi-
> tor! Are you in favor of Colonization! If you are, my language is plain.[27]

The letters of Martin Freeman, James Holly, and Loudon Langley illustrate not only the diversity of ideas among people of color but
also the excellent education that these men had received. Freeman was
schooled in Rutland and attended Middlebury College. James had been

tutored in Washington, D.C., and furthered his education in Burlington by studying the classics, a high-status subject in preparation for the clergy. Loudon was schooled on the Hill, having been born and raised there. Clearly, living in the rural area of the Hill did not hinder his (or his relatives') education or isolate him from the issues of the day. The people of the Hill were actively engaged in the wider world and keenly interested in the issues affecting blacks in the country.

Other black activists lived in Burlington at the time and were intimately acquainted with their fellow activists in Hinesburgh. Evidence of this is the fact that two men from the Hill married women from the Anthony family, who were also documented as having harbored fugitives from slavery.[28] We have no way of knowing how they met. However, it is easy to imagine the cousins Charles Clark, Loudon Langley, and George Williams attending a colonization debate between the Holly brothers in Burlington. Tony and Eliza Anthony and their daughters, being from Burlington must have taken an interest in attending such a gathering. Activists on both sides of the debate would have been there — some perhaps for no other reason than to heckle James Holly! Others may have attended who were interested in receiving free copies of *The African Repository*, a colonizationist publication, and "willing to Read and circulate it amongst their friends."[29] Imagine the fireworks that might ensue among these strong-minded people during a debate of these issues. Certainly Loudon would have forcefully made his views known — and a young Jane Anthony would have taken notice of the articulate, five-foot-nine Langley as he rose and filled the hall with his voice.[30]

What we know to be true is that in 1859 Loudon Langley and Jane Anthony were married in nearby Winooski Falls, Vermont. Loudon's cousin, George Williams, attested to the date and place years later when helping Jane get her widow's pension for Loudon's service in the Civil War.[31] George eventually married Jane's sister, Nettie, and had a barbershop business in Burlington with her brother, Abial Anthony, who years later recalled his parents harboring fugitives from Virginia and New Orleans.[32]

George and Loudon were living away from the Hill at the time of their marriages, perhaps in Winooski. Those still on the Hill were continuing their farm chores in the midst of social unrest, which does not mean they ignored the roiling social matters, it just means they also had to continue the work of Hill farmers to survive. They may have felt like William Cooper Nell, considered the first black historian, who wrote, "The white man . . . has come to think the colored man fit only for the menial drudgery to which the majority of the race has been so long doomed. This prejudice was never reasoned up and will never be reasoned down. *It must be lived down*."[33] For sixty years this community had been living their lives alongside their white neighbors and in the process had been living down the inferiority theories that had followed them to the Hill. What remains of their stories reveals their varying degrees of success.

### The Peters, Edwards, and Waters Families

Sustained family support to cope with the loss of property continued to be the theme at the bottom of the Hill. By this time, the Peterses, once on the cutting edge of farming practices, had only 12 acres, far fewer than the average farm in Vermont, which was 139 acres, of which 87 were improved acres.[34] However, Caroline Peters, who had married Henry Riley of Ridgefield, Connecticut, and moved there, still owned the 20 acres on lot 83 that she had bought from the elder Samuel in 1830. It would make sense in this family, who had lived together and farmed collectively for decades, that Josephus and his older sons would farm her acreage in order to supplement the family resources.

However, Josephus Peters no longer farmed as his sole means of survival; laboring for others had become his primary source of income by mid-century. We know that he sometimes worked in Hinesburgh for his wealthier farming neighbor, Augustus McEuen, and also for the town doing odd jobs, such as mending fences.[35] At a minimum though, he would still perform basic farming chores, turning the soil with his horse-drawn plow and harvesting with scythes. Josephus and his older sons were certainly chopping and sawing wood, caring for a horse, spreading and raking hay, binding the grain, husking and shelling corn, and the like. Josephus's sister, Sarah, and the younger boys had their hands full taking care of baby William and turning raw materials into items used by the family. They milked a cow or two, made soap and candles, spun linen and wool, and wove cloth. No doubt there was little money to buy manufactured goods. The women and children also sewed clothing, made butter, put food by, and cared for the kitchen garden.

There were two marriages in the Peters family this decade; one was Josephus's son George to Mary Jane Peters, born in Canada East (modern-day southern Quebec). I found no marriage record, but by 1858, they had two daughters. Josephus's first granddaughter was born one month before the Dred Scott Decision.[36] Picture the discussions on the Hill when they read the local papers proclaiming that blacks, whether slave or free, could never be citizens of the United States. Did the old fear of not being quite equal emerge from the recesses of their minds? They must have worried terribly for their children and grandchildren. If they read the text, they would have encountered these words:

> The question before us is, whether the class of persons described in the plea in abatement [African Americans] compose a portion of this people, and are constituent members of this sovereignty? We think they are not, and that they are not included, and were not intended to be included, under the word "citizens" in the Constitution, and can therefore claim none of the rights and privileges which that instrument provides for and secures to citizens of the United States. On the contrary, they were at that time considered as a subordinate and inferior class of beings, who had been subjugated by the dominant race, and, whether emancipated or not, yet remained subject to their authority, and had no rights or privileges but such as those who held the power and the Government might choose to grant them. . . .
>
> They had for more than a century before been regarded as beings of an inferior order, and altogether unfit to associate with the white race, either in social or political relations; and so far inferior, that they had no rights which the white man was bound to respect; and that the negro might justly and lawfully be reduced to slavery for his benefit. He was bought and sold, and treated as an ordinary article of merchandise and traffic, whenever a profit could be made by it. This opinion was at that time fixed and universal in the civilized portion of the white race.[37]

African Americans and many whites were outraged by the decision and fiercely disagreed that a "civilized portion" of any race would come to such a decision. According to Loudon Langley, slavery is "an institution of bondage that half-civilized nations are becoming heartily ashamed of."[38] The court, in the decision written by Roger Taney—a staunch supporter of slavery—also declared the 1820 Missouri Compromise unconstitutional. The result was that slavery was now permitted in the territories of the United States. The decision showed, in stark terms, the political power of the South, and it greatly increased the tensions in the country around the slavery issue. It certainly incensed the citizens of the Hill, who had long voted and actively participated in the civic, economic, and religious life of the community. Did they worry about their own places in the wider Hinesburgh and Vermont society, or did they assume that the decision by slaveholders would not affect them in Vermont?

The debate in Vermont was settled the following year when the Vermont General Assembly passed resolutions relating to the Supreme Court's decision. In part, the resolutions stated:

> Resolved, That all laws of Congress which recognize the right of property in man, or deprive any person of liberty without due process of law and a jury trial, or provide that any person shall be delivered up, as owing service to another, without such trial, are unconstitutional, void, and of no effect.
>
> Resolved, That these extra-judicial opinions of the Supreme Court of the United States are a dangerous usurpation of power, and have no binding authority upon Vermont, or the people of the United States.
>
> Resolved, That no ingenious sophistry of the judges of that court can make it appear that the citizens of each State are not citizens of the United States, and citizens when in the other States; and entitled, as such, to all rights and privileges of citizens in the several States.
>
> Resolved, That, whenever the government or judiciary of the United States refuses or neglects to protect the citizens of each State in their lives or liberty, when in another State or territory, it becomes the duty of the sovereign and independent States of this Union to protect their own citizens, at whatever hazard or cost.[39]

Feeling secure in his rights as a citizen of Vermont, that same year Josephus Peters's son John took the Freeman's Oath in Hinesburgh. The Vermont Constitution provided that any man who was a citizen of the United States and "of a quiet and peaceable behavior" should take the oath, swearing to always vote his conscience, in order to gain suffrage in the state.[40] By accepting John, the town clerk in Hinesburgh signified his acceptance of him as a citizen of the United States, disregarding the Supreme Court ruling. Soon after, Joseph Peters and Loudon Langley traveled into town one fall day to take their Freeman's Oath as well.

The three men were continuing in the tradition of their fathers, who had long been voting citizens of the Hill. Conceivably William Langley and Josephus accompanied their sons to town with a feeling of stubborn pride as they took part in civic activities denied other African Americans in the country. One wonders how they felt as they neared the village of mostly white people. Did they feel vulnerable? Did old fears of being looked at as "somehow flawed," lump in their stomachs?[41] Of course, their families' years of farming in the community and good relations with their white neighbors on the Hill provided them with some armor against the racism of the times, perhaps enough to approach the town clerk's office with as much confidence as in the past.

A newcomer to the Hill, farm laborer Henry Prince, twenty-one, from St. Albans, accompanied Joseph and Loudon to take his Freeman's Oath too. The Princes and the Peterses also had a family relationship. Sometime during the decade, Josephus married Amy Prince, originally from St. Albans. She was the daughter of another Henry Prince, who had deep roots in the Swanton–St. Albans area. Amy was fifteen years younger than Josephus, with enough energy to help raise his boys. In all probability, they met through the younger Henry Prince, who worked at the Lemuel E. Livermore farm on the Hill. It would be natural for Henry to become friends with other young African American men on the Hill and socialize with them and their families.

Livermore, a white farmer and businessman, first appeared on the Hill in 1852 owning some buildings in District 11 on the school lot near the Clark farm. Over the decade, he gradually accumulated about 60 acres on the Hill and large parcels elsewhere in town. With two white partners, he acquired over 400 acres in District 11. Some of the expanding Livermore land had been traditional Peters farmland bought from Caroline Peters's children, and thus passing into white hands for the first time. Only the Abenakis and the Peters had ever lived there.

At the end of January 1857, a lawyer by the name of Hiram Scott, from Ridgefield, Connecticut, appeared in Hinesburgh to sell Caroline's property. Both Caroline and her husband, Henry Riley, had died, leaving the twenty acres to their two children, who had no interest in keeping it. This was the same land that Samuel Peters had deeded to Caroline in 1830 – part of lot 83. In April, Livermore bought the piece for $300. The Peterses still owned a small part of lot 83, deeded to Prince and the younger Samuel Peters, and another part leased to a neighbor, but with the sale, their property was dwindling, even as the family was growing.[42]

Josephus must have felt a sinking feeling as the land that had been in the family for sixty years changed hands – but unfortunately, he had no money to buy the plot at that time.[43] The country was in a depression, and similar sales of lands were occurring among whites. The dwindling land meant that not all of Josephus's sons could support families on the Hill as farmers, and his son Henry and wife Cynthia moved away to farm in nearby Colchester. However, George, the only other son who ever married, decided to stay on the Hill with his wife, Mary Jane, to raise their young children.

In addition to the growing number of people with the surname of Peters at the bottom of the Hill, there were two other related families in the neighborhood. Maps and the federal census reports show that in addition to George's family, Josephus's sister Sarah Edwards and her husband and Calista Peters and her husband all lived nearby in the growing Peters community.[44] In 1850 Sarah and her children had been living with Josephus, with no sign of her husband, Charles Edwards. But by 1860, Charles was again living with her and their two sons. One child had died during the preceding decade. By this decade, the Edwards family joined the extended family on the land inherited by Sarah that had first been settled by Prince and Hannah more than sixty years earlier.

A mysterious family living nearby is Charles and Calista Waters. Charles first appeared on the grand lists for 1855 with a four-acre lot and a building, and then on an 1857 map with his house just north of Josephus (see figure 1.3). Charles, fifty at the time, was born in Maryland. The only other black non-New Englander on the Hill was Edward Williams at the top of the Hill, also born in Maryland. This seems too much of a coincidence; they must have known each other before their migrations to Vermont. Perhaps the men traveled north together, or Charles followed Edward. At any rate, Charles was married to Calista, fifty-four, and they had joined the communal living arrangements begun by Samuel, Prince, and Hannah decades earlier.

There is no official evidence that Calista Waters's maiden name was Peters, but in my research the people on the Hill who seemed unrelated at first glance usually turned out to be directly related through the women. Family support was important, and living closely together gave them an intimate social network. Moreover, earlier there had been a Calista Peters who belonged to the same Hinesburgh Baptist Church as others from the Hill. A piece of evidence that this Calista became Mrs. Waters is the naming of the Waters's children. Their older son was Charles, named after his father. Their second son was named Samuel.

Perhaps Calista was a child of the elder Samuel Peters and named her son after his grandfather. There is a tradition on the Hill of the same family names being used generation after generation, but we have no further evidence on this question. In any case, there was a growing community of people of color at the bottom of the Hill, as well as the top, interrelated by lineage and rural traditions. The Peterses had little in the way of material goods or land, but they had a growing family around them for support on a portion of their traditional farmland.

Although the growing Peters clan was losing economic status, it appears that they had always paid their debts. Since Samuel's legal problems for nonpayment of debts in 1820, the town never again attached their land for any reason during this period.[45] The same cannot be said for the Clark-Langley-Williams families at the top of the Hill. During the 1830s and 1840s, they had been better off than the Peterses, but by the 1850s, they were not in good shape financially. To be sure, it was a period of uncertainty, considering the increasing problems between the North and South, and the state was deep in a depression by 1857.

## The Clark, Langley, and Williams Families

The most telling document concerning the situation at the top of the Hill is the Hinesburgh Record of Writs and Executions of 1829–1853 (table 4.1). Through 1850, the families never appeared in it. Beginning in 1851, however, some of them were having a hard time paying their debts. The worst offenders were Jerry and Henry Langley and Edward Williams. Because of the Langley brothers' debts, their father's farm was attached a number of times from 1851 to 1853. One wonders about the conversations within the household between their father, William, and his two twenty-something sons. They owed money at Alexander Fergusen's store and to white neighbors, including Daniel Ray.

The land records of Hinesburgh for this period are also instructive concerning their finances. The Langleys, who started the decade with land in Huntington but none in Hinesburgh (even though their house was there on Clark land), eventually acquired land on the west side of the Hill in Hinesburgh. In May 1851, Lewis W., Jeremiah N., and Henry C. Langley, all of Hinesburgh, bought the "Clark Farm," where the Langleys resided, for $1,300. They signed a mortgage deed on the same day to the Peterses' neighbor, Daniel Ray. They had to pay four

TABLE 4.1
*Hinesburgh Record of Writs and Executions*

| Date of writ | Names & amounts | Officer's return |
|---|---|---|
| Aug. 17, 1850 | George Peters v. Allen Sweet for $20[a] | Attached all of Sweet's land & hay |
| July 1, 1851 | Alexander Fergusen[b] v. Henry Langley for $75 | Attached the "farm on which Wm. Langley now lives as the property of the defendant." |
| July 1, 1851 | A. Fergusen v. Edward Williams for $60 | Attached the "coal pit in the Shubil Clark farm in Hinesburgh as the property of the defendant" |
| July 1, 1851 | A. Fergusen v. Jeries[?] Langley for $25 | Attached his property in Hinesburgh and left a copy of the writ "at the last and usual place of abode of the defendant in the care of his Father." |
| July 14, 1851 | Daniel Ray v. Jerius[?] Langley for $20 | Attached property and real estate of JL, "most particularly the farm formerly occupied by said defendant." |
| Dec. 27, 1851 | Elias Flen[?] v. Edward Williams for $20 | Attached all his land and left a copy of the writ "with his wife." |
| Feb. 6, 1852 | Alexander Fergusen v. Edward Williams for $59.25 | Attached all his land. |
| June 21, 1852 | M. Hull[c] v. Violet Clark for $50 | Attached all her real estate "most particularly her title and interest and the use of said estate." |
| Nov. 6, 1852 | G. D. Wells v. Edward Williams | Attached all his property & real estate. |
| Mar. 14, 1853 | Nathan Peck v. W. Langley et al. for $60 | Attached the property of all the defendants. |
| Mar. 4, 1853 | Wm. J. Dauylan[?] v. Henry Langley for $30 | Attached all his real estate in Hinesburgh |
| Mar. 15, 1853 | A. Fergusen v. J. & H. Langley for $99 | Attached all their real estate in Hinesburgh |

SOURCE: Hinesburg Town Clerk, *Record of Writs and Executions for Hinesburgh*, 1829–1853.

[a]These are small amounts compared to others — they range from these small amounts into the hundreds and thousands of dollars.

[b]In the 1843 grand lists for Huntington, Fergusen owned two stores. In the 1850 federal census for Huntington, he is a merchant with a wife, Marancy, and nine children, all born in Vermont.

[c]Marcus Hull established a store in Hinesburgh in 1826.

notes on October 1 for the next four years, but they had difficulty making the payments and eventually lost the land.

Jeremiah (aka Jerry, Jeries, Jerius) left the Hill during this time of trouble, leaving behind many debts, including the mortgage to Ray. We know he left soon after the May land transaction, because in July 1851 Daniel Ray attached "the farm formerly occupied" by him (table 4.1). At the same time, Fergusen left a copy of his writ against Jeries "at the last and usual place of abode of the defendant in the care of his Father."[46] In 1852, Jeremiah finally sold his portion of the farm to his brother, Newell, for $200. Jeremiah appeared in Rensselaer, New York, to sign and seal the deal and was never again taxed for land in Hinesburgh. He had left the Hill for good, pushed out by an increasingly gloomy economic situation.

Lewis, Henry, and Newell, along with their father, struggled on their land for two more years and finally sold it to their white neighbor George Smedley for $1,125. That amount was surely enough to pay their debts and get the family out of trouble with the town merchants. The 1857 Wallings' map for Hinesburgh (figure 1.3) clearly shows the transition from the original large Clark farm to small Clark holdings next to Smedley, who also appears to have owned the house that the Langleys lived in. Smedley, however, seemingly lived across the road in the other house designated as his.[47]

In 1854, we see more attempts by a Langley brother to hang on to the Clark family farm on which their mother, Almira, had grown up. This time, Newell was working alone. First, he got in touch with his aunt, Sybil Clark Loudon, who was living in Ravenna, Ohio, and who still owned a piece of property she had inherited from her father, Shubael. She sold that to Newell. The next year, he bought forty-four acres from Daniel Ray: "A part of the Shubel Clark farm (so called) and is all the shares set off from said farm to Charles Clark, Harriette Clark, and Phebe Clark (which three shares wer set off in common) except 5 acres off the north end of said shares now owned and occupied by Edward Williams."[48] Even twenty years after he had died, the farm was still called the "Shubael Clark farm" in the records. Newell received a mortgage from Ray for $205 to buy his grandfather's land and had four years to pay it back. In 1856, Newell sold the land back to Daniel Ray, with the caveat that he "reserves the hay now on the premises."[49] Newell must have been despondent to let go of the old family homestead that he had tried vigorously to keep. Newell had farming in his veins and farmed for the rest of his life, but not in Hinesburgh. He and his wife, Harriet E. Butler, soon moved to nearby Charlotte.

That left two Langley brothers, Lewis and Henry, still on the Hill with their father, William, who was sixty-two by this time. William must have agonized over the continual loss of the land and the loss of his wife and children to help him in his old age. However, Lewis married Pamelia Storms from Vergennes in 1857, and they moved into the little house with William. She was the Vermont-born daughter of a formerly enslaved couple from Fishkill, New York, who lived nearby in Vergennes. Pamelia had a good job as a cook in Vergennes, and in March 1860, she bought some of the traditional land back in both Hinesburgh and Huntington for $1,200. One piece was part of the old Lewis Clark farm, and another piece "being the Lewis Clark house lot . . . three and three tenths acres."[50] In the 1860 census, Lewis was listed as a farmer with $1,800 in real estate and $800 in personal estate, thanks to his wife's ability as a cook and her salary. This was a significant piece of land for them to own, both economically and psychologically, since it not only was the means of their survival as an extended family, but it also held the bones of their ancestors. They did not let go of it easily, but constantly struggled to keep it in the family by mortgaging it, selling it, and buying it back when they could.

None of these dramas of Hill life involved Jane or her brother, Loudon Langley. Jane was twenty-one and had left home by this time to marry James Greene and live in Cleveland, New York. Loudon was also living elsewhere. When Loudon wrote an 1854 letter to the *Green Mountain Freeman*, he was eighteen and mentioned "the infrequency of my visits to Hinesburgh."[51] He was most likely working in Burlington or Winooski Falls, where he and Jane Anthony married in 1859. He may have been living with Jane's brother, Abial, who many years later wrote, "For several years [we] occupied the same house, engaged in manual labor together and were in the most intimate terms possible."[52] It seems that Loudon had already decided to leave the Hill for good; he just did not know how far from the Hill, physically and mentally, that he would travel in the next couple of decades.

The Williams family represented another branch of the Clarks who were struggling to pay debts and keep their land. Edward Williams had his land attached in the 1850s, along with his mother-in-law, Violet, who was in her late seventies. In the 1850 census, Edward, his wife Harriet, and his two children were still living on the five acres that he and Phoebe had received from Shubael and Violet many years before. Violet continued to live on her thirty acres near the Williamses, along with her sons Hiram (described as "idiotic" in the federal census) and Charles Clark, a shoemaker.

This decade before the Civil War, however, was not easy for any of them. In February 1851, Harriet and Edward mortgaged their land for seventy-five dollars with Daniel Ray. In July, Alexander Fergusen attached Edward's coal pit on the Clark farm. Edward likely paid his debts by giving Fergusen coal or kerosene oil, produced from coal, to sell at his store. He most likely also paid Violet's debt. At any rate, he seemed to have paid off everyone and still owned the farm worth $800 on the eve of the Civil War.

In 1857, Harriet Williams lost her niece and household helper, as Edward's daughter Rachel, seventeen, married Aaron Freeman, the farm laborer occasionally found working on the Rokeby farm in Ferrisburgh. The Rokeby account book shows Aaron doing odd jobs, such as filling ditches and harvesting pumpkins.[53] Rachel, the daughter and granddaughter of Baptists, married Aaron in the Congregational church in Charlotte. Neither was a member there, so why they chose that church is a mystery.[54]

Rachel and Aaron Freeman moved to Massachusetts, most likely to find work, and were living there by 1859. Their first child, Clark (Rachel's mother's maiden name), was born there. Four years later, they were back in Vermont, and their daughter Gertrude was born in Hinesburgh. Loudon Langley also returned to Hinesburgh by 1860 along with his sixteen-year-old-wife, Jane Anthony, and their eight-month-old baby, Edward. Loudon, who wrote letters filled with beautiful prose, was listed as a day laborer, the most unreliable occupation, since one never knew from day to day if work would be available. They were most likely living on the old Clark farm in the traditional Langley house along with Loudon's father, brothers, and sister-in-law. The family again provided security at a time of economic depression and looming Civil War. Many of the children who left the Hill returned at some point. It was a magnet for three generations of Clarks and more generations of Peterses, who all found comfort and support in the place their families had carved out and improved over many decades of patient and skillful farm work.

Violet Clark, the matriarch of the community, must have rejoiced in her grandchildren's return to the Hill and the births of her great-grandchildren. Once again, family surrounded her. It is likely that Vio-

let, who lived across the road from the Langley house, rocked baby
Edward to sleep on occasion, perhaps humming traditional African mel-
odies. Unfortunately the child would not live long. He soon became
gravely ill with enteritis, an inflammation of the small intestine caused
by contaminated food or drink that can cause fever, cramps, diarrhea,
and dehydration, especially in babies.[55] Edward died on November 9,
1860.[56] Violet had seen death come before, and she must have been a
consoling presence for Loudon and Jane as they buried their first child
in the old family cemetery.

Although there had been many such painful episodes in her life, Violet had also lived to see the space that she and Shubael had shaped flourish to support a large, extended family. We can see how successful the
farm was from the agricultural census taken in 1860. During the mid-
1800s, the state of Vermont took a number of agricultural censuses, but
in only one year do we find the African American neighborhood from
the Hill enumerated. Only those with important marketable produce
were included—those highly visible to the market culture in town.[57]
Examined as separate farms, the Langley-Williams-Clark plots do not
compare favorably to the individual white-owned farms on the Hill of
Ray, Weed, and Livermore (table 4.2). However, the relatives surely
worked the three farms collectively, and analyzing the farms together
shows that the original Clark farm was quite prosperous into the mid-
nineteenth century. The second generation was collectively farming 170
acres, almost the same as the wealthier Lemuel Livermore toward the
bottom of the Hill. The land was still quite fertile—the Hill families
produced more corn, potatoes, and orchard products than the wealthier white farms nearby. Their sheep were producing at top capacity for
merino rams: four pounds per sheep.[58] With only six cows, their butter production was impressively higher than most. Their cows were also
producing at top capacity: 500 gallons of milk per year with a three-to-
one ratio of gallons to pounds of butter.[59] Animals slaughtered exceeded
all but those of Anson Weed, and their production of maple sugar
exceeded all but Ray's, the wealthiest farmer. With four oxen and three
horses among them, they had plenty of power for plowing, planting,
harvesting, and hauling buckets full of sap, as well as renting out their
oxen and labor to neighbors for heavy work. The number of people supported on their farms was also higher than those of nearby white farms.
This was high-yielding land under their hands, and yet their collective
farms were worth much less than those of their white neighbors.

TABLE 4.2
1860 Vermont Agricultural Census for Black-Owned Farms Compared to White-Owned Farms on the Hill

| FARM ITEMS | White-owned farms | | | | Black-owned farms | | |
|---|---|---|---|---|---|---|---|
| | Daniel Ray (8 people) | Anson Weed (5 people) | L. E. Livermore (7 people) | Old Clark Farm Composite (10–12 people, plus any fugitives) | Lewis Langley[a] (5–7 people) | Edwin Williams[b] (2 people) | Hiram Clark[c] (3 people) |
| Improved acres | 300 | 300 | 175 | 170 | 60 | 40 | 70 [?] |
| Unimproved acres | 210 | 25 | 35 | 45 | 15 | 10 | 20 |
| Farm's cash value | $15,000 | $13,000 | $8,500 | $4,500 | $1,800 | $1,000 | $1,700 |
| Milch cows | 4 | 16 | 28 | 6 | 2 | 2 | 2 |
| Sheep | 120 | 250 | 0 | 8 | 0 | 8 | 0 |
| Value of livestock | $2,000 | $500 | $1,000 | $425 | $150 | $175 | $100 |
| Ind. Corn (bushels) | 50 | 20 | 50 | 165 | 50 | 25 | 90 |
| Oats (bushels) | 400 | 500 | 300 | 100 | 0 | 0 | 100 |
| Wool (lbs) | 760 | 825 | 0 | 32. | 0 | 32 | 0 |
| Irish potatoes (bushels) | 100 | 400 | 100 | 450 | 100 | 200 | 150 |
| Butter (lbs) | 450 | 2,000 | 700 | 1,800. | 600 | 700 | 500 |

|  | White-owned farms | | | Black-owned farms | | | |
|---|---|---|---|---|---|---|---|
|  | Daniel Ray (8 people) | Anson Weed (5 people) | L. E. Livermore (7 people) | Old Clark Farm Composite (10–12 people, plus any fugitives) | Lewis Langley[a] (5–7 people) | Edwin Williams[b] (2 people) | Hiram Clark[c] (3 people) |
| Cheese (lbs) | 0 | 0 | 8,000 | 0 | 0 | 0 | 0 |
| Hay (tons) | 54 | 100 | 70 | 58 | 20 | 20 | 18 |
| Maple sugar (lbs) | 1,200 | 0 | 300 | 450 | 100 | 150 | 200 |
| Wheat (bushels) | 45 | 0 | 60 | 45 | 10 | 20 | 15 |
| Value of animals slaughtered | $110 | $200 | $150 | $168 | $50 | $18 | $100 |
| Number of animals: | | | | | | | |
| horses | 10 | 8 | 2 | 3 | 0 | 2 | 1 |
| oxen | 0 | 2 | 0 | 4 | 2 | 2 | 0 |
| swine | 2 | 4 | 4 | 3 | 1 | 1 | 1 |
| Value of orchard products | $50 | $75 | $60 | $170 | $50 | $20 | $100 |

SOURCE: Agricultural Census for Hinesburgh, Vermont, 1860 Microfilm at the University of Vermont.

[a] Part of S. Clark original farm
[b] Part of S. Clark original farm
[c] Part of S. Clark original farm

The main differences lay in the number of acres and types of animals the farms had, and their degree of specialization. The Rays had accumulated the most land, 510 acres. They were managing 120 sheep and owned 10 horses and 4 cows, all worth $2,000 — compared to livestock worth only $450 at the old Clark farm. The Rays were also producing a good supply of wool and maple sugar for resale. They needed to buy their cheeses and additional hay from their neighbors. The Weeds had 325 acres and were still heavily into sheep farming with 250 sheep producing wool for resale. With their 16 cows, they were producing only a bit more butter for resale than the women on the Clark farm with their 6 cows. They needed to buy their maple sugar and wheat products from their neighbors. The Livermores had no sheep, but were moving more and more toward dairy farming, keeping 28 cows. They were heavily into the production of cheese, later to become a major industry in Hinesburgh. Because of their cheese specialization, the Livermores apparently needed to buy hay and wool products from their neighbors.

Specialization was the wave of the future, and businesses began to crop up to support this wave. As early as 1855, Loren Murray, a white businessman, had begun to manufacture cheese boxes for the budding Hinesburgh dairy industry. By 1866 the Valley Cheese Factory in town was receiving milk from 300 cows and manufacturing about 60,000 pounds of cheese annually.[60] Sugaring, once an activity to supply only the family needs, was becoming an important industry, partly because of the boycott of slave-produced sugar from the Caribbean. By 1863, a Hinesburgh business was manufacturing sap buckets and pails in support of the move to more specialization in maple products.

While the Clark farm had more diverse products than their neighbors, their mixed farm did not produce the profits that specialization did, leaving them without enough capital to expand.[61] They also had fewer animals, and to continue to be competitive, they needed more cows to produce dairy products and more animals of all kinds to keep the farm fertile. While the nearby farms with many animals were being well manured and staying productive, the Clark farmers needed to buy manure from their neighbors or buy bat guano from South America, an expensive proposition. It was no longer the friendly rural economy where neighbors loaned their animals; the Clarks needed cash, not only to buy more land, but also to buy fertilizer. Without the capital to do this, their farms would begin to fail. On the eve of the Civil War, the changing culture of farming, the poor economy, and their lack of ability to specialize and expand to compete with large-scale farms foreshadowed disastrous days to come for the community on the crest of the Hill.

The nearby farms owned by whites, both those who had been there for decades like the Rays, Rosses, and Nortons, and newcomers like the Livermores, Smedleys, and Harveys, thrived or at least survived during these difficult times. Therefore, perhaps "racism" can be added to the list of forces that pushed the Clarks off the Hill—however the records fail to show any evidence of this. Perhaps the white farmers more readily adapted to the new capitalist culture than the people descended from very different African traditions. In any event, many societal forces were at work, and together they would spell the end of the community at the top of the Hill in the coming decade.

In an 1856 speech before the U.S. Congress, Vermont's representative Justin Morrill described the country as suffering under the burden of slavery. "I think our country weeps beneath the yoke—It weeps, it bleeds; and each new day a gash is added to her wounds."[62] The looming Civil War would finally cauterize this deep wound, but also bring many unwanted changes to the Hill, as some of her sons and daughters would scatter to places unimagined by them in the 1850s. One such place was Beaufort, South Carolina—a steamy southern town on the shores of the Beaufort River that flowed into the nearby Atlantic.

Robert Smalls, who would later become a friend and colleague of Loudon Langley, was born in Beaufort in a slave cabin in 1839. In the early 1850s, his owner sent him to Charleston to hire himself out to work and send money back. He lived there for a decade, working, marrying, and raising a family. In 1861, he was hired as a deckhand and soon became the pilot on board the steamship *Planter*, positioning him to become an early hero of the Civil War.[63] On June 14, 1862, *Harper's Weekly* described Smalls's dash past Confederate forts in Charleston Harbor, bringing the steamboat to the Union side:

> One of the most daring and heroic adventures since the war commenced was undertaken and successfully accomplished by a party of Negroes in Charleston on Monday night last. Nine colored men comprising the pilot, engineers and crew of the rebel gun-boat "Planter" took the vessel under their control, passed the batteries and forts in Charleston Harbor, hoisted a white flag, ran out of the blocking squadron, and thence to Port Royal,

via St Helena Sound and Broad River, reaching the [Union] flagship "Wabash" shortly after ten o'clock last evening.[64]

The Beaufort–Port Royal area was in Union hands at this time, therefore, they had delivered the *Planter* to the Union Navy. With the $5,000 award he received from the government, Smalls later bought the house in Beaufort where he and his mother had been enslaved. Loudon Langley eventually fought in the Civil War, stayed in Beaufort during Reconstruction, and bought the house next door to the Smalls family. That decision to stay in Beaufort placed his family in an environment enormously different from their Hill in the Green Mountains, and Loudon's friendship with Robert would ultimately take him into the halls of power in post–Civil War South Carolina.

## CHAPTER FIVE

#  The Civil War Years, 1861–1865

Slavery is a "stain on the face of the republic. . . . The whole world has been steadily marching in the opposite direction, until even the despotisms of the ages refuse no longer to bear such a reproach.
—Justin Morrill, U.S. Congressman from Vermont[1]

they make them that have got on boots go out in thair bair feet in the thistl and dril then they set on thair horses and laf at us. that ant right. —Aaron N. Freeman, Vermont soldier, Massachusetts 54th

If one believes in nature foreshadowing human events, an 1858 storm in Hinesburgh and Huntington provides fodder for one's imagination. That July,

it had been dry and sultry for several days preceding the 3rd, and about 3 o'clock in the afternoon the storm which Nature had been brewing began to descend. Dark, heavy cloud banks came up from the west and northwest, turning the day to almost the darkness of night, and emitting their electric fluid in blinding, zigzag streaks of flame. Soon the rain began to descend, gently at first, but gradually increasing to a perfect deluge, continuing to pour down with an intensity rarely exceeded by tropical showers, for two hours and a half without cessation; and when at length it did abate it was soon renewed for a shorter period. The effect of this deluge soon raised the waters of the river and its tributaries far above their usual height, and at sunset they were bearing huge masses of driftwood and whole trees upon their angry breasts, and at ten o'clock had attained a height never before reached by any previous freshets. Bridges, fences, and all within the sweep of the current were borne away, besides in some places cutting out huge pieces of land with their standing crops.

. . . [W]hen the swollen current subsided it left a scene of devastation that was appalling.

. . . [Four men had climbed nearby Camel's Hump, when] the storm came upon them so suddenly that they were obliged to encounter its fury with no shelter but the clouds. The atmosphere was so dense and the rain descended in such torrents that they could only breathe by placing their hands upon their mouths and nostrils . . . until it became too dark too see at all, the clouds below them resembled the waves of the ocean, rolling and seething, as though, as they in their fright imagined, the whole earth were covered with a mighty deluge as in the days of Noah. After total darkness had settled over them the vivid flashes of lightning continued to dart through the inky blackness, followed by deafening peals of thunder that seemed to shake the mountain upon its base. From the effects of this night of terror Mr. Rood never recovered, but died about two years after from results of the exposure.[2]

Little did the country know in 1858 that a torrential fury of gunfire, anger, and terror would roll over the country to shake its very core. Many people, including some from the Hill, would never recover from the terror and devastation as North against South, family against family, waged war on each other. This was not only the conventional wreckage of war, but also a storm of total destruction that descended on parts of the South. The final plunge into violent conflict began on March 4, 1861, when Abraham Lincoln took the oath of office as the sixteenth president of the United States. Seventy-five percent of Vermont's voting men, perhaps including the men on the Hill, had voted for him. Angry that the country had voted for a Republican president, South Carolinians attacked Fort Sumter in April, and the country soon plummeted into civil war.

Both Union and Confederate governments had to create armies practically from scratch, and local governments formed militias all over the country. In Vermont, a total of 34,000 men eventually fought in the war, and 15 percent never returned home, having died of wounds, accidents, or diseases. Men of the Hill were among them. Every African American family from the Hill sent sons or grandsons into the military during this time — but not immediately. Many people counseled Lincoln to avoid raising black regiments or allowing blacks to enlist for fear of forcing border states to side with the Confederacy. Although many African Americans were eager to engage the Confederates, and some did unofficially, they could not do so officially until the fall of 1862.[3]

With the war going badly for the Union after General George McClellan's troops retreated from Richmond in June 1862, talk began anew concerning the raising of black regiments. In July, Congress passed two acts allowing the enlistment of African Americans, but enrollment could not start until after the issuance of the Emancipation Proclamation in September. There was still much debate in the country among whites about whether or not black men could fight well, but in October 1862, the First Kansas Colored Volunteers silenced the cynics by driving back the Confederates at the Battle of Island Mound in Missouri.

At the 1863 battle of Port Hudson in Louisiana, African American soldiers again proved their mettle as they advanced steadily over open ground in the face of deadly artillery fire. That same year, at Honey Springs, Indian Territory (now Oklahoma), the First Kansas U.S. Colored Troops (USCT) again fought with courage. After a two-hour bloody engagement, Confederate soldiers began to retreat. The First Kansas, which had held the center of the Union line, advanced to within fifty paces of the Confederate line and exchanged fire for twenty minutes until the Confederates broke and ran. General Blunt wrote after the battle, "I never saw such fighting as was done by the Negro regiment. . . . The question that negroes will fight is settled; besides they make better soldiers in every respect than any troops I have ever had under my command."[4] By August 1863, fourteen black regiments were in the field and ready for service, including the Massachusetts Fifty-fourth, formed in January of 1863. Approximately 180,000 African Americans comprising 163 units ultimately served in the Union Army during the Civil War, and another 18,000 African Americans served in the Union Navy, including Robert Smalls in South Carolina.[5] Both free men and those escaping slavery joined the fight, not for nation but for freedom and the final abolition of slavery. The completion of the Revolution for people of color had begun.

### Farmers to Soldiers

Use of the telegraph during the Civil War, made news travel quickly. Reports of black regiments and their battles surely reached the Hill soon after they occurred, and by the fall of 1863, several men from the Hill had decided to join the first Northern black regiment, the Massachusetts Fifty-fourth. Henry Prince, a farm laborer, was first to go; he didn't actually *decide*, however, but was one of the men drafted into the militia to fill Hinesburgh's quota of soldiers. According to the March 1863 Enrollment Act:

> All able-bodied male citizens of the United States, and persons of foreign birth who shall have declared on oath their intention to become citizens under and in pursuance of the laws thereof, between the ages of twenty and forty-five years, except as hereinafter excepted, are hereby declared to constitute the national forces, and shall be liable to perform military duty in the service of the United States when called out by the President for that purpose.[6]

Blacks had long been citizens in Vermont with all the rights and responsibilities of their gender. For men, that now meant eligibility for the draft. The men from the Hill had to register for military duty along with every other man from age twenty to forty-five in Hinesburgh. In August 1863, Henry Prince mustered into the Massachusetts Fifty-fourth Infantry as a private in Company (Co) H. He mustered out exactly two years later, having served his country honorably. Other men from the Hill either enrolled in the militia for Hinesburgh or volunteered for the Massachusetts Fifty-fourth.

Harlo Prince, twenty-two, a black laborer, enlisted in the Enrolled Militia for the Town of Hinesburgh. Three Peters men joined him: Cornelius, George, and John, grandsons of Prince Peters, who had fought in the Revolutionary War for his own freedom and the hoped-for freedom of all African Americans in the new nation. He and many others in the country had returned home deeply disappointed. Now, his grandchildren worked to complete the dream. However, what they did during the war is a mystery, since I find no letters, pension records, or other documents for them. They are on the grand lists as paying poll taxes during the war, so perhaps they stayed in Hinesburgh as members of the local militia. They begin to show up in the land records again after the war in 1865. The Clark descendants, on the other hand, left both letters and a pension record.

William Langley saw three sons off to join the Massachusetts Fifty-fourth: Newell, Lewis, and Loudon. Edward Williams's son-in-law, Aaron Freeman, joined his wife's Langley cousins in the Fifty-fourth. They all signed up in the fall of 1863 and traveled together in January 1864 to Brattleboro to muster into their unit. The flurry of men signing up in 1863 was due to Lincoln's call for 200,000 more troops to be in the field by January 5 of the next year. In July 1863, three regiments of the Second Vermont Brigade had cut off Picket's Charge during the Battle of Gettysburg, securing a Union victory in Northern territory. Success for the North gave the Union new hope for winning the war, and Lincoln made his call for more soldiers soon after.

For each town, this meant either volunteer enlistments to meet their quotas or a draft. In hopes of avoiding the despised drafts, there were federal, state, and local bounties offered to those who voluntarily enlisted. In the fall of 1863, Vermont towns began trying to fill their quotas. In addition to the federal bounty of $302 and the state's of $125, Rutland offered $500 more to residents and nonresidents alike to enlist in that town.[7] For farm laborers, the $927 was the equivalent of about two years' pay, and seventeen new volunteers from Rutland enlisted. Among them was Loudon Langley from the Hill, who was accepted as being from Rutland so they could meet their quota. With a baby, a pregnant wife, and an aging father, the money would certainly help the folks back home. By December 28, 1863, Rutland had met its quota without a draft.

It was more than money, however, that spurred blacks to enlist. Many felt they must prove their courage, determination, and abilities to a country that believed in their inferiority. Frederick Douglass felt the time was ripe for blacks "to rise in one bound from social degradation to the plane of equality" by fighting bravely for victory over the South.[8] Douglass had great hopes that black soldiers would once and for all prove their humanity and their courage to the white race, once each had "an eagle on his button, a musket on his shoulder and the star-spangled banner over his head."[9] The Langley and Freeman men answered the call.

### Destruction of the Clark Farm

While a determination to disprove inferiority theories and to abolish slavery were certainly the overriding reasons for fighting in the war, the money was needed in the families. In 1860 Lewis and Pamelia Langley had mortgaged their fifty-seven acres lying north of the road, which was to be paid in seven notes at Lewis Langley's dwelling house by 1868. By November 1862, however, Pamelia and Lewis decided to sell most of their land in Hinesburgh and Huntington. Due to the terrible economy of the war years, perhaps they needed the money to make their mortgage payments. Or Pamelia may have wanted to live nearer her work, because the family moved to Ferrisburgh after the sale.

In addition to the land, they also sold cows, steers, one sheep, three yokes, one plow, one drag, one pair "travers" [*sic*] sleds, and all the hay and grain in the barn and house. It appears they were giving up the farming way of life, and the Langleys never again lived on the Hill. William, who had lived there for almost forty years and raised his children there along with his wife, Almira, left the Hill to live with Lewis and Pamelia. One can imagine their visiting the cemetery to say painful goodbyes to generations of family members. In all likelihood, they returned for a time to care for the burial ground first prepared by Shubael and Violet over sixty years previously.

However, they could no longer fight the changes in the Vermont economy. By the time of the Civil War, Vermont farmers were in agricultural turmoil, as many found they could no longer compete with western farmers or large-scale operations. Sheep, once so plentiful on the Hill, were scarce. The nearby wealthy white farmer, Augustus McEuen, who once had 450, was down to 170, and other white farmers had gotten rid of their sheep herds altogether, replacing them with cows and beef cattle. Those who could afford it bought out smaller farmers. The world had changed. Many farmers of means were no longer satisfied with the simple comforts of self-sufficiency in friendly, rural neighborhoods. They were moving to larger, more scientific, competitive, and impersonal farming approaches with a more luxurious lifestyle.

The families on the Hill were caught in this web of change. With fewer and fewer farm animals, they could not keep their pastures fertile. In earlier times, their neighbors gladly loaned them animals for that purpose, but in the more competitive atmosphere, they were more likely to buy them out. The home manufactories, like those of Violet Clark, Almira Langley, and Eliza Peters, who had woven wool and linen and churned butter in their households for extra cash or store credit, were also disappearing. They could not compete with the commercially made items of the mills, factories, and creameries. As a result, the farmers at the top of the Hill could no longer find a way to survive on their ancestral lands, and they sorrowfully began selling out to wealthier farmers.

The last surviving member of the pioneering generation, Violet Clark, lived to see her world being torn apart by the changing economy. Then, in early 1863, Violet had an accident common among old folks — she fell and broke a "limb."[10] Soon after, she died of complications of the fracture. Surely she was buried next to Shubael in the family cemetery on the top of the Hill. Her death certificate says she was eighty-eight years old and an "aged mother."[11] Perhaps she welcomed death when it came, having witnessed the death of her husband, daughters, great-grandson, and others, as well as the emigration from the Hill of her son, Lewis Clark, and the Langley branch of the family. She must have mourned the changes in their way of living as they struggled with fierce competition from big, impersonal farms.

On the other hand, living long enough to hear the Emancipation Proclamation must have been a profound day of joy for her, similar to twenty-first-century people watching Barack Obama inaugurated as the nation's first black president. In 1862, blacks all over the northeast gathered on New Year's Eve to await freedom for all people enslaved in the Confederate states. In Boston people burst into song at midnight, singing "Blow ye trumpet, blow, Jehovah hath triumphed, his people are free."[12] Prayer meetings and celebrations continued for days in the North. The people of the Hill likely joined in celebrations as well. Perhaps the Free Will Baptist church to which Violet and her children belonged organized prayer meetings on January 1 to thank Jehovah for the freedom of their Southern brethren. The next month, friends and family gathered to lower Violet into her final resting place on the Hill.

For sixty-eight years, she had lived on the same land and raised nine children. She milked cows, churned butter, cared for the house garden, put up the orchard products, spun wool, sewed clothes, and lit the lanterns in the evenings in addition to myriad other farm chores. She faithfully attended Baptist meetings with Shubael in churches on both sides of the Hill and helped transform Hinesburgh from old-growth forests to frontier town to industrialized farming community. Violet was a founding mother of the community and lived on the Hill longer than any other member of the African American neighborhood. Though we are not sure where she was born, we know she lies for eternity at the top of the Hill surrounded by family. Many artifacts, the shards of her life, such as stone walls and a barn foundation still dot the landscape at the top of the Hill bearing silent witness to her life.

There was also loss in the Peters family during the 1860s. Josephus's second wife died in September 1862. At forty-three years of age, Amy Prince Peters died of ovarian tumors. It must have been a painful death, and Josephus was left to bury her in "West Hill Cemetery" on lot 83.[13] There is no West Hill Cemetery in Hinesburgh; however, part of the Hinesburgh Cemetery has a hill on the west side that is sometimes referred to as "West Hill." Perhaps she is there, although there is no stone for her. The Peters land was on the west side of the Hill, so the burial document could be referring to a hidden cemetery on lot 83 where the elder Peterses might be buried as well. The next year, Josephus and John, in separate transactions, bought back parts of lot 83 that the elder Samuel had sold to Asa Weller in 1835. Weller was now dead, and they bought the land back from his estate. This piece of land was clearly of vital importance to this family, more evidence that it might be where their relatives are buried.

Two years later, in January, Josephus, sixty, married Sarah Jane Freeman, thirty-five, from Vergennes. She was born in Burlington, the daughter of John Jackson, a soldier in the Massachusetts Fifty-fourth, and Polly Freeman.[14] This time, his wife was twenty-five years younger than he was. Over the next four years, they had two children, Clara, and a child unnamed in the records.

The community of the Peters, Waters, and Edwards families was not devastated by the war years as were the families at the top of the Hill. They had already given up on farming as their primary means of survival and had become laborers on the McEuen farm or servants for nearby white families. Even so, they owned some of the land of their ancestors and stayed there much longer than the community at the top of the Hill, well into the twentieth century. We do not know for sure where the earliest Peterses are buried, except for Charlot, but their progeny have prominent markers in the local cemetery.

*Discrimination on the Battlefront*

In January 1864, not quite a year after burying their grandmother, the Langley brothers—Loudon, Newell, and Lewis—and Aaron Freeman were among the new Massachusetts Fifty-fourth recruits who marched to Brattleboro, Vermont, to muster in before their deployment to the South.[15] The *Rutland Herald* reported that every man there signed his articles of enlistment—no one made an X signifying illiteracy. They first marched to Boston, then continued to New York City, where they boarded a steamer for Folly Island, South Carolina. In February, the

Fifty-fourth steamed by sea to Jacksonville, Florida, for their first engagements with the enemy.

The heat of Florida in their wool uniforms must have been grueling for the eager recruits, followed, of course, by the terrors of battle. However, in addition to these miseries, black soldiers had others to contend with. Both Aaron Freeman and Loudon Langley wrote letters to people in Vermont and to editors of papers describing and complaining about their experiences in the war. One issue was that of unequal pay. Despite the proven bravery of black soldiers, the Militia Act of 1862 stated that soldiers of African descent were to receive only $10 a month, plus a clothing allowance of $3.50. This was much less than the pay for whites of $75 a month. As a result, many regiments continually struggled for equal pay, some refusing any money until they were granted the same pay as whites.

Loudon began his letter writing almost immediately upon mustering in. One is from Park Barracks in City Hall Park, New York City, in January 1864. He sent this to the *Anglo-African Paper*:

Mr. Editor: . . . Nine-tenths of the boys had been informed by selectmen, who were very anxious to fill their town quotas, that the colored recruits received from the U. S. the same pay and bounty as the white recruits. The writer had warned and told all those who had been thus informed, that such was not the case; but the boys preferred to believe the misrepresentations with which the officers (either from ignorance or a love of falsehood) had filled their ears.

They had confidently expected to receive the seventy-five dollars that the U. S. pays their white recruits until a couple of hours before their departure, when we were ordered to "fall in," after which we were informed by Lieut. Phillips, the officer in charge of us, the real facts of the case.

The intelligence, as might have been expected, was received with (I am sorry to state it) much cursing and swearing, accompanied with the declaration that they never would have enlisted had they been truly informed, and that they would not leave the camp until they had been paid the seventy-five dollars. The officers, apprehensive of more trouble, deemed it expedient to resort to more falsehood, so we were told that we would be paid as much as any recruits, and that our pay had been sent to our regimental headquarters, at which place we would be paid on our arrival there.

This course, it was alleged, was necessary, because we were going to a regiment from another State. This falsehood the boys believed and took courage, until to-day, when, with the aid of your paper, I have convinced them that what I had previously told them was true. I verily believe that but for the reconciling remarks of Lieut. Phillips, the boys (although having no arms) would have shown a spirited resistance to marching. Not only Capt. J. F. Brannan, but Maj. W. Austin positively stated falsehoods with reference to our pay. But let the sin rest where it belongs—on the U. S. government and not on its officers. The latter were between two fires—the honor of the State, and the requirements of the National government. Both must be preserved, and hence personal honor must be sacrificed. The boys feel somewhat down-hearted, but hope for the best, and have some faith in the justice of Congress. . . . Mr. Editor, may we hope that Congress, for the sake of the honor of the country, and for the sake of the families of a portion of its able and true defenders, will soon remove this disgraceful distinction from the military statute of this great nation?

Loudon S. Langley<br>A Colored Vermont Recruit[16]

The letter shows a young man well brought up and with a good education. Loudon was polite, smart, and honorable. He put the blame on the impersonal government, instead of his officers, while still insisting that the United States was a "great nation." His signature gives us insight into his own identity—the way he wanted to be seen by those reading the paper. He was a man of color but also a Vermonter. Born and raised in the hills of northern Vermont, of Vermont-born parents who farmed in the Green Mountains, he must have been proud of his birthplace. At the same time, he was proud of being part of a "great nation." Black, Vermonter, American—all equal parts of one man's identity and certainly of others in his regiment as well.

Three months later, Aaron Freeman wrote from Jacksonville, Florida, to complain about the conditions and lack of pay. He wrote to George Robinson at Rokeby in Ferrisburgh, Vermont to see if he could do something about the unequal pay. The letter showed he was not as fluent in writing as Loudon, but he certainly got his point across.[17]

i think that we shant get eny money from the government. they say that they ant pay but 7 dolars a month. That what the Caurnal said . . . they paid to colard troops and he said that we had beter right home and see about it. he said that he could not do eny thing about it then I thought I

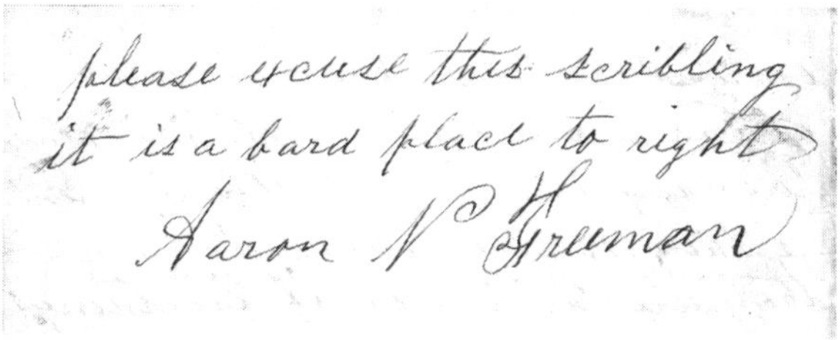

FIGURE 5.1 Aaron N.
Freeman's signature.

had beter right home and see what could be done about it. i dont want to
stay down here and git knathing for it and be killd or git my limes brake
then git nothing to help my self with . . . i want to hav my pay or get home.
i dont wan to wark for nothing

. . . i dont get fair play here. they dont treat this rigment as they do the
others rigment. they are the poorer off far things. they dont pay them eny
thing they dont want to pay them eny thing. i cant stand that. i want my
pay and i know I shant get it. they say it is a fraid under a falce potence
that they hav got us down here. i think that they cant hold us thair. can
they? I want sum one to find out whather they can or not and get us away
or get our pay. I can get sum things then that will make me beter off. if
should be sick i should hafter suffer. I hafter sufer a nuf . . . yours truly
Aaron Fr.

Please excuse this scribbling. it is a hard place to right

Aaron N Freeman[18]

Aaron also shined a light on some of the trials he faced under the
white officers of the Fifty-fourth. Some conditions were the same for
the white soldiers, such as few clothes, bad food, lice and fleas. However, the black recruits always had the added problems of racism and
discrimination.

thaught that i wood inform you how we are treated here. i hav work
all night and then had to drill all day. they make them that hav got on
boots go out in thair bair feet in the thistl and dril then they set on thair
horses and laf at us. that ant right. i hant had but one shirt for more then
a month. when I git my shirt wash I hafta tak it af and let it [dri crossed
out] dry then put it on a gain. sumtimes I haf to catch lise sumtimes they
are as thik as the hair on a dog and flease with them to boot. cant get eny
thing that is fit to eat here then I hav had a cold every sens i have ben here
. . . i want to get home as soon as i can.[19]

Like any soldier, Aaron was homesick and dreamed of returning to the hills of Vermont. It was bad enough being away from home and drilling for battles that might take life or limb, as white soldiers did, but drilling in bare feet and being laughed at by officers on horses because of the color of his skin must have been almost more than he could bear. And black soldiers did it for one-seventh the pay. Vermont must have seemed like a far-away paradise to him. Loudon also thought about Vermont and described his memories in a letter from Jacksonville to the *Burlington Free Press*:

> The weather here for the past few days has been very cool, but to-day it is very warm, and owing to the sudden change the heat is somewhat oppressive. The pretty and odoriferous flowers that almost everywhere greet the eyes, remind one of June weather in Vermont. The country around this city has been stripped, and both man and beast the swine in particular bear evidence of great scarcity and want, all that presents a striking contrast to the thrift and abundance that everywhere greet one in Vermont.[20]

At home in Vermont, people were doing what they could to support soldiers in the field. Some of the harvest of hay and potatoes was sent to the troops. People fasted in order to preserve food and dispatch as much as possible for the cause. Women took knitting everywhere with them: on wagon trips to town, to church, and to lectures, making socks and other clothing to send to their men in the army. Ladies' aid societies collected the knitting, as well as maple sugar, food, and bandages to transport on trains to the troops.[21]

The women of the Hill surely were among those who sewed and sacrificed, especially since their men had less pay and fewer resources than white soldiers. At the same time, these women were caring for their families alone and with much less pay coming from the battlefront. For Harriet and Jane Langley things were even harder, for not only were they taking over the men's chores and caring for their older relatives and children, but also both were pregnant when their husbands marched away to Brattleboro. In June 1864, Harriet gave birth to her third child. The next month, Jane Langley gave birth to her second. Pamelia and Lewis Langley had no children. All of these women were living in Charlotte.[22] Pamelia was with her father-in-law, William Langley, and certainly would have assisted at the births of her niece and nephew. Exactly where the families were living at the time is unknown—but it is a distinct possibility that this close-knit family of women and children shared a household in Charlotte.[23] Rachel Freeman was the only woman of this generation living on the Hill. While Aaron was away; she lived with her father, Edward Williams, Aunt Harriet, and her two children.[24] It would be a long time waiting for their husbands to return home—if they returned.

## Action on the Battlefront

The first action for the men from the Hill in the Massachusetts Fifty-fourth was at the Battle of Olustee in February 1864. The ranges of central and south Florida provided cattle in the tens of thousands that Confederate armies desperately needed for leather and beef. The demand for Florida beef became even more critical in 1863, following the Confederate defeat at Vicksburg, which cut off supplies from Texas and Arkansas.[25] The Union campaign to cut off the Florida supply line, as well as attract more black recruits to the Union cause, climaxed at Olustee. It was a defeat for the Union, but the black regiment from Massachusetts "stood alone under intense fire as the Union line crumbled in disorder. As a result, the 54th earned more plaudits for its stubborn defense among the pines."[26]

Loudon Langley provided a close-up look at the action by describing the battle in a letter, this time to the *Burlington Free Press*.

> On Wednesday the 16th ult. we left our camp, with a sufficient force, as we supposed, to crush all opposition, but the rebels having been largely reinforced from Georgia, were ready to give us a warm reception. On Saturday the 20th ult., we came up to the extreme front. It was about three P.M. when our regiment with a hearty cheer went into the fight. The enemy were strongly entrenched behind a breastwork of earth, which greatly protected them from the effect of our fire. Before we came up the rebs succeeded in capturing one of our batteries of six guns, and soon after we went into the fight they had endeavored to flank us by a regiment of rebel cavalry. We wheeled and paid our respect to them, which soon set them to a "right about face." We fought bravely (i.e. the regiment, I was not in the fight, having been ordered to the rear by the Colonel, to guard the knapsacks of our men) until we were ordered to retreat.

But the men had no idea of obeying the firm order, and it was repeated by Col. Hallowell three times before the order was obeyed. The 54th was the last regiment that left the field, and they retreated in good order, as did other regiments that participated in the fight. The loss to our regiment in killed, wounded and missing, was 97 men. Among the wounded was Private Emery Anderson of Hinesburgh, who received a ball through his leg just above the ankle joint. Many of our wounded were left on the field, from which place they crawled along into the thick bushes to hide themselves, and afterward were discovered and captured by the enemy. However, quite a few were brought off, and those whose wounds were in the flesh only about the head and arms, retreated with the rest of our army. . . . As our men left the field, the rebs rent the air with cheer upon cheer. It was after 8 P.M. when we left the vicinity of the battle, and before we could rest, we must march back to the place we had encamped the night before, which was a distance of 15 miles. . . . It was about 5 A.M. before the stragglers all came in, or when the rear guard of the army came up. The men were tired and foot-sore, having marched that day 32 miles, and had fought one battle and sustained a defeat.

. . . [We] have lost one [Vermonter] by death, private John H. Freeman, whose family reside in your village, and one has been missing since the battle of Olustee (Saturday 20th ult.) — Private Charles E. Nelson of Bristol — and is supposed to have been captured by the enemy.[27]

After Olustee, the Fifty-fourth remained in the South, fighting in a number of actions, including the battles of Honey Hill and Boykin's Mill. In mid-April, they returned to South Carolina. Aaron Freeman was ill at that time and admitted to a field hospital that served black soldiers in Beaufort, South Carolina. The Union had taken Beaufort earlier in the war and confiscated the plantations, homes, and churches of the Confederates to use as army offices, officers' quarters, and hospitals.[28] The survival rates in these hospitals were not high; however, Aaron recovered and returned to duty at the end of the month.

While in the Port Royal–Hilton Head area, Loudon Langley became familiar with the South Carolina Thirty-third USCT, also on duty at Port Royal. He requested to be transferred to that regiment in April 1864, evidently out of admiration for them; as he explained, "Being the first colored regiment raised in the United States, we were regarded as experimenters, upon whose success or failure the weal or woe of our whole race depended."[29] I have no evidence he knew anyone from the regiment prior to his transfer request, but his transfer was granted. The move to the Thirty-third was fateful for Loudon. At the end of June, the regiment went on an expedition to James Island, South Carolina, to join operations against Charleston. On July 2, they battled the Confederates on James Island not far from the city. Loudon described it in a letter to the *Anglo-African Paper*:

> We were not long in finding our way to James Island, and continuing to advance, we soon encountered the rebel picket, which however, were soon drove in; but we succeeded in capturing one cavalry man (picket) together with his horse. . . . Nearing the enemy, he soon opened a raking fire of grape and canister from a two gun battery, known as Fort Laniar. At about this time, Col. Hartwell, who was in command of the brigade, came to our regiment and ordered us to "fire in retreat," and at the same time, Lt. Col. Fox, who was in command of the 55th MA, which was at this time a little to the rear, commanded his regiment to "forward! double-quick!" Our major, who was in command, inferring from the maneuvering of the 55th MA that the order to retreat was countermanded, immediately gave the order to "forward! double-quick!" and away we all rushed toward the fort, arriving there with the 55th MA., and capturing two brass field pieces, one of which the rebels left loaded, not having time to discharge it at us. . . . There was a peculiar fitness in the fact that the Star Spangled Banner of the first colored regiment raised, should be the first to float its bright stars and red stripes over the parapet of the captured position.[30]

Loudon loved the appropriateness of having the stars and stripes of the Thirty-third, the first black regiment to fight against the Confederates, fly over the fort they had just captured. He did not mention, however, an injury that would plague him for the rest of his life. In his pension records, a fellow soldier, Bristow Eddy, said that after that July battle, Loudon suffered from sunstroke.[31] Some of the men took him to the shade of a tree and bathed him in cold water. The regiment was then ordered to Coles Island, and they had to cross a stream on a plank to get there. Loudon was still suffering from the heat and fell off the plank, plunging about twelve feet into the stream. Several men carried him to the regimental hospital where he was treated for an injury to his back. After this, he was able to do only light duty around the camp, whereas beforehand he was able to do full duty as a soldier.

We know what his job was after the injury because of his signature on letters after that day: "L. S. Langley, Clerk at Hd'qrs." They had evidently found a use for his education and writing skills and had made him a part of the field staff. In November, he was promoted to sergeant major, the highest rank possible for an African American at that time. The Thirty-third saw duty all over South Carolina and Georgia until 1866, and Loudon was always with them, but he never again engaged the enemy. He mustered out with the regiment on January 31, 1866, in Beaufort, where he and Jane and their children settled and lived for the rest of their lives.

While Loudon was clerking for the Thirty-third USCT, his brothers and cousin in the Massachusetts Fifty-fourth had varied fates. The Fifty-fourth was also in South Carolina and Georgia for the remainder of the war. In 1864, they were defeated at Honey Hill, South Carolina, and continued fighting between Charleston and Savannah in order to disrupt Confederate troop supplies. In February 1865, companies B and F of the Fifty-fourth, including Newell Langley, were among the initial troops to enter Charleston after its fall. The remainder of the regiment, including Lewis Langley and Aaron Freedom, arrived soon after. They must have been exultant to be part of the victorious army entering the city that had so long been a Union target.

In March, they tramped to Savannah for three weeks of garrison duty before going to Georgetown, South Carolina, for their last campaign. During April, the Fifty-fourth fought the enemy in skirmishes from Dingle's Mill to Singleton's Plantation, from Camden to Boykins Mills. Aaron Freeman, Newell and Lewis Langley, and the rest of the regiment marched twelve to twenty-three miles a day, destroying such infrastructure as trains, mills, and trestles and releasing 6,000 contrabands.[32] How they reacted to these thousands of fellow African Americans reduced to dependence on the Union is unknown, but they probably felt a mixture of pride and horror at the scenes of their liberation from the conditions of slavery.

The men from Hinesburgh must have been war-weary to their very core by this time and longing for springtime in Vermont. Even though General Lee had surrendered his army to the Union on April 9, 1865, battles continued for the Fifty-fourth and other regiments in the South. During these final skirmishes, they heard the terrible news that Lincoln had been assassinated on April 14. We have no letters from the Langley brothers or Aaron Freeman about how they felt, but their Colonel, Worthey Hooper, wrote:

On the 23rd a cloud settled upon us; rumors reached us that our President had been foully murdered; we at first could not comprehend it, it was too overwhelming, too lamentable, too distressing. We said quietly, "Now there is no more peace, let us turn back, again load our muskets and if necessary, exterminate the race that can do such things."³³

Were Aaron, Newell, and Lewis as angry as their leaders? Or did they simply long to return home? There is no doubt they participated in the resulting devastation as the Fifty-fourth destroyed railroads, bridges, shops, mills, and a large quantity of cotton. How could they not feel an unleashed fury as they tore through Georgia demolishing everything in their path? Hooper's letter does not discuss the numbers of people "exterminated" during this time, but one wonders if the farmers from the Vermont Hill had nightmares afterward, a normal postwar experience.

By May, the remaining Confederate Army had finally surrendered, and the Fifty-fourth regiment returned to Charleston for garrison duty. In August 1865, the men were finally discharged from duty at Mount Pleasant, South Carolina, and steamed to Boston Harbor, arriving on September 2. Among the men was Aaron Freeman. He was finally getting closer to Vermont and must have been eager to continue the journey. A local Boston paper described the event:

The Fifty-Fourth Massachusetts Regiment . . . recruited at a time when great prejudices existed against enlisting any but so-called white men in the army, when a colored soldiery was considered in the light of an experiment almost certain to fail, this command—which now returns crowned with laurels . . . hav[ing] fought themselves into public esteem—had such a reception to-day as befitted an organization the history of which is admitted to form so conspicuous a part of the annals of the country.³⁴

They had "fought themselves into public esteem," and no doubt they enjoyed the admiration and the tumultuous reception in Boston. After the regiment disbanded, Aaron finally came home to the Hill to be reunited with Rachel and their children at the top of the Hill. Newell and Lewis had stayed behind in South Carolina, both hospitalized on Hilton Head due to diseases. Newell eventually recovered enough to travel and transferred to a New York City hospital to fully recuperate before returning to Harriet and their children in Charlotte. Loudon also returned to Jane

FIGURE 5.2    Pamelia Langley's gravestone in the left foreground, next to her formerly enslaved parents, Primas and Pamelia (the next two stones), and her sister in Basin Harbor, Vermont.

and their children in Charlotte with tales of his duty in the Thirty-third USCT. One can imagine the weary men setting eyes on the Green Mountains of Vermont again, smiling with joy as they reunited with their families. Each man had a child he had never seen, and Harriet and Jane doubtless welcomed their husbands with cries of relief.

One wife was not waiting for her husband to return, however. Pamelia Langley, Lewis's wife, had died in August 1865 in Charlotte. She was fifty-seven and had never borne children, having married later in life. Because the sisters-in-law were all living in the same town, it is likely they were living together along with their elderly father-in-law during the war. This was a phenomenon replicated numerous times all over the country as men marched off to fight in the Civil War and left many women performing the traditional duties of both husband and wife. For many this was the beginning of role changes, as women felt their potential power in the managing of finances, farm chores, and other obligations usually reserved for the men. It would be natural for the bonds among women to strengthen as they helped each other survive the devastating war years. Surely, Jane and Harriet were at Pame-

FIGURE 5.3 Pamelia
Langley's signature on
her will.

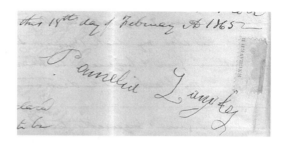

lia's side at her death. She was buried according to her wishes next to her parents in Basin Harbor, Vermont.

Pamelia's will was the first woman's "voice" that I found in the records of these families, and it documents her close relationship with the Langley women as well as with other women in the area. From it we can get a sense of the intimacy and devotion that existed between them. She bequeathed to her sister-in-law, Jane Langley, "my purple silk dress," and to Mary Ann Henry "my black merino dress and also my black merino Shawl." To Harriet Langley she left "my black silk dress." To Rachel Freeman, she gave "my double merino wrappers" and to Clara Freeman "now in Ohio my blue and white merino shawl." She also left to Jane Green (Lewis's sister) in Cleveland, New York, "either my large blanket shawl or a [coverlet?], whichever my husband Lewis Langley may elect."[35] Pamelia's silk and merino dresses and shawls were cherished possessions, and she passed them on to women beloved by her. All but one of the women were on the Langley-Clark side of the family. Pamelia had found an extended family dear to her. She was a woman in the same situation as they—alone with her husband fighting a far-away war—and they leaned on each other for support. They were family.

Pamelia's husband probably never heard about her death. Lewis had been too sick to travel back home with the Fifty-fourth and was left behind on Hilton Head Island, South Carolina. The day after the regiment arrived back in New England in September, Lewis died of fever and disease; he was forty-two years old. They buried him at Hilton Head, along with many others who died there of injuries or disease during and after the war. He was later reburied at the National Cemetery in Beaufort, South Carolina, along with other comrades of the Fifty-fourth who never made it home.

On December 6, 1865, the Thirteenth Amendment to the Constitution was ratified, and slavery was finally officially abolished in the

FIGURE 5.4 Lewis Langley's gravestone in the Beaufort, South Carolina, National Cemetery. All the stones of soldiers of the Fifty-fourth in the Beaufort National Cemetery say "MASS." regardless of their home states. © Stephen Wise.

United States. William Langley had survived to see slavery abolished in the United States, but it must have been a bittersweet event for him. He had lived for over seventy years with the burden that slavery conferred on all people of color—now they were free of that weight, and his sons had participated in securing the victory. What an indescribably exhilarating feeling that must have been to feel for the first time the sense of living in the land of the free. At the same time, he had lost both a son and daughter-in-law during the war. William seems to have been particularly close to Pamelia. When she knew she was close to death, "though infirm in body yet, as I believe, of disposing mind and memory," one of her priorities was to provide for William:

> I give wish and bequeath to my dear husband Lewis Langley now in the army of the United States and his heirs all the remainder of my estate both real and personal Provided he . . . shall take such proper care of his father William Langley & support him in such manner as his condition in life shall require during his natural life.[36]

Unfortunately, having died in service to his country, Lewis could not take care of his father in his old age. Loudon could not help either, since he and Jane had decided to return to South Carolina. However, Harriet and Newell welcomed William into their household, moving to nearby Williston in 1865. Although Newell had been disabled by rheumatism while in the service, his six-foot frame weakened with disease, he nevertheless returned to farming with his father and brother, Henry.[37] In November 1865, William and Newell bought $9\frac{1}{4}$ acres in the western part of Williston north of the old Winooski Turnpike.[38] The families never again had anywhere near the 175 acres that Shubael and Violet worked in the 1790s.

Even after they moved to Williston, the Langleys still owned some of Violet's real estate on the Hill. In 1868, Newell and Harriet sold that land to William Ross of Huntington for $800. That same year, Loudon and Jane Langley and Loudon's sister from Cleveland, New York, also sold their rights to their grandmother's land in Hinesburgh and Huntington to William Ross, for $16.75. Loudon and Jane were identified as being from Williston in the land records, and they appeared personally to sign the deed for the final turnover of their ancestral land. Loudon, however, was on the school board in Beaufort, South Carolina, by then, so they must have been staying with their family in Williston at the time.[39]

In April 1869, William Langley seemed to relinquish all hope of living on the Hill again and sold his interest in the land of Lewis W. Langley and Jeremiah N. Langley, both deceased, to William Ross as well.[40] His son, Henry, living in Huntington as a farm laborer, sold his rights at the same time and moved into the Langley household in Williston. The Langley family, therefore, reproduced a small part of the Hill community a few miles away in the Champlain Valley, and they ended their lives there, continuing to farm for over thirty more years. They were able to do this because of the perseverance and determination of their parents and grandparents, who had taught them how to thrive on a nineteenth-century farm.

The only family who had stayed on top of the Hill during the war was Edward and Harriet (Clark) Williams, in spite of everything still succeeding at farming on land that had belonged to Harriet's parents. Edward's daughter, Rachel Freeman, and granddaughter, Gertrude, lived with them while Aaron was fighting in the war.[41] It must have been lonely with everyone else from their extended family gone. Edward was about fifty years old in 1863, when the call went out for men to sign up for a possible draft. But when Aaron volunteered the family benefited from his bounty money, about double what he could have made as a farm laborer for two years. Just after Aaron mustered in, Edward bought back forty-four acres of the original Clark farm from Daniel Ray. Aaron and Rachel may have hoped to resume life on the Hill with their children after the war.

Somehow the family managed to survive on the Hill through the war years, even though their relatives, who had been through so much with them, were no longer there to help. By some means, the farm, along with Edward's coal pit, had supported them. But the friendly farm economy of Violet and Shubael's day was gone, replaced by a more commercial and competitive one. That was apparently the final push that resulted in the Clarks, Langleys, and Williamses all leaving the Hill by the end of the Civil War. In 1865, the Williamses decided to sell out to their neighbor William Ross, who had bought all the rest of the old Clark farm by this time.[42] With the profits, the Williamses and Freemans bought a small farm in nearby South Burlington, and the two families moved there together.[43] Never again would the clan from the Hill live collectively—being strewn now all over the United States from Vermont to South Carolina to Ohio.

Nature, a changing economy, and a competing large-scale farmer had won out over the Hill farmers who had been there for generations. William Ross now owned all the former Langley-Clark-Williams land on the Hill. If you visit the top of the Hill today, you will see a sign for "Ross Hill" just over the line into Huntington. There are no signs for the Clarks or the Langleys who first cleared and then farmed the ancient land and who are there still in the old burying ground. Similarly, we find no signs for the Peterses who cleared and farmed the bottom of the Hill even longer—into the twentieth century—and whose forbears fought in the American Revolution.[44]

Even though the Williamses and Freemans found land nearby, it must have been extremely difficult to leave behind the old homestead and the remains of their relatives in the old burying ground at the top of the Hill. With everyone gone, there would be no one left to care for the cemetery first cleared seventy years ago when Shubael and Violet arrived to start a new life. But times had transformed the nature of farming, and an individual farm worked by fewer family members was the new way of agriculture. Also, it is possible that they felt they did not need the safety of the isolated Hill during Reconstruction—hopes were still high for an end to prejudice and discrimination based on race.

The Civil War era had emancipated those enslaved in the South but it had also had devastating consequences for the African American community on top of the Hill. Those who survived the war emigrated far and wide. An attraction unknown to us pulled Charles Clark, the shoe-maker, to Morristown in northeastern Vermont after his mother died. The Langleys were drawn to a farm in nearby Williston, the Williamses to South Burlington in close proximity to them to continue farming as well. The farmland in those neighboring towns was not hill land, but good valley property, and both families stayed on their farms for the rest of their lives. Their share in the Vermont way of life, passed down to them from the Revolutionary generation, made it possible for them to live out their days tilling the soil in the state of their choice. Most had been born and raised in Vermont and understood the traditions of hill farmers in the Green Mountains. They could claim the identity of "real Vermonters."[45]

## CHAPTER SIX

The Post–Civil War Years

> All profound changes in consciousness, by their very nature, bring
> with them characteristic amnesias. Out of such oblivions . . . spring
> narratives. —Benedict Anderson, *Imagined Communities*

After the Civil War, an exhausted nation began the task of reconstruct-
ing the destroyed South. Gaining suffrage for those recently freed
became a priority of both blacks and northern whites. Historian Mia
Bay claims that much of the Northerners' eagerness for civil rights was
based on their desire for blacks to stay in the South and grow cotton for
Northern mills. Passage of the Fourteenth and Fifteenth Amendments
and military rule in the South was meant to stabilize the economy and
ensure there would be enough Southern farm workers and raw materials from the South to stimulate further Northern industrialization. The
struggles of Reconstruction and the whites' need to return to some sem-
blance of normalcy "ultimately exhausted their very limited enthusiasm
for black civil rights."[1] Whites seized on new pseudoscientific data, such
as longer arm measurements of black soldiers, as yet another sign of
black inferiority, and fears of race mixing again took center stage. Frederick Douglass's hopes that people of color would "rise in one bound" to
equality with whites through service in the war were dashed. Even the
bravery of black soldiers was forgotten and reinterpreted by northern
General Jacob Cox to mean that they were "most easily ruled."[2]

As the myths about black intellectual inferiority persisted, blacks
returned to their argument that the whole idea of outward appearances
signaling intellect was "born of absurdities" and that if there was such
a thing as a racial defect, it was white behavior, specifically their inhu-
mane treatment of people of color. Bay claims that blacks' "intellectual
resistance to racism's relentless ideological assault was in many ways as

historic and difficult as the protest actions against slavery."[3] Perhaps it was more difficult after the war, because their hopes had been so high after emancipation and the constitutional amendments granting equal rights. They must have been desperately asking themselves how their hopes for justice and equality could be dashed yet again.

In the post–Civil War years, as in the post–Revolutionary War period, conservative forces doused the fire of real reform and the hoped-for transformations in power structures. The Reconstruction era began with high hopes by abolitionists, white and black alike, as new ideas for equal rights and racial justice abounded. But meaningful reform was short-lived as whites from the North and the South colluded to ensure that blacks did not gain a foothold in the halls of power. As in the post-Revolutionary period, people in power washed away all memory of problematic truths as they reinterpreted the reasons for the war and invented new racial ideologies. Historian Eric Foner claims, "The war was 'remembered' not as the crisis of a nation divided by antagonistic labor systems and political and social ideologies, but as a tragic conflict within the American family, whose bloodshed was in many ways meaningless but that accomplished the essential task of solidifying a united nation."[4]

White soldiers from both sides were reimagined as fighting for the noble principles of either *union* (the North) or *self-determination* (the South). The war's legacy lay in the valor of the soldiers, "not in any ideological causes or purposes."[5] As such, the dreams of a socially transformed nation with racial justice and equality were abandoned in the rush to reunite whites from the North and South to rebuild the economy. As Frederick Douglass said, liberty and justice for blacks was doomed from "the hour that the loyal north began to shake hands over the bloody chasm."[6] The lives of the residents of the Hill illustrate the lowering expectations of people of color in the aftermath of the war.

*Bottom of the Hill: Descendents of Hannah and Prince Peters*

The Peters's descendants, who made their living largely by working their acreage and becoming servants and farm laborers for local white families, survived longer on the Hill than those of the Clarks, many of whom continued the farming tradition elsewhere. Hannah and Prince's children and grandchildren were present to see the Hill receive a new name after the war: Lincoln Hill.[7] Josephus Peters, who had been born and raised on the Hill and nurtured a large family there, along with his three wives, died at his home November 28, 1869, at sixty-seven years of age. His death certificate says he is buried in West Hill, either a part of the town cemetery, or a designation for lot 83 on the west side of Lincoln Hill. I have never found his stone. At his death, he had twenty acres on the Hill according to the inventory of his estate, and his land was surrounded by that of four of his sons, his sister Sarah Edwards's family, and the family of Charles and Calista Waters. The Peters part of the Hill was at its greatest numbers at this point, and Josephus surely had a large funeral as his widow, children, sister, and in-laws gathered to mourn him.

Josephus's third wife, Sarah, had trouble with her widow's dower. In June 1876, she continued the tradition on the Hill of turning to the courts to settle disputes by complaining to the probate court that her "interest in the Estate are neglected by Sidney Ray and imperiled and . . . she has had no account rendered to her."[8] Sidney Ray was from the same family that had paid for Prince's medicines and helped Prince's widow after he died in 1832. The families still had a connection, but Ray needed to be called into court to finally give his accounting. Sarah received some household furniture, cash support, and the homestead. In 1871, Ray sold all of the real estate, except the house, to Josephus's sons, John and Cornelius; it was bounded on the west by more of John's land.[9] Sarah lived at the old homestead "containing one half acre more or less being all of the real estate whereof the said Sarah Peters widow of Josephus Peters died seized" sometime in the 1870s.[10]

Josephus and Charlot's sons George, John, Joseph, and Cornelius, lived on the Hill into the twentieth century and owned about thirty acres altogether. In the 1870 census, John and Cornelius, in their thirties, were listed as farm laborers on the Augustus McEuen farm. McEwen was valued at $18,000 real estate and $15,000 other possessions. In 1872, Augustus McEuen died. A typed sheet on the back of a picture in his former home states:

> He [McEuen] selected four colored boys who had worked for him, more or less, as had their father before them, sons of Cephus Peters, as pall bearers. They were to carry the body to the grave which was on his own farm, and lower it to its last resting place, fill the grave with earth and then walk back to the house, where they were to find each a letter, sealed

FIGURE 6.1    McEuen driveway with Peters men (ca. 1880s).

and directed to them, in which was the money to pay for this last service which he had required of them. They did the work, and received the sealed letters; but what sum of money was therein has not yet transpired.[11]

The Peterses were an integral part of the McEuen family in life and death. Augustus, brother to Carlton, who was at Charles Bowles's deathbed many years before, likely attended Josephus's funeral three years earlier to pay his respects to his longtime neighbor and farmhand.

By 1880, John, Joseph, and Cornelius, all bachelors, were living together at the old homestead, while George lived next door with his wife, Jane, and their three sons. They owned property, but are all listed as farm laborers in the census reports and business directories for the late nineteenth century. Family history records that George took care of his neighbor's race horses, and Jane cooked for them. George's bachelor brothers were nicknamed the "three fiddlers" because they were all musicians who played the violin.[12] The four brothers lived on the Hill together into the twentieth century. The last of the brothers to die was

Cornelius in 1922. Josephus and Charlot's numerous descendants were an integral part the local economy and the Hill farm community, continuing the traditions first brought to the Hill in the eighteenth century. They had lived and worked on the Hill for almost 200 years.

The Edwards family, another link back to Hannah and Prince Peters, also had a home on the Hill for many years. Sarah Peters and husband Charles Edwards had a dwelling on "the houselot of Josephus Peters," continuing the tradition of having their homes on the same lot, regardless of whose name was on the deed.[13] The 1880 census states they were living with a boarder, Grant Peters, age 10. Charles, age seventy, was listed as a farm laborer in the Hinesburgh Business Directory, and their sons were farm laborers for the Livermores.[14] Sarah was sixty-seven by this time. Their son Henry stayed single and lived at the old homestead for a time after his parents died sometime before 1890 and worked as a farm laborer. In 1890, he spent time in jail and mortgaged the homestead, which he had bought from Josephus's estate, in order to pay the claim on the lot and get out of jail. He eventually disappeared from the Hinesburgh records.[15] His brother, Warren, also a farm laborer, and his family eventually moved to Rhode Island Corners, another section of Hinesburgh, in 1891, and their descendants lived there for many years.

Charles and Calista (Peters) Waters were another link back to the earliest Peters pioneers. Charles Waters, originally from Maryland, needed a guardian in 1867 for some reason. On March 12, the Probate Court in Burlington gave his guardian the authority to sell Waters's real estate "as shall be most beneficial of said ward."[16] He sold the land, part of lot 83, to John Peters. The Waterses disappear from the records after this.


*Top of the Hill: Descendants of Violet and Shubael Clark*

Unlike the Peterses, the Clark descendants did not stay on the Hill, although their relatives are buried there in the family cemetery, which is not recognizable as a burial ground today. In 1865, Lewis Clark was living in Orange, Massachusetts, Charles in Ferrisburgh, Vermont, and Sybil Clark Loudon in Ohio. They sold all of Violet's dower land, which they had inherited two years earlier at her death, to William Ross.[17] The transfer was complete — Ross owned all the land cleared and worked for decades by the first settlers at the top of the Hill. He owned the Clark-

Langley-Williams land, coal pit, and cemetery, and benefited from the work of these black pioneers who had cleared the old-growth forest and worked the Hill for seventy years.

As far as I can tell, the surviving Clark men were never again property-owners in Vermont. By 1870, Lewis Clark, who twenty years earlier had owned hundreds of acres on the Hill and had been proudly listed as one of the top landowners in the Baptist church records, seemed to be living in Worcester, Massachusetts, and working as a "jobbing laborer."[18] His wife, Ruth, had died in 1863.[19] Perhaps his land went to his children, who could probably pass as white, and he moved to Massachusetts after his wife died. However, what happened to his assets is a mystery. He died of old age in September 1876. Charles Clark, forty-seven, who cared for his mother for many years, was living in Morristown, Vermont, with his wife, Maria, in 1870. He was still a shoemaker, and they had no children.

The Clark-Langley women and their families have varied stories going into the twentieth century. Historian Nina Silber asserts that "the war required many women to take on new economic and political challenges and to assume a greater degree of autonomy in running their households," which transformed their lives and had long-range implications for them.[20] Despite the fact that their lives generally reflected lowered expectations due to racial discrimination, changing gender roles were becoming apparent in some of the Clark-Langley family records. In 1880, Rachel Freeman had left her father's South Burlington farm and was working as a cook in Burlington.[21] Sybil Clark Loudon was living in Ravenna, Ohio, with her husband and children. She was listed in the census as a widow, seventy-four, living with her son (a music teacher),[22] daughter (a dressmaker), and daughter-in-law (a teacher). These women had professions, unlike the women of the Hill, who had always worked on the farm with their husbands. The first Langley woman with a profession had been Pamelia. Her role in her family was first seen when they repurchased traditional Clark land that the family had lost in the 1850s. She had been able to help buy the land because of her job as a renowned cook at the Stevens Hotel in Vergennes, a trade she had learned from her mother.[23] Her much-needed salary gave her power in the Langley family that most women did not have at that time.

Lewis Langley's estate inventory of 1865 also shined a light into Pamelia's activities, depicting more of the interior of their 1865 home, Pamelia's sphere, than his activities (document 6.1). Apart from a few farm implements, the rest was in the feminine realm. It seems that Lewis, twelve years her junior, had moved in with her after they sold all the Hill possessions and had brought little with him. The contents of the house show expensive items for the kitchen: pots, pans, and kettles; silverware; glassware; and crockery. The kitchen had a table and chairs with a tablecloth. The three bedrooms were well equipped with sheets, pillows, and pillowcases; blankets and comforters; bedsteads; beds and ticks; and curtains. They also had a clock and a looking glass, perhaps on the bureau in a bedroom. Pamelia would have put her silk dresses

DOCUMENT 6.1
*Inventory of the Estate of Lewis Langley, 1866*

| | | | |
|---|---|---|---|
| 6 Large Silver Spoons | $12.00 | Amount Brought Forward | $86.30 |
| 11 Silver Tea Spoons | 8.00 | 6 Cotton Pillow Cases | 2.00 |
| 1 Set Knives & Forks | .75 | 4 Prs Cotton Window | 2.00 |
| 1 Pr Shears | .34 | Curtains | |
| 7 Sheets | 14.00 | 20 Yards Carpeting | 5.00 |
| 9 Pillows | 6.75 | Ladies Under Clothing | 6.00[a] |
| 5 Bed Comfortables | 6.50 | 1 Sewing Bird | .20 |
| 2 Bed Blankets | 7.00 | 5 Ladies Dresses | 5.00 |
| 1 Linen Table Cloth | 1.00 | 1 Knit Shawl | 1.50 |
| Crockery & Glass Ware | 12.00 | 2 Shawls | 2.00 |
| 12 Tin Pans | 2.00 | 4 Ladies Skirts | 3.00 |
| 1 Brass Kettle | 5.00 | 1 Small Brass Kettle | .75 |
| 2 Sad Irons | .75 | 1 Parlor Stove | 2.50 |
| 1 Dinner Pots | 1.50 | 3 Beds & Ticks | 16.00 |
| 1 Fry Pan | .25 | 1 Clock | 2.00 |
| 1 Clothes Bar | .50 | 1 Looking Glass | 1.50 |
| 3 Bed Stead | 2.25 | 1 Bureau | 5.00 |
| 1 Rocking Chair | 1.00 | 1 Table & Cover | 3.00 |
| 1 Wood Bowl | .37 | 1 Stand & Cover | .75 |
| 1 Side Hill Plow | 4.00 | 3 Kitchen Chairs | .75 |
| 1 Shovel | .34 | 2 Cows | 70.00 |
| | $86.30 | 2 Chains | 3.00 |
| | | 2 Tons Hay | 16.00 |
| | | | $234.25 |

SOURCE: Probate Court of Chittendon County, Vermont, Estate Inventory for Lewis Langley, *Probate Court Records*, v. 50, 1866 (Burlington, VT: Chittenden County Court).

[a]Normally only the man's possessions were on inventories, which included everything except the woman's very personal possessions. Everything else could be sold to pay his debts. Because Pamelia died first, his estate now included her clothing.

and merino shawls on the clothing rod and her everyday clothes in the bureau. The twenty yards of carpeting may signal that she was preparing to have new rugs installed in her home. As a woman with a good job, she could have afforded it, even during the war. Clearly she was a force in this household, illustrating the status that some women with economic power were able to achieve at that time.

Land records also depict the advancement of women's rights. On the Hill, the names of women were never found on land deeds unless they were single or widowed. However, the Langley land records in Williston in 1875 show that Harriet E. Langley bought a piece of property for $1,000.[24] Newell signed a mortgage for the property, but it was always in Harriet's name after that, even though they remained married. These bits of evidence show that these families experienced gender role changes along with the rest of the country after the war.[25]

Newell and Harriet Butler Langley continued to farm the same land in Williston for the rest of their lives. They had five children. Four daughters predeceased them; two died as babies and one at age fifteen. Their other daughter, Mary, lived to adulthood, married and had two children. But Mary and her children all died in 1877. Only their son, William, named after his grandfather, survived them. The elder William lived with them and died in 1876. He was eighty-two years old. Newell's brother, Henry, who also lived with them, died in 1881, and Newell died in 1892 of heart disease at age sixty-five. By this time, Harriet was alone. Everyone she loved had died except her son, and he had married Addie Hazzard from a long-established black family of Woodstock, Vermont, and moved to Saint Armaud, New York.[26] For whatever reason, they did not care to stay on the Williston farm, and he worked instead as a "day laborer," hiring himself out to perform manual labor as opportunities arose.

In 1905, Harriet could no longer live alone and she leased her farm of ten acres for five years to a man from Ireland. The lease stated that he must occupy it for a farm and garden and "in a good husband-like manner" or she could throw him off the property.[27] Harriet lived for four more years. She and Newell had often mortgaged the farm through the years, but they always paid their debts, and she was debt free at her death. Her son was her only heir, but he did not want the farm. The ten Williston acres that had been in the Langley family for forty years was sold and the proceeds sent to William in Saranac Lake, New York.[28] Harriet's place of death was Saranac Lake, so she evidently lived her last years with William. So ended the eighty-year history of the Hinesburgh Langleys in Vermont.[29]

Rachel Williams Freeman, the daughter of Phoebe Clark, who had lived on the Hill her entire life, and Edward Williams, perhaps formerly enslaved in Maryland, also survived to see twentieth-century Vermont. Rachel farmed with her children, her father, and her Aunt Harriet on their South Burlington farm right after the war. At some point in the late 1860s, Rachel's husband, Aaron, moved to New York City looking for work and became a coachman.[30] In September 1869, he died of an aneurism of the aorta while walking down Fulton Street toward the ferry. The Civil War veteran is buried in an unmarked grave in Potter's Field on Hart's Island, a New York City cemetery begun that year. Rachel's father, who had likely escaped slavery in Maryland to live the life of a free farmer, died in 1877 of lung congestion. His death certificate identified him as a laborer, not a farmer.[31] Rachel, her brother George, and Aunt Harriet mortgaged the farm that same year. I presume that Harriet lived there until she died. This was the family who had originally drawn me to this research and who led me to their relatives on the Hill. Unfortunately, I have not been able to find where any of them are buried, but often imagine that they were reunited with relatives in the Hill cemetery.

After the deaths of her father and aunt, Rachel and her daughter moved to Burlington to live with her brother, who was a barber, and his wife. The 1900 census says that Rachel had given birth to four children, but that only one was living by that time.[32] Ten years later, she was seventy, her only surviving child had died, and Rachel V. Freeman was living with her granddaughter in Burlington.[33] She must have passed away in the house where she and her granddaughter rented rooms. This was my first hint of Rachel's middle name. Could the *V* stand for her grandmother's name, Violet?

Rachel's younger brother, George T. Williams, worked with his brother-in-law, Abial Anthony. They were listed in city directories from 1869 until 1891 as having a barbershop opposite the City Hall.[34] The 1910 census continues to identify George as being a barber with his own shop. For over forty years he walked to the same shop on Church Street. Barbering was one of the best jobs available to African American men, and they thrived as long as their clients were white. An indication that they catered to well-to-do white men is the longtime location of their business across from the halls of power in the largest city in the state.

By 1920 they were elderly. George was seventy-six and Nettie was sixty-nine, and they had moved to Medford, Massachusetts, to live with their son's family. George W. worked at the U.S. Arsenal, and his sisters, both single, also lived with them — one doing laundry in private houses.

An important question to ask about these families is why there was such a downturn in their social and economic mobility, given the fact that they had come from a prominent farming family that had persisted in the Green Mountains since the 1790s. Newcomers, such as the Irish and French Canadians, had shaken off the prejudice of their early days and were becoming better off economically, even socially prominent in the case of the Irish, as the century advanced.[35] Their differing experiences suggest that skin color and its attendant prejudice and discrimination made it difficult for children and grandchildren from the Hill to take advantage of their ancestors' prosperity and long roots in the community.

## The South Carolina Langleys

The family that best illustrates the highs and lows of the nation's adherence to its principles is that of Loudon Langley, the sixth child of Almira Clark and William Langley. In addition to his becoming an educator after the war, Loudon was one of the over 1,000 black men who served in public offices in the South during Reconstruction (1867–1877) and was one of the founding fathers of radical Republicanism in South Carolina during the postwar period.[36]

After Loudon mustered out of the Thirty-third USCT in South Carolina, he stayed and immediately began to work for the Freedmen's Bureau in Beaufort. One of the Bureau's tasks was to educate the thousands of freedmen who had flowed into the county during the war, because early on it was in the hands of the Union. At some point, certainly because of his excellent writing skills and good education, Loudon was appointed to the Beaufort County School Board. Historian Monica Tetzlaff tells us that Loudon, called "Landon" in the Southern literature, hired Abbie Holmes Christensen, a Northern white teacher, to teach African American children. After many difficult months of trying to manage her class, "Superintendent Langley praised her in a lecture to a group of teachers."[37] He said she had "better order in her school than anyone else he had visited, and Abbie considered this praise 'a feather in my cap.'"[38]

A look into the land records of post–Civil War Beaufort revealed the name of "L. S. Langley" in numerous places in the books. He had become the auditor of accounts for the county and often confiscated the land and homes of Confederates for nonpayment of taxes. He sometimes sold the properties to his wife, Jane, and their small children. Evidently this is why historian Eric Foner called him a "black carpetbagger."[39]

The 1870 census gives us some clues as to his relationship with an important politician from South Carolina. At that time, Loudon, thirty-two, had a house next to one of the heroes of the Civil War, Robert Smalls. With the bounty Smalls had earned by capturing the Confederate ship, *Planter*, he bought the house in which he and his mother had been enslaved and lived there for the rest of his life as a free man and a representative from South Carolina in the U.S. Congress.[40] In the Langley household next door were twenty-six-year-old Jane and their two small children, as well as four other seemingly unrelated people, including a schoolteacher from Massachusetts. Loudon served with Smalls on the Beaufort school board and was also elected with him to the 1868 Constitutional Convention, which wrote a new, futuristic constitution guaranteeing racial equality.[41]

Loudon was an active and outspoken member of the convention, which included sixty-seven blacks, many of them newly freed, and fifty-eight whites. A correspondent for the *New York Times* described a delay of several days in getting down to serious business due to the wide variety of people attending:

> The antagonistic opinions and incongruous interests which entered into the compositions of the body made it wise that the crucible should stand, and its contents settle, so that its surface could be known from its sediment. Men have learned somewhat of their motives and influence. Those who represent intelligence, moderation and patriotism have taken their places at the front. The ignorant, the vicious and impracticable are laid away to rest. (Therefore) this Convention . . . exhibits a larger share of ability, and with ability, tact of that type which wins, than any other body of Southern Reconstructionists yet assembled.[42]

The reporter went on to say that the convention president made excellent committee appointments, "The best men of the Convention were chosen — the 'ragtag and bobtail' of both colors being ignored." Loudon

Langley was appointed to the education committee, signaling that he was one of the "best men," not one to be ignored. According to the proceedings of the convention, during which Loudon spoke 165 times, his main passions were three: protecting the rights of rural areas and agricultural interests against urban and mercantile interests (i.e., Charleston); protecting the laboring man against property owners, labor being the only property of the poor; and ensuring an equal, free, and compulsory education for all.[43]

As a member of the education committee, Loudon argued that all schools, including colleges and universities, should be open to everyone regardless of race or color. The *New York Times* reporter wrote that most white men at the convention "object to the affiliation of their children with negroes under the same roof and teacher." He warned that if nonsegregated education was mandated by the constitution, it would so inflame "the prejudices of the people and so unanimously will they oppose it, that the entire instrument may fail in being ratified." Loudon lost that fight with both blacks and whites voting against him. Apparently he was a radical minority on that issue.

His interests in protecting agricultural and labor interests and providing free and equal education hearken back to his life in Vermont. Members of his family were still farming in rural areas of Vermont, and he had once been a farm laborer who had enjoyed a free and nonsegregated education on the Hill. He doubtless thought of home as he argued passionately for the same rights for the newly freed men and women in South Carolina. It must have been heady times for the family, as they lived in a place where most of the leadership was black and a state that went further than any other state to "provide freedmen with land and encourage the breakup of the plantation system."[44]

However, the hopes of freedmen were dashed with the exit of U.S. soldiers from the South in 1877, as whites waged an "extraordinary campaign of defiance and subversion against the new biracial social order" that had been imposed on them by the federal government.[45] White South Carolinians violently cast out the last black government in the state, and across the South white men organized themselves into militias and vigilante groups to intimidate and control blacks and Union agents through lynching and various other types of violence. This included a system of neoslavery: scouring the countryside for black men to arrest and sell to the highest bidder as forced labor in mills, mines, and lumber camps.[46]

FIGURE 6.2    Loudon Langley's gravestone at the Beaufort National Cemetery in South Carolina. © Stephen Wise.

For Southern whites, this was a time of "redemption." For blacks, it was condemnation into a labyrinth of racial injustice, neoslavery, and terror. By 1879, Loudon Langley was no longer a prosperous Beaufort politician, and he applied for a pension due to his back injury during the war. He claimed he was in need of help since he could not do manual labor, apparently the only work open to him by that time. He was denied the pension. One wonders if the reason may have been connected to prominent South Carolinians' losing property to him when he was the auditor of accounts for Beaufort. But Jane received a pension for his service some years later.

By the next year, the Langleys had lost their house in Beaufort and were living on St. Helena Island; Loudon worked as an assistant lighthouse keeper on nearby Hunting Island. Jane and Loudon had four children to support by this time and a servant who lived with them. Because of his back injury, he may have been doing paperwork at the lighthouse, but more likely he was lugging fifty-pound oilcans up ninety-five stairs to fuel the light. There is some evidence this may have caused his final illness.

The next year, Loudon became sick, and his friends Middleton W. Brown and Peter H. Dais visited him frequently during his illness. They "acted as nurses upon several occasions, and were so acting at the time of his death. . . . The said Landon S. Langley departed this life at his residence at Oakland . . . about seven miles from Beaufort on the 28th day of June 1881 in their presence."[47] He was forty-three years old. Brown and Dais said that for the past fifteen years Loudon had suffered "from an affliction of the back suffered in battle during the Civil War," and they believed that he died from that.[48] No physician was called because his death was quite sudden and the nearest medical help was seven miles away in Beaufort. At the National Cemetery in Beaufort, not far from his brother Lewis's grave, Loudon's final resting place is marked with a stone inscribed "Sgt. Maj. L. S. Langley." The initial *S* of his middle name honored his grandfather, Shubael Clark.

After Loudon's death, Jane began her quest to receive a widow's pension, since she believed that he had died from injuries suffered in the war. Her children under sixteen, who still needed to be cared for, were a toddler and nine-year-old, Ida St. Clair Elizabeth Ann (figure 6.3).[49] Jane established her right for a pension, even though Loudon failed at the same task, and began receiving twelve dollars a month sometime in the 1880s. By 1883, freedom for blacks had deteriorated even further as the U.S. Supreme Court struck down the Civil Rights Act of 1875 "opening the door for the eventual triumph of Jim Crow laws across the south," and neoslavery was firmly established in the "Black Belt" from South Carolina to Texas.[50]

In the 1900 census for Beaufort, Jane is listed as a dressmaker, age fifty-six, and living with her daughter Nettie and her son-in-law, a preacher.[51] Nettie had given birth to eleven children, and ten of them from ages eighteen to two were living with them, including a pair of twins. One child had died. All were unemployed at the time.

On December 7, 1902, Jane died, most likely surrounded by her large family in Nettie's Beaufort home. Her gravesite is unknown. Jane Anthony Langley had traveled many miles from Burlington to Beaufort and light years away from the world of her parents and Loudon's family in terms of geography, politics, and culture. She and Loudon had lived through peaceful times on the Hill, the frightening times of separation during the Civil War, the exhilarating times of South Carolina Reconstruction politics, and the terror of post-Reconstruction.

One wonders if Jane died full of hope for her grandchildren or full

FIGURE 6.3   Ida Langley, daughter of Loudon and Jane, with her husband, Harry
Proctor, married in Ohio. The connection to Ohio was undoubtedly through her
great aunt, Sybil Loudon, who grew up on the Hill. Courtesy of Langley Proctor,
a descendant.

of despair, since by 1895, the futuristic Constitution that Loudon had
helped write had been rewritten for one purpose: to disenfranchise
blacks. All the modern educational and political elements were retained,
but only for whites. A new racist ideology based on social Darwinism
and ideas of black degeneracy took control on the South.[52]

Through the use of violence, poll taxes, and unfair literacy tests in six
Southern states, including South Carolina, blacks who dared attempt
registration to vote were more often than not denied their suffrage
rights, terrorized, and, perhaps arrested on flimsy charges.[53] Their
short few years of using political power and the ballot in the South were
ended, and seventy years of fighting to regain their human and civil
rights ensued.

It would not be until 1945 that the system of convict labor would
begin to unravel. Not until twenty years later would the U.S. Congress

pass the Voting Rights Act to ensure that the Fifteenth Amendment was enforced throughout the nation, as it had been during Reconstruction. This time both men and women of color took their fight for equality to the ballot box. Little did they know they were fighting for rights that had been realized long ago by farmers of color on a Hill in northern Vermont.

Some Conclusions: Vulnerable Spaces

Identities and memories are not things we think *about* but things we
think *with*. — John Gillis, quoted in Blight, *Beyond the Battlefield*

While scholarship on urban black communities and identities is ubiquitous, rural areas have been so understudied that we cannot make generalizations about them. This story adds not only to our knowledge of
rural black history but also to little-studied contacts between rural blacks
and whites.[1] Through intimate stories of small places we can start to
understand real people, such as these Hill families, who often created
their own way of living in their biracial community despite a racist culture. By doing labor-intensive research on a small geographic area like
the Hill, historians can uncover real, complex relationships among individuals and between groups. That is the beauty and the worth of this
type of history. Uncovering how people of the past have struggled to
live together day-to-day can help us as we struggle with the same issues
today. This is just the beginning of a more complex understanding of
our rural and biracial history.

    This story demonstrates that despite the relatively low numbers of
African-descended people throughout Vermont during the antebellum
period, there were higher percentages in many places in the state including this rural hillside.[2] An examination of where the spouses of the Hill
people originated also uncovers a widespread network that reached into
many areas of the state, as well as into New England, New York, Canada, and the South. Draping this once invisible network of people of
color over our traditional histories stimulates us to rethink the past and
modify the stories we tell about ourselves.

    The history of the Peters, Edwards, Waters, Clark, Langley, Wil-
liams, and Freeman families, will help to eliminate the idea advanced

by some historians, that only "scattered and isolated African American families struggled quietly (in rural areas) to survive the harsh realities of their hard-won freedom."[3] In the past, there has been little room for successful black settlers in the images or written histories of white Yankees who battled the northern wilderness and built nineteenth-century farming communities. It is past time to return them to the historical terrain they occupied.

Expanding our traditional histories to include these rural farmers reminds us that our heroic past includes people of color who successfully negotiated a racialized society and passed their knowledge and skills for doing so on to the next generations. It also shows us how vulnerable their situations were. They may have overcome to some extent the racial injustices of the eras in which they lived, but disappointment always seemed to follow. Despite the revolutionary generation's hopes of an increasingly better world for their children, the second generation was left trying to hold back a flood of rising racism. By the third generation, they still remembered the past of their grandparents, but their lives turned tragic as the community at the top of the Hill crumbled and the Peterses' land dwindled. Not even their bravery in the Civil War was remembered and celebrated. Many felt betrayed by their country once again, and some of the descendants of the Hill farmers retreated into whiteness to protect themselves.

One aspect of their lives that that eludes determination is how much rural racism they encountered on a daily basis. Their apparent acceptance on the frontier and cross-racial relations on the Hill make this a complicated endeavor. Historian Elizabeth Bethel discussed the "undelivered democratic freedom" in the country between the Revolution and the Civil War.[4] However, it appears it *was* delivered in some small, out of the way places like this Hill, because a few people insisted on it. The founding mothers and fathers of the Hill lived through times of constantly resisting dehumanization to episodes of exhilarating freedom to putting their stake in the ground and risking the hazards of life on the Hill alongside their white neighbors. All the while they insisted on an equal chance in life as they helped build new cultural ideals in their neighborhood on the Hill. It might have been easier for a small minority to create such a place. White people of the time, fearful of revenge for the brutality of slavery, often imagined all sorts of terrifying things attached to people of color, but this small group may have posed no foreseeable threat to them.

Their acceptance also might have been connected to shifting social class status as the century advanced and racial theories changed. In the nineteenth century, the Connecticut Colonizationist Society described societal prejudices against people of color as "prejudices which neither refinement, nor argument, nor education, nor religion itself can subdue."[5] On the contrary, archaeologist Robert Paynter discovered that blacks in Massachusetts who were educated and economically successful became the targets of physical and mental assaults, since many whites felt that "the practices of gentility were out of bounds" for people of color.[6] Since hill farming was not a genteel life and revolutionary egalitarianism was in the air, the earliest Hill people were most likely accepted by their white neighbors, who were all of a similar social class. As the century advanced and the Peterses' economic position declined, they were accepted into town life as hard-working small farmers, laborers, and servants.

The Clarks and Langleys, on the other hand, stretched the boundaries at the top of the Hill, boundaries that had been set up for people of color by white racism. Their farm was successful for a time, Shubael was a leader in the church, and their children were well educated. Lewis Clark expanded the family holdings with his own farm in the middle of the Hill, entering the middle class at a time when the advancement of blacks frightened whites. Soon after land-ownership and high economic achievements passed to the next generation, often a sign that families would stay and become civic leaders, Lewis and his family migrated to an even more rural part of the state. Perhaps it had become too uncomfortable for a successful biracial family to continue living on the Hill.

The rest of the extended Clark-Langley-Williams family eventually migrated to other parts of the state or to southern New England, the Midwest, or South Carolina, leaving behind their ancestral lands. On the other hand, many white farmers from mid-century who owned land on the Hill or in the vicinity, enjoyed many generations of life in Hinesburgh, and some of their descendants are still there benefiting from their reputations as long-standing members of the community today. White descendants had no need or desire to hide their lineage.

For most of our country's history, people have been forced by societal pressures to identify by race.[7] But at least for a time, the people of the Hill and their friends and colleagues in the surrounding towns may well have personally identified by gender, religion, education, profession, and socioeconomic status. They were not a monolithic group, as shown by their varying lifestyles and different views on issues such as colonization. Through the stories of this Hill, one can see a constant struggle by people of color to survive and advance as men and women, as rural farmers, and as members of the middle class. Eventually, however, they were thwarted in their attempts to self-identify, forced by societal pressures into a binary world of white and black.

Still, this history reminds us how vulnerable racism might be to the march of time. Paynter contends that "racial identities as parts of social systems of oppression are phenomena of our recent past and not a social principle extending back to time immemorial."[8] Doctrines of racial inferiority and superiority seeped into Western culture with the beginning of the slave trade. We are still in that era. If nothing else, however, history has taught us that progress is not a straight upward climb, but a series of peaks and valleys followed by more peaks and valleys. Therefore, someday, the world will climb out of the valley of the slave-trade era and into a more enlightened age.

One of the privileges of whiteness has been that white people can choose to be ruled by members of their own race.[9] In the nineteenth century, Shubael Clark's committee work showed a time on a Hill in Vermont where whites chose a black man to lead them. On election day in November 2009, Vermont was the first of the contiguous states to declare for Barack Obama, demonstrating that that spirit is still alive in the Green Mountains. The election of a black president might signal that the United States has entered an era of increased acceptance of difference. One can hope. But we must never rest in our struggle against racist ideologies, because as Bethel reminds us, "Disillusionment inevitably followed each moment of heightened hopes and expectations" by people of color and their allies.[10]

We will know the world has changed when people can choose their own complex identities across racial distinctions and be treated as such. One way to keep the heightened hopes alive is to find more stories like those of these Hill people, where coalitions of blacks and whites were successful, at least for a time. The story of this Hill demonstrates that times and places of greater equality once existed in the antebellum period. However, they plunged back into valleys of injustice, and it was left to another generation to start the long climb to regain what was lost. Such stories are often excluded from our grand historical narrative because they cannot be integrated easily into the American myth of steady progress toward liberty and justice for all. The Hill families expose the fiction of that traditional narrative and illustrate that striving for our democratic ideals is a grueling, complex, and never-ending task full of victories and defeats.

More histories like that of the Clarks and Peterses in Hinesburgh need to be brought out of the shadows and celebrated as *a city upon a hill.*[11] This rural community and others like it could be a beacon to those who see racism "as vulnerable, as a mere upstart in the world's long history, and one challenged by unending human desires to live, play, create and work together."[12] These families, for a time, satisfied their souls' yearnings. They lived freely and created a place for themselves on this Hill where they not only lived and played together, but also loved and worshipped in a biracial community in the Green Mountains of Vermont.

# Acknowledgments

This project could never have been accomplished without the dedicated people who oversee archival materials, and I am indebted to them for their help: Vermont town clerks: Olga M. Hallock and Heidi Racht of Huntington, Melissa Ross and Cheryl Hubbard of Hinesburg, Helen McKinlay of Pittsford, Carmelita Burritt of Monkton, and Deborah Beckett of Williston. I am also indebted to the UVM Special Collections staff: Nadia Smith, Chris Burns and Jeff Marshall; as well as Debby Brunelle of the Chittenden County Probate Court; Vermont state archivists Gregory Sanford and Kathy Watters; Superior Court of Chittenden County. Also welcoming and helpful were people at the New York City Archives and New York historian Thomas McCarthy; Christine Kwasney, Tyron Keels, and Jean Nudd at the National Archives in Pittsfield, Massachusetts; and the Beaufort, South Carolina County Court. I am also grateful to Dave Allen for his help with old maps.

There were many people outside of archives who freely gave their time and expertise, and am grateful to them: Judy Dow, Suzanne Richards, Dona Brown, Amani Whitfield, Jim Peterson, Alan Berolzheimer, Jerry Fox, Carolyn Stone, Jane Williamson, Gerhard Speiler, Jim Davidson, Eric Ross, Don Wickman, Don Papson, Allen Yale, and Sue Roberts. Thanks also go to Langley Proctor and Debbie Van Dyne for family information and photos.

Others shared their knowledge of the land in Hinesburg and walked the Hill with me in all kinds of weather: Scott McLaughlin, Walter Poleman, Britt Haselton, Ann Thomas, Mary Crane, Paul Wieczoreck, Jane Dorney, and Steve Leffler. Thanks also go to University of Vermont professors, Judith Aiken, Willi Coleman, Charles Rathbone, and Sherwood Smith and St. Michael's College professor Susan Ouellette, for giving me invaluable advice and encouragement. I am also grateful to the Flow of History and the Chittenden County Historical Society for supporting my research.

My thanks to Eliot Lathrop for preservation of the Huntington District 8 schoolhouse and permission to take a picture of it (fig. 2.1). Thanks to Stephen Wise for providing the photos of the gravestones of Loudon and Lewis Langley in the Beaufort National Cemetery (figs. 5.3 and 6.2) and to Mr. Otis Daies, a groundskeeper at the cemetery, for helping me to find Loudon's gravesite. Thanks to Helen and David Nagel for permission to print the photo of the Peters men at the McEuen home (fig. 6.1). Thanks also to Langley Proctor for permission to use the photo of Ida Langley (fig. 6.3) and to John Reynolds for the photo of the Langley house on the Hill and reflections on Shubael's death.

I appreciate the time and effort of Carl Bridges, John Leppman, and Fran Delwiche for medical information. My thanks also to Kari Winter, Bob Walsh, Amy Demarest, Janet E. Carter, Tess Taylor, and John Peterson for their support.

Personal thanks go to the Houlihan family for providing me with a quiet space to write with a friendly dog for company. A special thank-you, David, for supporting me every step of the way and giving me valuable feedback on the manuscript. And finally, thank you, Sarah, for reading to me so I could type faster!

# Notes

## Introduction

1. Named "Lincoln Hill" after the Civil War. Since this story is antebellum, I call it simply the Hill. I also use the original spelling for the town, with an *h* on the end throughout the text (except when referencing the modern-day Hinesburg Town Clerk's Office as a source in notes).

2. Henry Louis Gates Jr., introduction to *The Bondwoman's Narrative* by Hannah Crafts (New York: Warner Books, 2002), p. xi.

3. Toni Morrison, *Playing in the Dark, Whiteness and the Literary Imagination* (Cambridge, MA: Harvard University Press, 1992), p. 46.

4. Joanne Pope Melish, *Disowning Slavery: Gradual Emancipation and "Race" in New England, 1780–1860* (Ithaca, NY: Cornell University Press, 1998), p. 3.

5. David Roediger, *History against Misery* (Chicago: Charles H. Kerr, 2006), p. 170.

6. Anonymous, personal communication with the author.

7. For example, in 1779, nineteen enslaved men in New Hampshire presented a petition to the legislature using the Revolutionary rhetoric of inalienable rights: "The God of nature" gave us life and freedom, and that freedom "is an inherent right of the human species, not to be surrendered but by consent." Benjamin Quarles, *Black Mosaic: Essays in Afro-American History and Historiography* (Amherst: University of Massachusetts Press, 1988), p. 54.

8. J. Saillant, *Black Puritan, Black Republican: The Life and Thought of Lemuel Haynes, 1753–1833* (New York: Oxford University Press, 2003), p. 153. See also Bruce R. Dain, *A Hideous Monster of the Mind: American Race Theory in the Early Republic* (Cambridge, MA: Harvard University Press, 2002); James Brewer Stewart, *Abolitionist Politics and the Coming of the Civil War* (Amherst: University of Massachusetts Press, 2008).

9. Native peoples were seen as somewhere in between: free and virile but also savage and history-less.

10. For more on blackness and whiteness see Mia Bay, *The White Image in the Black Mind: African American Ideas about White People, 1830–1925* (New York: Oxford University Press, 2000); Ira Berlin, *Generations of Captivity* (Cambridge, MA: Belknap Press of Harvard University Press, 2003); Elizabeth R. Bethel, *The Roots of African American Identity: Memory and History in Antebellum Free Communities* (New York: St Martin's Press, 1997); Matthew Frye Jacobson, *Whiteness of a Different Color: European Immigrants and the Alchemy of Race* (Cambridge, MA: Harvard University Press, 1998); Melish, *Disowning Slavery*; Robert Paynter, "The Cult of Whiteness in Western New England," in *Race and the Archaeology of Identity*, ed. Charles E. Orser Jr. (Salt Lake City: University of Utah Press, 2001), Roediger, *History against Misery*, especially section 3; David R. Roediger, *Black on White: Black Writers on What It Means to Be White* (New York: Schocken Books, 1998); David R. Roediger, *How Race Survived U.S. History* (Berkley: University of California Press, 2002); Saillant, *Black Puritan, Black Republican*.

11. For people of color, negative stereotypes of whiteness grew in reaction to their treatment by whites and included characteristics such as hypocritical, brutish, violent, destructive, unjust, aggressive, domineering, immoral, and avaricious. Positive stereotypes of people of color included gentle, peaceful, long-suffering, moral, religious, pious, benevolent, and affectionate. See Bay, *The White Image in the Black Mind*; Paynter, "The Cult of Whiteness in Western New England."

12. For an interesting discussion of "Who is an American?" see chapter 7 in Eric Foner, *Who Owns History? Rethinking the Past in a Changing World* (New York: Hill & Wang, 2002).

13. In his 1794 history of Vermont, which ignores black Vermonters in the body of the text, Samuel Williams included an appendix entitled "A Dissertation on the Colours of Men." For twelve pages he analyzed his observations and explained his rules governing how long it would take for blacks to turn into whites. He decided that it would take 125 years with intermarriage and the influence of cold winters. He could not conceive of how long it would take if no intermarriage occurred. He stated that black is "the most durable of any colour whatever and that white is more soon sullied, and changed." His use of the word "sullied" shows his negative attitude toward blackness. Samuel Williams, *The Natural and Civil History of Vermont* (Walpole, NH: by author, 1794), p. 389.

14. Other New England states also have a very white image, but research has begun to break down those images. For example, see Maureen E. Lee, *Black Bangor: African Americans in a Maine Community, 1880–1950* (Hanover, NH: University Press of New England, 2005); Gary B. Nash and Graham R. G.

Hodges, *Friends of Liberty: Thomas Jefferson, Tadeusz Kosciuszko, and Agrippa Hull* (Philadelphia: Basic Books, 2008); M. J. Sammons and V. Cunningham, *Black Portsmouth: Three Centuries of African-American Heritage* (Durham, NH: University of New Hampshire Press, 2004).

15. Elise A. Guyette, "The Working Lives of African Vermonters in Census and Literature, 1790–1870," *Vermont History* 61, no. 2 (1993).

16. In 1790, these percentages represented only fourteen people of color in Vergennes and twelve in Ferrisburgh, since the numbers of whites were also miniscule. In 1800, there were twenty blacks in Braintree, and in 1810 there were thirty-two in Windsor (as well as thirty-two blacks in Hinesburgh [2.5 percent]). In 1820, there were seventy-one blacks counted in Burlington and twenty-five in Hinesburgh. When one walked around the town in those days, there was more diversity than there is now.

17. There is reason to hope for more examination of these pockets of African American populations in the state. My research on this hill in Hinesburgh, Laroe's research in St. Albans, and Whitfield's in Burlington are thus far the only published investigations into African American communities in Vermont. However, they have all been completed since 2007. Surely more will follow. See Dawn Laroe, "The Prince Family: A Community History of Life in Franklin County Vermont" (BA thesis, Burlington College, 2008); Harvey Amani Whitfield, "African Americans in Burlington, 1880–1900," *Vermont History* 75, no. 2 (2007).

18. Kevin Thornton, "A Cultural Frontier: Ethnicity and the Marketplace in Charlotte, Vermont, 1845–1860," in *Cultural Change and the Market Revolution in America, 1789–1860*, ed. Scott C. Martin (Lanham, MD: Rowman & Littlefield, 2005).

19. Daniel Chipman was fighting this myth in 1849 as he wrote, "It has been said that the soil of Vermont was never polluted by Slavery, but this is a mistake; there was slavery in all the New-England Colonies, and some of the slaveholders moved into the Grants and brought their slaves with them." Daniel Chipman, *A Memoir of Thomas Chittenden* (Middlebury: by author, 1849), p. 82.

20. By the turn of the twentieth century 14 percent of Vermonters and 15 percent of the rest of the nation were foreign born. See Elise A. Guyette, "Behind the White Veil: A History of Vermont's Ethnic Groups," in *Many Cultures, One People: A Multicultural Handbook about Vermont for Teachers*, ed Gregory Sharrow (Middlebury: Vermont Folklife Center, 1992).

21. Thornton, "A Cultural Frontier," p. 62.

22. Thornton, "A Cultural Frontier," p. 62.

23. Foner, *Who Owns History?* p. 204.

24. Yentsch tells us that family homes remembered and family homes forgotten, in reality, tell us more of social structure and hierarchy within the community than about the history of the community. Anne Elizabeth Yentsch, "Legends, Houses, Families and Myths: Relationships between Material Culture and American Ideology," in *Documentary Archaeology in the New World*, ed. Mark C. Beaudry (Cambridge: Cambridge University Press, 1993), p. 11.

25. Blight talks about historical/collective memories as the "prize" in a struggle for rival versions of the past—those who win the prize have an important instrument of power in their hands to shape their political ends. David W. Blight, *Beyond the Battlefield: Race, Memory and the American Civil War* (Amherst: University of Massachusetts Press, 2002), p. 279.

26. "Petition of 1788 by Slaves of New Haven for the Abolition of Slavery in Connecticut," available from www.hartford-hwp.com/archives/45a/023.html (accessed 2007).

27. Elise A. Guyette, "Black Lives and White Racism in Vermont 1760–1870" (MA thesis, University of Vermont, 1992), p. 89. The numbers are admittedly small—this represents 112 white households with one or two servants, representing 178 people. The assumption I have made is that blacks living in white households were working for them. The census sheds no light on relationships in the household until 1850. There were only 23 households recorded as being headed by blacks in 1790, representing 93 people.

28. Guyette, "Black Lives and White Racism," pp. 97–98. For an excellent first-person account of indentured servitude in the North, see H. E. Wilson, *Our Nig; or Sketches from the Life of a Free Black, in a Two-Story White House, North. Showing That Slavery's Shadows Fall Even There. By "Our Nig."* (Boston: by author, 1859; reprint, New York: Vintage Books, 1983).

29. "An Act Pertaining to Negroes and Mollatoes" (1791), in *Journals and Proceedings of the General Assembly of Vermont*, v. 3: 80, ed. W. H. Crockett (Bellows Falls, VT, 1932). I am grateful to Caroline Stone for pointing out this act.

30. Until the 1990s, the journal *Vermont History* had only five articles dealing exclusively with blacks in Vermont, mostly about slavery, and twenty-six other articles that mentioned blacks briefly. See Katherine E. Conlin, "Dinah and the Slave Question in Vermont," *Vermont History* 21, no. 4 (1953); Henry G. Fairbanks, "Slavery and the Vermont Clergy," *Vermont History* 27, no. 4 (1959); Elsie B. Smith, "William J. Anderson: Shoreham's Negro Legislator in the Vermont House of Representatives," *Vermont History* 44, no. 4 (1976); Marshall True, "Slavery in Burlington? An Historical Note," *Vermont History* 50, no. 4 (1982). For a romanticized view of black-white relations, see Sharon

Carbonti Davis, "Vermont's Adopted Sons and Daughters," *Vermont History*
31 (1963). The *Journal of Negro History* has had one article set partly in Vermont about Prince Saunders, raised in Thetford and later attorney general of
Haiti: A. O. White, "Prince Saunders: An Instance of Social Mobility among
Antebellum New England Blacks," *Journal of Negro History* 60, no. 4 (1975).
There had been one book on the free black experience in Vermont: B. Katz and
J. Katz, *Black Woman* (Toronto: Pantheon Press, 1973), a fictionalized biography of Lucy Terry Prince, now out of print. The bulk of articles I found were all
about antislavery efforts in Vermont, not about blacks living in the state.

Starting in the 1990s, the literature is a bit more inclusive. For children's
literature see Michael T. Hahn, *Alexander Twilight: Vermont's African American Pioneer* (Shelburne, VT: The New England Press, Inc., 1998); Michael
Medearis and Angela S. Medearis, *Daisy and the Doll* (Middlebury, VT: Vermont Folklife Center, 2000); Mildred P. Walter, *Alec's Primer* (Middlebury,
VT: Vermont Folklife Center, 2005). For adult books see Gretchen Holbrook
Gerzina, *Mr. and Mrs. Prince* (New York: Harper Collins, 2008); David Proper,
*Lucy Terry Prince: Singer of History* (Deerfield, MA: Historic Deerfield, Inc.,
1997); Saillant, *Black Puritan, Black Republican*; Jeffrey Brace, *The Blind African Slave or Memoirs of Boyrereau Brinch, Nicknamed Jeffrey Brace*, ed. Kari
J. Winter (Madison: University of Wisconsin Press, 2004). In addition, there
is an out-of-print source, John W. Lewis, *The Life, Labors and Travels of Elder
Charles Bowles of the Free Will Baptist Denomination* (Watertown, NY: Ingalls
and Stowell's Steam Press, 1852). These all focus on the individual in history,
not community history.

Civil War literature hints at the existence of black communities in Vermont,
since we can make some assumptions about neighborhood networks by studying the men who mustered into Civil War regiments together. See J. Fuller, *Men
of Color, to Arms! Vermont African Americans in the Civil War* (Lincoln, NE:
iUniversity Press, 2001); D. Wickman, "Their Share of Glory: Rutland Blacks
in the Civil War," *Rutland Historical Society Quarterly* 22, no. 2 (1992); Jane
Williamson, "'I Don't Get Fair Play Here': A Black Vermonter Writes Home,"
*Vermont History* 75, no. 1 (2007). Underground Railroad literature includes
Vermont Historical Society, *Yours in the Cause of a Slave* (Montpelier, VT:
Vermont Historical Society, n.d.); Jane Williamson, "Telling It Like It Was
at Rokeby," in *Passages to Freedom*, ed. David W. Blight (Washington, D.C.:
Smithsonian Books, 2004). Historical fiction of poor quality that takes real his-
torical characters who never came to western Vermont (e.g., Harriet Tubman)
and places them in Burlington is Louella Bryant, *The Black Bonnet* (Shelburne,
VT: The New England Press, 1996). My own book, published before my

research into black Vermonters began, did not mention blacks out of the context of the Underground Railroad: Elise A. Guyette, *Vermont: A Cultural Patchwork* (Peterborough, NH: Cobblestone, 1986).

31. For journal articles that offer tantalizing clues to a black community history in Vermont, see Guyette, "The Working Lives of African Vermonters"; Whitfield, "African Americans in Burlington." See also Laroe, "The Prince Family." Jane Williamson at Rokeby Museum in Ferrisburgh, Vermont, is researching blacks in Addison County. Caroline Stone is researching blacks in Montpelier. For examples of efforts to correct romantic visions of the Underground Railroad, see Katherine Paterson, *Jip, His Story* (New York: Lodestar Books, 1996), a young-adult novel; Williamson, "Telling It Like It Was at Rokeby"; Ray Zirblis, *Friends of Freedom: The Vermont Underground Railroad Survey Report* (Montpelier, VT: Division for Historic Preservation, 1996).

32. Melish, *Disowning Slavery*, p. 3.

33. For a discussion of the "world-as-lived" and "world-as-thought," see Yentsch, "Legends, Houses, Families and Myths," p. 17.

34. There are many stories of blacks penetrating the Vermont frontier with their masters or on their own. See Guyette, "Black Lives and White Racism"; Guyette, "The Working Lives of African Vermonters."

35. See for example, J. Deetz, *In Small Things Forgotten: The Archaeology of Early American Life* (Garden City, NY: Anchor Press, 1977); Graham R. Hodges, *Slavery and Freedom in the Rural North: African Americans in Monmouth County, New Jersey, 1665–1865* (Madison, WI: Madison House, 1997); M. S. LoRusso, "The Betsey Prince Site: An Early Free Black Domestic Site on Long Island," in *Nineteenth- and Early Twentieth-Century Domestic Site Archaeology in New York State*, ed. John P. Hart and C. L. Fischer (Albany, NY: New York State Museum Bulletin, 2000); S. A. Vincent, *Southern Seed, Northern Soil: African American Farm Communities in the Midwest, 1765–1900* (Bloomington: Indiana University Press, 1999).

36. French Vermonters, and others, changed their names and abandoned their mother tongues to become fully "American." See Thornton, "A Cultural Frontier."

37. For other studies of rural black communities, see Deetz, *In Small Things Forgotten*; Melvin P. Ely, *Israel on the Appomattox: A Southern Experiment in Black Freedom from the 1790s through the Civil War* (New York: Alfred A. Knopf, 2004); Kathryn Grover, *Make a Way Somehow, African-American Life in a Northern Community, 1790–1965* (Syracuse, NY: Syracuse University Press, 1994); Hodges, *Slavery and Freedom in the Rural North*; LoRusso, "The Betsey Prince Site"; Vincent, *Southern Seed, Northern Soil*.

38. David B. Danbom, *Born in the Country: A History of Rural America* (Baltimore, MD: Johns Hopkins University Press, 2006), p. 90.

39. Jefferson believed that city dwellers bread corruption, but that rural farmers were righteous. In his *Notes on the State of Virginia* (1787) he wrote, "Those who labour in the earth are the chosen people of God, if ever he had a chosen people, whose breasts he has made his peculiar deposit for substantial and genuine virtue." Thomas Jefferson, *Notes on the State of Virginia*, Query XIX, available from http://xroads.virginia.edu/~hyper/HNS/Yoeman/qxix.html.

40. See Joanne Bowen, "Seasonality: An Agricultural Construct," in *Documentary Archaeology in the New World*, ed. Mark C. Beaudry (Cambridge: Cambridge University Press, 1993); Danbom, *Born in the Country*; Deborah Fitzgerald, *Every Farm a Factory: The Industrial Ideal in American Agriculture*, Yale Agrarian Studies (New Haven, CT: Yale University Press, 2003); S. McMurry, *Families and Farmhouses in Nineteenth-Century America* (New York: Oxford University Press, 1988).

41. Berlin, *Generations of Captivity*, p. 99.

42. Langley Proctor, personal communication with the author, 2006.

43. Philip S. Foner and Robert James Branham, eds., *Lift Every Voice: African American Oratory 1787–1900* (Tuscaloosa: University of Alabama Press, 1998), p. 160.

44. Quarles, *Black Mosaic*, p. 54.

45. Enslaved men were not allowed to enlist in any state prior to 1777–1778.

46. Foner and Branham, *Lift Every Voice*, p. 59.

47. Sidney Kaplan and Emma Nogrady Kaplan, *The Black Presence in the Era of the American Revolution* (Amherst: University of Massachusetts Press, 1989), p. 4.

48. Commonwealth of Massachusetts, *Massachusetts Soldiers and Sailors in the War of Revolution*, vol. 12 (Boston: Wright and Potter Printing Company, 1896), p. 239. This source states that Prince enlisted in 1781, but his pension record states 1780, as does Carlton E. Fisher and Sue G. Fisher, *Soldiers, Sailors, and Patriots of the Revolutionary War, Vermont* (Rockland, ME: Picton Press, 1992), p. 404.

49. I searched the land records and vital records of Northampton, Massachusetts, but found no *Prince* Peters. However there were many other Peterses in the records. In the neighboring county there are also many named Peters, some of them enslaved, some free, but no Prince. See Joseph Carvalho III, *Black Families in Hampden County, Massachusetts, 1650–1855* (Boston: New England Historic Genealogical Society, 1984).

50. From other sources, we know that this was Silas Pierce, a grocer from Boston. See Town of Lexington, *Proceedings at the Centennial Celebration of the Battle of Lexington, April 19, 1875* (Boston: Lockwood, Brooks, and Co., 1875), p. 94; Zachariah Whitman, *The History of Ancient and Honorable Artillery Company* (Boston: John H. Eastman, Printer, 1842), p. 405.

51. By the time Prince left the service in 1783, the case of *Brom and Bett v. John Ashley, Esq.* had been settled by the Court of Common Pleas in Great Barrington, which ruled that slavery was illegal under the new Constitution (1781). The Supreme Judicial Court of Massachusetts also found slavery unconstitutional in the Quock Walker case in 1783. Slavery did not suddenly disappear, however, but lingered in some places through the end of the century. See Massachusetts Historical Society, *The Legal End of Slavery in Massachusetts*, available from www.masshist.org/endofslavery/?queryID=54 (accessed April 10 2009); Nash and Hodges, *Friends of Liberty*, pp. 84–86.

52. Lewis, *The Life, Labors and Travels of Elder Charles Bowles.*

53. U.S. National Archives, Revolutionary Pension #S41943, 1818, for Prince Peters.

54. Lewis, *The Life, Labors and Travels of Elder Charles Bowles*, p. 6.

55. William Cooper Nell, *The Colored Patriots of the American Revolution: With Sketches of Several Distinguished Colored Persons: To Which Is Added a Brief Survey of the Condition and Prospects of Colored Americans* (electronic edition) (Boston: Robert F. Wallcut, 1855), p. 380, available from http://docsouth.unc.edu/neh/nell/nell.html.

56. David R. Roediger, *Colored White: Transcending the Racial Past* (Berkeley: University of California Press, 2002), p. 133.

57. Gustave de Beaumont, *Marie, or Slavery in the United States, a Novel of Jacksonian America* (France: 1835), p. 4.

58. Beaumont, *Marie*, p. 5.

59. H. Nicholas Muller III, "Freedom and Unity: Vermont's Search for Security of Property, Liberty and Popular Government," in *The Bill of Rights and the States: The Colonial and Revolutionary Origins of American Liberty*, ed. Patrick T. Conley and John P. Kaminski (Lanham, MD: Rowman & Littlefield, 1992). However, John N. Shaeffer argues that the twenty-seven changes made by the Vermont convention were substantial and produced markedly different systems. John N. Shaeffer, "A Comparison of the First Constitutions of Vermont and Pennsylvania," in *In a State of Nature*, ed. H. Nicholas Muller and Samuel B. Hand (Montpelier: Vermont Historical Society, 1982).

60. George W. Pierson, *Tocqueville and Beaumont in America* (New York: Oxford University Press, 1938), p. 515.

61. Alexis de Tocqueville, *Democracy in America* (1835; repr. Garden City, NY: Doubleday, 1969), pp. 343–44, 356–62.

62. Edward Strutt Adby, *Journal of Residence and Tour in the United States of North America, from April, 1833 to October, 1834* (London: 1835), p. 374.

63. James. W. C. Pennington, *A Textbook of the Origin and History, Etc, Etc, of the Colored People of the United States* (Hartford, CT: L. Skinner, 1841), p. 78.

64. Pennington, *A Textbook of the Origin and History of the Colored People*, p. 13.

65. H. Easton, "A Treatise on the Intellectual Character, and Civil and Political Condition of the Colored People of the United States; and the Prejudice Exercised Towards Them: With a Sermon on the Duty of the Church to Them," in *Negro Protest Pamphlets, a Compendium* (Boston: Isaac Knapp, 1837), p. 33.

66. Adby, *Journal of Residence*, p. 117.

67. Adby, *Journal of Residence*, p. 216.

68. Guyette, "The Working Lives of African Vermonters," pp. 97–98.

69. Yentsch, "Legends, Houses, Families and Myths," p. 17.

70. Paul Searls, "America and the State that 'Stayed Behind': An Argument for the National Relevance of Vermont History," *Vermont History* 71 (2003): p. 85. One can see similarities in identity development as far away as Hawaii. For example, see Hunani-Kay Trask, "From a Native Daughter," in *The American Indian and the Problem of History*, ed. C. Martin (New York: Oxford University Press, 1987).

71. Grand lists were lists of taxable property created by "listers" who worked for the town and visited households annually. They are invaluable in discovering year-to-year changes in peoples' lives.

72. Sigurdur G. Magnusson, "Social History as 'Sites of Memory'? The Institutionalization of History: Microhistory and the Grand Narrative," *Journal of Social History*, Spring (2006): 907.

*Chapter One: Founding Mothers and Fathers of the Hill*

1. My thanks to anthropologist Scott McLaughlin for the description of the trees in the old-growth forest on the Hill and to historian Allen Yale for his advice on the early Vermont landscape.

2. Adapted from Luigi Castiglioni, *Viaggoneglistati uniti dell' America settentrionale, fatto negli 1785, 1786, e 1787*, translated by Armand Citarella (Milan: Giuseppe Marelli, 1790). Quoted in T. D. S. Bassett, *Outsiders inside Vermont* (Canaan, NH: Phoenix Publishing, 1967), p. 41.

3. Hinesburgh Town Clerk, *Hinesburgh Land Records*, v. 2: 576.

4. There is a 1798 land survey showing that Huntington selectmen surveyed and laid out a road "beginning at Shubal Clarks land in the Town line Between Hinesburgh and Huntington." It is a bit unclear; however, it may be connecting to and improving upon "the Old road from Hinesburgh." An electronic version of the survey is in the hands of the author.

5. Hamilton Child, *The Gazetteer and Business Directory of Chittenden County, Vt., 1882–83* (electronic version) (Syracuse, NY: The Journal Office).

6. Hinesburgh Town Clerk, *Grand Lists for the Town of Hinesburgh*. These are fragile rolls covered with leather and tied with cloth ribbons found in boxes in the town vault. They list all the taxable property.

7. Child, *The Gazetteer and Business Directory of Chittenden County.*

8. Hinesburgh Town Clerk, *Hinesburgh Land Records*, v. 8: 446. A man from Connecticut, Moses Sash, sued Samuel two decades later to reimburse him for the care of his mother. See Edmund Baldwin, *Moses Lash [sic] v. Samuel Peters*, in *Hinesburgh Land Records*, v. 6: 80 (June 30, 1821). Sash was originally from Cummington, Massachusetts, near Prince Peters in Northampton, according to Sash's Revolutionary War pension. U.S. National Archives, Revolutionary Pension #s36291, 1818–1820, for Moses Sash.

9. Hannah may have been white; in later census reports their children are designated as "mullato." She also could have been Abenaki. Judy Dow, an Abenaki historian, tells me that Peters is a name associated with Abenaki people. According to genealogist John Moody, Abenaki oral tradition holds that fugitive blacks were living at Missisquoi as early as the seventeenth century, and intermarriage between blacks and native people was common. John Moody, lecture given at the University of Vermont–Burlington, September 24, 1991.

10. Prince was not on a federal census until 1820, although he was probably included in the line item for 1810. However, we know he was there by 1799, as recorded in *Grand Lists for the Town of Hinesburgh*. We know Hannah was his wife because of their son's marriage certificate. Middlesex, Vermont, Vital Statistics, Microfilm # 30337.

11. Child, *The Gazetteer and Business Directory of Chittenden County.*

12. The research of Vermont historian Allen Yale shows that kinship did not preclude marriage among whites. He found that first cousins married on occasion. Allen Yale, personal communication with the author, spring 2009.

13. There was also a Joseph Peters from Warren, Connecticut, who bought seventy-five acres in nearby Monkton in 1791. The census report for Litchfield County in 1790 put Joseph in the white column. I have no other information about him, but the same last name is tantalizing; perhaps there was a connection of some sort.

14. Edgar McManus suggested that census takers undercounted blacks constantly, not seeing them as important members of the population. See E. J. McManus, *Black Bondage in the North* (Syracuse, NY: Syracuse University Press, 1973).

15. Child, *The Gazetteer and Business Directory of Chittenden County*.

16. Some of the descriptions of travel in the winter are adapted from Seth Hubbell, *A Narrative of the Sufferings of Seth Hubbell and Family* (Rutland: Vermont Heritage Press, 1824); available from www.rootsweb.com/~vermont/LamoilleWolcott.html (accessed 2006).

17. Roger N. Parks, *Roads and Travel in New England, 1790–1840* (Sturbridge, MA: Old Sturbridge Village, 1967), available from www.teachushistory.org/detocqueville-visit-united-states/articles/roads-travel-new-england-1790-1840 (accessed September 15, 2008).

18. Parks, *Roads and Travel in New England*.

19. Parks, *Roads and Travel in New England*.

20. Although there had been free people of color before the Revolution, the massive number of emancipations during the Revolutionary era created a new class of free blacks, unheard of before this time.

21. William D. Piersen, *Black Yankees: The Development of an Afro-American Subculture in Eighteenth-Century New England* (Amherst: University of Massachusetts Press, 1988).

22. Piersen, *Black Yankees*, pp. x, 22.

23. Monkton Town Clerk, *Monkton Land Records* 2: 103 (January 13, 1791). There are two page 103s, this is the second one, after page 108. Shubael was not in 1790 census for New Milford; he may have been living in a white household, and therefore would not have been named.

24. Lorenzo J. Greene, *The Negro in Colonial New England, 1620–1776* (New York: Columbia University Press, 1942), pp. 89–92; McManus, *Black Bondage in the North*, pp. 15 and 169.

25. He also could have owed Ferris his labor or crops, but there was no note about other considerations in the land record. By comparison, Agrippa Hull in Stockbridge, Massachusetts, bought a half acre for nine pounds in 1784. See Nash and Hodges, *Friends of Liberty*, p. 89.

26. For discussions of the numbers of blacks in Connecticut, see Greene, *The Negro in Colonial New England*; McManus, *Black Bondage in the North*. However, some of Greene's numbers have been disputed in Bruce Stark, "Slavery in Connecticut: A Re-Examination," *Connecticut Review* 9 (November 1975).

27. Guyette, "Black Lives and White Racism," p. 5.

28. U.S. National Archives, Revolutionary Pension #S41943, for Prince Peters.

29. See note 51 of the introduction for information about the end of slavery in Massachusetts.

30. Jeffrey Brace, *The Blind African Slave, or Memoirs of Boyrereau Brinch, Nick-Named Jeffrey Brace* (electronic edition) (St. Albans, VT: Harry Whitney, 1810), ) available from http://docsouth.unc.edu/neh/brinch/brinch.html (accessed 2001).

31. Michael Sherman, Gene Sessions, and P. Jeffrey Potash, *Freedom and Unity: A History of Vermont* (Barre: Vermont Historical Society, 2004), p. 175.

32. Thornton, "A Cultural Frontier," p. 51.

33. Thornton, "A Cultural Frontier," p. 43.

34. See Brace, *The Blind African Slave*; Gerzina, *Mr. and Mrs. Prince*.

35. Piersen, *Black Yankees*, pp. 97–101. He concentrated on Rhode Island, Massachusetts, and Connecticut. Archaeological studies of the Hill could verify whether or not African traditions operated there.

36. According to her death certificate, Violet was born in Massachusetts: Hinesburgh Town Clerk, *Hinesburgh Births, Deaths and Marriages*, 1795–1906, v. 1: 48. Census records also mention Connecticut as her birthplace. No extant records clarify her place of birth.

37. The land record is not clear about how much acreage changed hands. Hinesburgh Town Clerk, *Hinesburgh Land Records*, v. 1: 105.

38. Hinesburgh Town Clerk, *Hinesburgh Land Records*, v. 8: 446. The Clarks paid for their land in pounds three years earlier. At this time many types of specie were accepted as payment.

39. Hinesburgh Town Clerk, *Hinesburgh Land Records*, v. 1: 447.

40. Hinesburgh Town Clerk, *Hinesburgh Land Records*, v. 3: 354–55.

41. Hinesburgh Town Clerk, *Hinesburgh Land Records*, v. 4: 201.

42. Later spelled "Ray."

43. Girdling a tree meant cutting off a large swath of bark all the way around in order to kill the tree and remove its canopy. Crops could then be planted among the skeleton trees.

44. Horace Greeley, *Recollections of a Busy Life* (New York: J. B. Ford & Company, 1868), pp. 55–60.

45. Elias Smith, *The Life, Conversion, Preaching, Travels, and Sufferings of Elias Smith* (Portsmouth, NH: Beck and Foster, 1816), pp. 35–43.

46. Hodges, *Slavery and Freedom in the Rural North*.

47. Nathan Perkins, "A Narrative of a Tour through the State of Vermont from April 27 to June 12, 1789," in *Outsiders inside Vermont*, ed. T. D. S. Bassett (Canaan, NH: Phoenix Publishing, 1967), pp. 23–32.

48. A. Kessler-Harris, *Out to Work: A History of Wage-Earning Women in the United States* (New York: Oxford University Press, 2003).

49. Kessler-Harris, *Out to Work.*

50. Superior Court of Vermont, *William Langley v Amanda Norton & Joseph Marsh*, (May 18, 1846), 471–75

51. Sherman, Sessions, and Potash, *Freedom and Unity.*

52. Hinesburgh Town Clerk, *Grand Lists*, 1799.

53. Huntington Town Clerk, *Huntington Land Records*, v. 3: 314. According to the Vermont 1787 Specific Tender Act, a creditor will accept only those specific items mentioned in the contract to repay a debt, so it was always spelled out exactly in terms of cattle, wheat, linens, and the like.

54. Melish, *Disowning Slavery.*

55. U.S. National Archives, Revolutionary Pension #s41943, Prince Peters.

56. Probate Court of Chittendon County, Estate Probate File #1093, for Shubael Clark, 1842 (Burlington, VT: Chittenden County Court).

57. Hinesburgh Town Clerk, *Grand Lists*, 1808.

58. This many improved acres in only two years is odd. Perhaps the Peters bought land already cleared; it is hard to say, because I find grand lists starting in 1799 but not before.

59. For similar practices, see Gerzina, *Mr. and Mrs. Prince*; P. Jeffrey Potash, *Vermont's Burned-Over District* (Brooklyn, NY: Carlson Publishing, 1991).

60. Potash, *Vermont's Burned-Over District*, p. 81.

61. Nash and Hodges, *Friends of Liberty*, p. 5.

62. Bethel, *The Roots of African American Identity*, p. 86. It is not surprising that Jeffrey Brace/Boyrereau Brinch published his memoirs in 1810. By then it was obvious that the end of the slave trade did not mean an end to slavery—once again hopes had been dashed. He explains in his book: "I have concluded it my duty to myself, to all Africans, to the church, in short to all mankind, to thus publish these memoirs, that all may see how poor Africans have been abused by a christian & enlightened people. . . . It is my anxious wish that this simple narrative may be the means of opening the hearts of those who hold slaves & move them to consent to give them that freedom which they themselves enjoy and which all mankind have an equal right to possess." Brace, *The Blind African Slave*, 200–1.

63. Although racism had not yet become the hardened scientific racism of the 1820s, it nevertheless created dangerous circumstances in early Vermont. For example, Helen T. Catterall reports the 1803 torture of a black man in Rutland in order to extort a confession from him. Two men accused Cato Jenkins of stealing a portmanteau with a number of bank bills in it. When he denied the charge, they hanged "him by a halter round his neck from the limb of a tree, until he was nearly suffocated, and . . . did then and there beat, bruise, torment, torture, and burn with fire." His life was spared, however, and he was brought

to trial and found guilty. His torturers were accused of a misdemeanor; one was found guilty and ordered to pay a fine to the State treasury. See Helen T. Catterall, *Judicial Cases Concerning American Slavery and the Negro* (Washington, DC: Carnegie Institute, 1936), p. 537.

64. Roediger, *History against Misery*, p. 136.

65. Nash and Hodges, *Friends of Liberty*, p. 202.

66. Roediger, *History against Misery*, p. 143.

67. "An Act Pertaining to Negroes and Mollatoes," p. 80.

68. "An Act Pertaining to Negroes and Mollatoes," p. 80.

69. *Journals and Proceedings of the General Assembly of Vermont*, v. 3: 327, ed. W. H. Crockett (Bellows Falls, VT, 1932).

70. Bay, *The White Image in the Black Mind*, p. 43.

71. According to William's death certificate, he was born William Page Langley in 1794 in Rutland. His parents were Richard and Abigail Langley. Williston Town Clerk, *Williston Marriages, Births and Deaths*, 1863–1883 and 1883–1947, p. 7.

72. Or perhaps Connecticut—his birthplace is listed in both states in various census reports.


*Chapter Two: Peaks and Valleys on the Hill Farms*

1. Guyette, "Black Lives and White Racism."

2. Bay, *The White Image in the Black Mind*, p. 14.

3. Bay, *The White Image in the Black Mind*, p. 35.

4. Bethel, *The Roots of African American Identity*, p. 7. See also Piersen, *Black Yankees*, chap. 10 for the importance of celebrating election days among blacks and Nash and Hodges, *Friends of Liberty*, p. 436.

5. Prince Saunders, *Documents Relative to the Kingdom of Hayti with a Preface* (London: 1816), pp. iii, 211. A year later, another Haitian, Pompee Valentin Vasty, wrote, "Men who call themselves philosophers, (are) willing to reduce human beings to an equality with brutes. . . . I can scarcely refrain from laughter at the absurdities which have been published on the subject." Bay, *The White Image in the Black Mind*, p. 37.

6. Lewis, *The Life, Labors and Travels of Elder Charles Bowles*, p. 9. One main difference between Calvinists and non-Calvinists was the belief by the former that God elected a select few for redemption, and all others were condemned for eternity. Non-Calvinists believed that people had free will and could gain salvation through repentance for their sins.

7. Hinesburgh Town Clerk, *Record of Writs and Executions for Hinesburgh,* 1829–1853, articles 5 and 7.

8. A. M. Hemenway, ed., *The Vermont Historical Gazetteer, a Magazine Embracing a History of Each Town, Civil, Ecclesiastical, Biographical, and Military,* vol. 1 (Burlington, VT: by author, 1868), p. 797.

9. *Records for the Baptist Church in Christ of Hinesburgh,* 1810-40 (Hinesburg, VT: Carpenter-Carse Library).

10. *Records for the Baptist Church in Christ of Hinesburgh.*

11. Potash, *Vermont's Burned-Over District,* p. 148.

12. Lewis, *The Life, Labors and Travels of Elder Charles Bowles,* p. 266.

13. Lewis, *The Life, Labors and Travels of Elder Charles Bowles,* p. 267.

14. Piersen, *Black Yankees,* p. 149.

15. Roediger, *History against Misery,* p. 151.

16. Bay, *The White Image in the Black Mind,* p. 41.

17. Bay, *The White Image in the Black Mind.*

18. Hinesburgh Town Clerk, *Hinesburgh Births, Deaths and Marriages.*

19. Richard S. Newman, "Faith in the Ballot, Black Shadow Politics in the Antebellum North," *Common-Place,* October 2008, available from www .common-place.org/vol-09/no-01/newman/ (accessed April 14, 2009).

20. Hinesburgh Town Clerk, *Hinesburgh Births, Deaths and Marriages.*

21. Hinesburgh Town Clerk, *Hinesburgh Town Records,* 1813–1830, v. 2: 158.

22. *Records for the Baptist Church in Christ of Hinesburgh,* p. 131.

23. Rutland, Vermont, Land Records, v. 8: 182, 9: 237, 10: 74, 95.

24. This was not unusual in Vermont. In the early nineteenth century, over half the farms carried mortgages. Bassett, *Outsiders inside Vermont,* p. 11.

25. Middlesex, Vermont, Vital Statistics, Microfilm # 30293.

26. Williston Town Clerk, *Williston Marriages, Births and Deaths,* p. 20.

27. I never found the Langleys being taxed for a house in either the Huntington or Hinesburgh grand lists, although from land and other records it is clear they have one. Later I discuss my theory about where the house is located.

28. Royal Hall, of Rutland, bought the farm for $300 and was to pay off a mortgage in two promissory notes in 1826 and 1827. "Rutland Land Records," v. 8: 182.

29. Huntington Town Clerk, *Huntington Land Records,* v. 6: 38, 40.

30. Piersen showed how traditions were passed down from those who remembered their days in Africa and were practiced in New England for many generations, some becoming a part of Yankee traditions. Piersen, *Black Yankees.*

31. Herbert G. Gutman, *The Black Family in Slavery and Freedom, 1750–1925* (New York: Vintage Books, 1976), p. 199.

32. Huntington Town Clerk, *Huntington School Records*, 1816–1858.

33. There is a Loudoun County in Virginia—perhaps his name signals a connection to that state through William's parents.

34. U.S. National Archives, Revolutionary Pension #s41943, for Prince Peters.

35. Sherman, Sessions, and Potash, *Freedom and Unity*, p. 153.

36. According to the grand lists. Potash found these lists extremely accurate in his study of nearby Shoreham and Cornwall. Potash, *Vermont's Burned-Over District*.

37. I assume this is the younger Samuel, who would have been about eighteen at this time, old enough to volunteer. The other Samuel must have been too old.

38. Vermont, State of; *Roster of Soldiers in the War of 1812–14* (St Albans, VT: The Messenger Press, 1933). A Samuel Peters was also listed as a volunteer for Plattsburgh from Shelburne. Men from Hinesburgh and Huntington were volunteers for the same battle as the "Huntington and Hinesburgh Company of Horse." See Byron N. Clark, *A List of Pensioners of the War of 1812 [Vermont Claimants]* (Baltimore: Genealogical Publishing Company, 1969), pp. 38–39. We know from Kate Kenny's research that African American soldiers were stationed at Burlington during this time, so Samuel would not have been unique. Kate Kenny, "Burlington's War of 1812 Soldiers' Burial Ground," in *The Center for Research on Vermont Research-in-Progress Seminar #190* (University of Vermont, 2005).

39. Sherman, Sessions, and Potash, *Freedom and Unity*, p. 164.

40. Nell, *The Colored Patriots of the American Revolution*, p. 313.

41. Nell, *The Colored Patriots of the American Revolution*, p. 313.

42. Nell, *The Colored Patriots of the American Revolution*, p. 314.

43. Potash, *Vermont's Burned-Over District*.

44. President Monroe signed the first pension bill March 1, 1818. Special courts were set up to help men apply who needed support. See Nash and Hodges, *Friends of Liberty*, pp. 247–48.

45. U.S. National Archives, Revolutionary Pension #s41943, for Prince Peters.

46. U.S. National Archives, Revolutionary Pension #s41943, for Prince Peters.

47. Deetz, *In Small Things Forgotten*, Graham R. Hodges, *Root and Branch, African Americans in New York and New Jersey, 1613–1863* (Chapel Hill: University of North Carolina Press, 1999), L. F. Litwak, *The Negro in the Free States, 1790–1860* (Chicago: University of Chicago Press, 1961), LoRusso, "The Betsey Prince Site."

48. Carol A. Raemsch and J. W. Bouchard, "The Henry Lehman Family Cemetery: A Unique Contribution to Nineteenth-Century Domestic Archaeol-

ogy," in *Nineteenth- and Early Twentieth-Century Domestic Site Archaeology in New York State*, ed. John P. Hart and C. L. Fischer (Albany: New York State Museum Bulletin, 2000), p. 116.

49. A. L. Hyde and F. P. Hyde, *Burial Grounds of Vermont* (Bradford, VT: Vermont Old Cemetery Association, 1992), p. 123.

50. This is according to the 1817 grand list. The 1818 one is too fragile to handle.

51. Baldwin, *Moses Lash v Samuel Peters*.

52. Baldwin, *Moses Lash v Samuel Peters*.

53. *Moses Sash v. Samuel Peters*, Vermont State Archives, Box PRA-00993, September 1820–September 1824, v. 2: 65–66, Chittenden County Court, June 30, 1821.

54. *Moses Sash v. Samuel Peters*.

55. At this time, the War Department had stopped pensions for all but the destitute. Moses had to prove that he was in "dire poverty" to keep receiving his pension. See Nash and Hodges, *Friends of Liberty*, p. 248.

56. U.S. National Archives, Revolutionary Pension #s36291, for Moses Sash.

57. According to U.S. census reports, Moses Sash had lived in Worthington, Massachusetts, in 1790 and in Hartford, Connecticut, by 1810. According to his pension, he died in May 1827. He was seventy-one.

58. According to the census reports of Huntington and Addison County, Gillet, a farmer, never reached the highest rungs of the socioeconomic ladder. This was the pattern, I have discovered, among those loaning money to the Hill farmers: They were not the richest people in town, but were people willing to make loans to those of more modest means.

59. John Demos, *Past, Present, and Personal: The Family and the Life Course in American History* (New York: Oxford University Press, 1986).

60. Huntington Town Clerk, *Huntington Land Records*, v. 5: 123, 301–2.

61. Nathaniel Dunham, *Hinesburg, Vermont, General Store Day Book*, 1827–1830 (Burlington: University of Vermont Special Collections), p. 145. Bohea was the last crop of the season, regarded as low quality by the Chinese, who often exported their worst products and saved quality items for internal use.

62. Dunham, *Hinesburg, Vermont, General Store Day Book*, p. 76.

63. Dunham, *Hinesburg, Vermont General Store Day Book*, p. 129.

64. Child, *The Gazetteer and Business Directory of Chittenden, County*.

65. It makes sense that they usually bought brandy. Many people were boycotting rum at this time because of its slave-labor connection.

66. Hinesburgh Town Clerk, *Grand Lists*, 1808–16. Also see Hinesburgh

Town Clerk, *Hinesburgh Town Records*, v. 2, 1813–1830 for years 1824 and 1826–29. There is evidence that black men voted in other northern New England states. See J. O. Horton and L. E. Horton, *In Hope of Liberty: Culture, Community and Protest among Northern Free Blacks, 1700–1860* (New York: Oxford University Press, 1997).

67. The Censors proposed three articles of amendment: creation of a state senate, clarifying a gubernatorial veto power (linked to creation of the senate), and a requirement that voters be U.S. citizens. The 208 town delegates quickly rejected the first two articles and adopted the third, which is now Sec. 42, Chapter II of the Vermont Constitution. Gregory Sanford, state archivist, personal communication with the author, 2007. The need to be a U.S. citizen to vote in Vermont becomes extremely important after the Dred Scott Decision in 1857 proclaiming that blacks are not citizens of the United States.

68. Matthew E. Hannon, "From Vermont to Liberia: An Examination of the Vermont Colonization Society" (MA thesis, University of Vermont, 2008), pp. 16–25, 61.

69. Martin Freeman, for example. See Russell W. Irvine, "Martin H. Freeman of Rutland, America's First Black College Professor and Pioneering Black Social Activist," *Rutland Historical Society Quarterly* 26, no. 3 (1996).

70. Blight, *Beyond the Battlefield*, p. 41.

71. The Second Great Awakening lasted from the 1790s to the 1840s. The first Great Awakening of religious piety in America was from the 1730s to the 1760s.

72. Lewis, *The Life, Labors and Travels of Elder Charles Bowles*, p. 9.

73. Hemenway, ed., *The Vermont Historical Gazetteer*, p. 817.

74. Huntington Town Clerk, *Huntington Ordinations & Public Notices*, 1817, p. 11.

75. Henry Crocker, *History of the Baptists in Vermont* (Bellows Falls, VT: P.H. Gobie Press, 1913), p. 610.

76. Lewis, *The Life, Labors and Travels of Elder Charles Bowles*, p. 135.

77. Lewis, *The Life, Labors and Travels of Elder Charles Bowles*, pp. 120, 150.

78. Lewis, *The Life, Labors and Travels of Elder Charles Bowles*, p. 104.

79. Lewis, *The Life, Labors and Travels of Elder Charles Bowles*, pp. 142, 173.

80. Lewis, *The Life, Labors and Travels of Elder Charles Bowles*, pp. 21–24.

81. Lewis, *The Life, Labors and Travels of Elder Charles Bowles*, p. 62.

82. Lewis, *The Life, Labors and Travels of Elder Charles Bowles*, pp. 73–74. It is not clear if they had others purposes in mind beyond disturbing the meeting.

83. Lewis, *The Life, Labors and Travels of Elder Charles Bowles*, pp. 116–17.

84. Bay, *The White Image in the Black Mind*, pp. 32 and 42.

85. Lewis, *The Life, Labors and Travels of Elder Charles Bowles*, p. 101.

86. Lewis, *The Life, Labors and Travels of Elder Charles Bowles*, p. 147.

87. Lewis, *The Life, Labors and Travels of Elder Charles Bowles*, p. 151.

88. Lewis, *The Life, Labors and Travels of Elder Charles Bowles*, p. 164. This and the previous quote.

89. *Records of the Baptist Church of Huntington*, 1828–1872 (Burlington: University of Vermont Special Collections).

90. D. Mullane, ed., *Crossing the Danger Water: Three Hundred Years of African-American Writing* (New York: Anchor Books, 1993), pp. 77–85. He ends by saying that he understands he may be murdered for saying the truth, but "what is the use of living, when in fact I am dead." On June 28, 1830, he was found dead outside his shop in Boston, perhaps poisoned.

*Chapter Three: Life and Death on the Hill*

1. Occupations were not enumerated in the census prior to 1850. However, the 1850–1870 census reports for Vermont show that blacks were almost exclusively relegated to service jobs and manual labor positions. See Guyette, "The Working Lives of African Vermonters."

2. Foner and Branham, *Lift Every Voice*, p. 181.

3. Bay, *The White Image in the Black Mind*, pp. 42–44. This is an example of how easily science can be used for social and political purposes.

4. Bay, *The White Image in the Black Mind*, p. 21. Some early black thinkers who fought against this idea, were Prince Saunders, Jeffrey Brace, Absalom Jones, Richard Allen, Benjamin Banneker, and James Forten.

5. Paynter, "The Cult of Whiteness in Western New England," p. 141.

6. Bay, *The White Image in the Black Mind*, p. 45. This quote is from a widely circulated 1836 history of the world written by Robert Benjamin Lewis in which he ignores whites, just as white histories ignored blacks. Bay documents well the existence of black racism. The major difference between white and black racist ideologies is that whites had the power to build systems to enforce their views.

7. Originally all-male gatherings, the 1848 Colored National Convention in Cleveland admitted women for the first time.

8. We know that Loudon Langley read the *Anglo African* magazine in the 1850s. Perhaps some of these publications reached the Hill earlier.

9. Hannon, "From Vermont to Liberia," p. 61.

10. J. K. Converse, "The History of Slavery, and the Means of Evaluating the African Race: A Speech before the Vermont Colonization Society" (Montpelier, VT: Chauncey Goodrich, October 15, 1840), p. 15.

11. Converse, "The History of Slavery."

12. There is no evidence that the society was integrated.

13. L. Ratner, *Powder Keg: Northern Opposition to the Antislavery Movement, 1831–1840* (New York: Basic Books, 1968), pp. 69, 72.

14. Randolph Roth, *The Democratic Dilemma: Religion, Reform and the Social Order in the Connecticut River Valley of Vermont, 1791–1850* (New York: Cambridge University Press, 1987), p. 183.

15. Nell, *The Colored Patriots of the American Revolution*, p. 321.

16. Foner and Branham, *Lift Every Voice*, pp. 181–82. Two years later Harris died at the age of thirty-one.

17. Zirblis, *Friends of Freedom*. In light of Williamson's contention about Vermont being a safe place for people escaping slavery, "harboring" people may not have been anything other than hosting people who needed a helping hand. Williamson, "Telling It Like It Was at Rokeby."

18. My mother, Louise Guyette, who lived through the Great Depression of the 1930s on a Kansas farm, tells me that those on small farms hardly noticed the depression; they had never had much anyway, but had enough to eat. Perhaps this was the same in the nineteenth century on the Hill.

19. Langley Proctor, personal communication with the author, 2009.

20. Christopher Harris, "Counting Sheep and Other Critters: Land Use, Soil Fertility and Population in Post–Civil War Vermont," in *Center for Research on Vermont: Research in Progress Seminar #202* (University of Vermont: October 2, 2006).

21. Hinesburgh Town Clerk, *Hinesburgh Land Records*, v. 8: 457.

22. Hinesburgh Town Clerk, *Hinesburgh Land Records*, v. 8: 241.

23. We don't know who actually wrote it; Eliza made her mark X; perhaps Calvin Wray or the town clerk wrote it for her.

24. The one-third of a man's estate inherited by his widow.

25. Probate Court of Chittendon County, Estate Probate File #844, for Prince Peters, 1832 (Burlington, VT: Chittenden County Court).

26. That it was a "pair" of oxen is important. It meant that they were trained to work together and, therefore, more valuable than a single ox.

27. Probate Court of Chittendon County, Estate Probate File #844.

28. For more information see David B. Davis, *Inhuman Bondage: The Rise and Fall of Slavery in the New World* (New York: Oxford University Press,

2006), p. 106; Bethwell A. Ogot and J. A. Kieran, eds., *Zamani: A Survey of East African History* (New York: Humanities Press, 1968). For precolonial traditions, see Francis Moore, Bartholomew Stibbs, and Leo Africanus, *Travels into the Inland Parts of Africa: Containing a Description of the Several Nations for the Space of Six Hundred Miles up the River Gambia; Their Trade, Habits, Customs, Language, Manners, Religion and Government; the Power, Disposition and Characters of Some Negro Princes* (London: E. Cave, 1738).

29. William Piersen found many African traditions were passed down and practiced elsewhere in New England. Piersen, *Black Yankees*. Hodges finds similar occurrences in Monmouth County, New Jersey. Hodges, *Slavery and Freedom in the Rural North*. He discovered an "African folk vernacular" there that suggested that "rural blacks clung to traditional beliefs" brought from Africa (p. 187). Included in this tradition was a collective mentality to support one another.

30. Charlot's last name comes from her son John's death record. My thanks to Deborah Van Dyne for this information.

31. The McEuen house still stands on Old Rte. 116 in Hinesburgh. The Peters and Clark houses are gone. This one effect of social class illustrates why it is easier to discover the artifacts of the social elites and, hence, easier to tell their histories.

32. Kathlyn Hatch and Nancy Engels, *Architectural Heritage Education: A Summary Report* (Washington, DC: NEH, 1982), p. 40.

33. This is also a traditional East African cooking vessel, described in Ogot and Kieran, *Zamani*, p. 115.

34. Charlot's death certificate indicates she was black. Middlesex, Vermont, Vital Statistics, Microfilm # 30337.

35. The 1840 census taker indicated this child was Cornelia, a female mulatto. Subsequent records say he was a male, voter, soldier, and laborer: Cornelius. In one census, he is listed as "Keeping House" for his brothers. His headstone bears the name *Corneles*.

36. A typed note on the back of a photo of two black men in the original McEuen home states that "Cephus" Peters had worked for him. (Photo in the hands of Helen and David Nagel.)

37. In contrast, those who did not farm moved more readily. One example is the blacksmith, Lyman F. Clark, a white man who lived in Hinesburgh for three decades, but presumably did not farm as his primary means of support. He and his wife, Mary B. Clark, immigrated to Potsdam, New York, in 1847, even though they were upstanding members of the elite Congregational church, had a house worth $550, and owned a blacksmith business. Their ties to Hinesburgh

were long, but not deep into the soil. Blacksmithing, keeping house, and Christianity are all easily portable. With the money made from selling their house and lot, they could buy another home in upstate New York with little trouble. High land prices, however, made it difficult for farmers to reestablish themselves.

38. Potash, *Vermont's Burned-Over District*, p. 81.

39. According to the 1830 census, there were six people in addition to Violet and Shubael in the household. My best guess is that they are: Hiram and Harriet in their early twenties; Phoebe and Minerva, twelve and eleven; and Caroline and Charles, under the age of ten. Lewis, thirty-six, who had a house of his own lower on the Hill, and Almira, thirty-three, who was married to William Langley, had moved out of the household. I believe that Sybil, twenty-five, had married Jeremiah Loudon by this time and moved to Charleston (and later Ravenna), Ohio. These wide variations in ages indicate that other children probably died young. Violet's first child was born when she was nineteen. It would be strange for Violet to have a burst of fertility in her forties after a decade of no births.

40. *Records for the Baptist Church in Christ of Hinesburgh*, p. 203.

41. *Records for the Baptist Church in Christ of Hinesburgh*, p. 203.

42. It may come as a surprise that the reaction was not harsher, but Vermont never had antimiscegenation laws and, in fact, in 1830, 4.2 percent of Afro-Vermonter households were mixed race.

43. J. V. C. Smith, M.D., ed, *The Boston Medical and Surgical Journal* 14 (1836), pp. 217–20. This article has a description of Shubael's autopsy, most likely performed in the Clark home. I am grateful to Sue Roberts for pointing out this source. The doctors and librarians I consulted came to the conclusion that this disease is caused by an injury or bacterial infection of the lungs, often as a complication of pneumonia. But since Shubael never mentioned being sick, perhaps a puncture wound to his lung, a lung abscess, or a pulmonary embolism (blocked artery) caused the initial infection that turned gangrenous.

44. Gerald Fox, personal communication with the author, December 15, 1996.

45. *Records for the Baptist Church in Christ of Hinesburgh*, p. 256.

46. *Records for the Baptist Church in Christ of Hinesburgh*, p, 265.

47. It is unknown where Shubael's sheep went—he had been paying taxes on some for years.

48. Probate Court of Chittendon County, Estate Probate File #1093.

49. Hinesburgh Town Clerk, *Record of Writs and Executions*, table 4.1, indicates a coal pit.

50. The people who now own the property told me they filled in a large cellar hole creating a front yard for the new home they built. So evidence of the

Clark life style is being held safely in suspended animation beneath the soil of the Hill.

51. The petition asked the court to pay Lewis $312.67 in order to pay off debts that had not been allowed by commissioners. Probate Court of Chittendon County, Estate Probate File #1093.

52. An undated list of members in the Huntington church records includes Charles. *Records of the Baptist Church of Huntington.*

53. *Records of the Baptist Church of Huntington.*

54. Probate Court of Chittendon County, Estate Probate File #1093.

55. Probate Court of Chittendon County, Estate Probate File #1093.

56. Gates makes a similar observation about Hannah Craft's handwriting in his introduction to *The Bondwoman's Narrative.*

57. Huntington Town Clerk, *Huntington School Records.*

58. Hinesburgh Town Clerk, *Hinesburgh Land Records*, v. 12: 137–38.

59. Piersen, *Black Yankees*, p. 159. Piersen contends that even though blacks were looking to assimilate, they were still shaped by a dual consciousness.

60. Zirblis, *Friends of Freedom.*

61. *Records for the Baptist Church in Christ of Hinesburgh.*

62. Hannah Crafts, *The Bondwoman's Narrative* (New York: Warner Books, 2002), p. 237.

63. Perhaps there was something else going on. It is probable that Lewis and Ruth's children were light skinned, since she was white, and all the Clarks were designated as "mullato" starting in the 1850s. It is possible that they were helping their children to pass as white in an increasingly racist country. However, Ruth and Lewis were again in the same household in 1860, once their children were grown and gone.

64. Lewis and Ruth's son was named Alonzo. The Yaws had a grandson named Alonzo. Could they have been related in some way other than geographical, and both passed on a family name? This is, of course, pure speculation.

65. Carlton and brother George had both moved to St. Lawrence County, New York, by this time.

66. Huntington Town Clerk, *Huntington School Records.*

67. In 1861, there was a Mitchell and Louisa Langley who had a child, Annett, born in Burlington. Mitchell was listed as being a farmer who had been born in Hinesburgh. So the Langleys may have had another child in the 1840s.

68. Superior Court of Vermont, *William Langley v Amanda Norton & Joseph Marsh.*

69. Superior Court of Vermont, *William Langley v Amanda Norton & Joseph Marsh.*

184 ※ Notes to pages 85–93

70. Superior Court of Vermont, *William Langley v Amanda Norton & Joseph Marsh*.

71. George Robinson, letter to his family (Middlebury, VT: Sheldon Museum, 1847). My appreciation to Jane Williamson for telling me about this letter.

*Chapter Four: Prelude to War*

1. Lewis D. Stillwell, *Migration from Vermont* (Montpelier and Rutland: Vermont Historical Society and Academy Books, 1948), p. 216.

2. Guyette, "Behind the White Veil," p. 19.

3. McManus, *Black Bondage in the North*, pp. 184–85.

4. Martin R. Delany, *The Condition, Elevation, Emigration, and Destiny of the Colored People of the United States* (New York: Arno Press, 1852; reprint 1968).

5. Nell, *The Colored Patriots of the American Revolution*, pp. 325–26.

6. J. Kevin Graffagnino, Samuel B. Hand, and Gene Sessions, eds., *Vermont Voices, 1609 through the 1990s* (Montpelier, VT: Vermont Historical Society, 1999), p. 165.

7. The Vermont Republican Party was formed in 1854, two years before the national party.

8. Roediger, *Colored White*, p. 126.

9. Bay, *The White Image in the Black Mind*, p. 64.

10. Delany, *The Condition, Elevation, Emigration, and Destiny*, p. 35.

11. Irvine, "Martin H. Freeman of Rutland," p. 81.

12. Irvine, "Martin H. Freeman of Rutland," pp. 80–81.

13. Irvine, "Martin H. Freeman of Rutland," p. 82.

14. Delany, *The Condition, Elevation, Emigration, and Destiny*, p. 183.

15. Schomburg Center for Research in Black Culture, "Canada, the Promised Land," in *In Motion: The African-American Migration Experience* (New York Public Library), available from www.inmotionaame.org/migrations/topic .cfm?migration=2&topic=9 (accessed April 29 2009); Schomburg Center for Research in Black Culture, "Migration to Haiti" in *In Motion: The African-American Migration Experience* (New York Public Library), available from www .inmotionaame.org/migrations/topic.cfm?migration=4&topic=5 (accessed April 29, 2009); Horton and Horton, *In Hope of Liberty*, p. 210; Library of Congress, "The African Mosaic: Colonization" (Library of Congress, 2005), available from www.loc.gov/exhibits/african/afam002.html (accessed May 18, 2009).

16. 1850 is the first census where all people in the household are named.

17. Mitchell is not in the household in the 1850 census.

18. Horton and Horton, *In Hope of Liberty*, p. 154.

19. Foner and Branham, eds., *Lift Every Voice*, p. 180.

20. L. S. Langley, Letter to the editor of the *Green Mountain Freeman*, February 8, 1855, in "Vermont African Americans: Letters of Louden S. Langley before and during the Civil War," available from Vermont Civil War Database: http://vermontcivilwar.org/units/afam/ll.php (accessed 2006).

21. Langley, Letter to the editor of the *Green Mountain Freeman*, April 27, 1854, in "Vermont African Americans: Letters of Louden S. Langley."

22. Irvine, "Martin H. Freeman of Rutland," p. 79. In 1863, Freeman resigned from the presidency of Avery. He went on a lecture tour for a year to raise money for his family's migration and for supplies for Liberia College. He started in Boston, then went to Maine, and finished the lecture tour mostly in New Hampshire and Vermont. He visited his mother in Rutland before going back to Pennsylvania. In 1864, he and the family finally set sail for Liberia. He was a professor there for over twenty-five years and kept a small farm. He visited Vermont one last time in 1887. Two years later, he died and was buried in Liberia. His wife immediately returned to the United States.

23. Carter G. Woodson, *The Mind of the Negro as Reflected in Letters* (New York: Negro Universities Press, 1969), p. 126 (emphasis in the original).

24. Zirblis, *Friends of Freedom*.

25. Woodson, *The Mind of the Negro*, pp. 126–27 (emphasis in original).

26. Woodson, *The Mind of the Negro*, p. 127. James Theodore Holly was sincere in his arguments advocating for emigration from the United States. However, he later became a missionary to Haiti and an Episcopal Bishop there in 1874. He died in Haiti in 1911.

27. Langley, Letter to the editor of the *Green Mountain Freeman*, April 27, 1854, in "Vermont African Americans: Letters of Louden S. Langley."

28. Zirblis, *Friends of Freedom*.

29. Woodson, *The Mind of the Negro*, p. 127.

30. Loudon's military records give his height. U.S. National Archives, Muster and Descriptive Roll of a Detachment of U.S. Volunteers for the 54th Reg't Mass. Inf. (Col'd) for Loudon S. Langley, (1864).

31. U.S. National Archives, Civil War Widow's Pension Request #222864 for Jane Langley, 1881.

32. William Siebert interviewed Abial in 1936 about his parents harboring fugitives. Zirblis, *Friends of Freedom*, p. 73.

33. Nell, *The Colored Patriots of the American Revolution*, p. 7 (emphasis in original).

34. Sherman, Sessions, and Potash, *Freedom and Unity*, p. 173.

35. Hinesburgh Town Clerk, *Check Stubs for Town of Hinesburgh*, 1859–67.

36. The case included his wife, Harriet Scott, about whom we read little since Supreme Court cases at the time had to be named after men. See K. C. Kaufman, *Dred Scott's Advocate: A Biography of Roswell M. Field*, Missouri Biography Series (Columbia: University of Missouri Press, 1996).

37. *Dred Scott v. Sanford*, 1857, available from www.tourolaw.edu/patch/Scott/ (accessed September 25, 2006).

38. Langley, Letter to the editor of the *Green Mountain Freeman*, February 8, 1855, in "Vermont African Americans: Letters of Louden S. Langley."

39. Graffagnino, Hand, and Sessions, eds., *Vermont Voices*, pp. 183–84.

40. Vermont State Constitution, Section 42.

41. Toni Morrison, *Sula* (New York: Alfred A. Knopf, 1974), p. 120.

42. Hinesburgh Town Clerk, *Hinesburgh Land Records*, v. 15: 65.

43. Ten years later, his sons bought the land back.

44. I had become increasingly convinced that Sarah Edwards was born Sarah Peters but had no evidence of it for many months. Then one day I decided to read ahead in the land records to try to figure out what happened to the Peters's land. There it was, while recording their sale of land to John and Cornelius Peters in 1889, the Edwards children had written that their mother had received her land on lot 83 from "the estate of her father Prince Peters." The land records had been unexpectedly informative on family genealogy. Hinesburgh Town Clerk, *Hinesburgh Land Records*, v. 21: 58.

45. In 1890, Henry W. Edwards mortgaged his land deed to J. J. Enright for one dollar and services received for the collateral that Enright put up for "my homestead . . . which I bought from the Josephus Peters Estate." The "services" to which he referred were for "my case . . . on which I am confined in jail." Hinesburgh Town Clerk, *Hinesburgh Land Records*, v. 21: 80.

46. Hinesburgh Town Clerk, *Record of Writs and Executions*.

47. My assumptions that the Langleys lived in the other house on the (by now) Smedley land are strengthened by the specific language of the writs and the land records. They never say "the William Langley farm," but simply "the farm on which Wm Langley now lives" or "the farm formerly occupied by said defendant." In the myriad records I have read, I never found a reference to the "William Langley farm," but I often encountered references to the "Shubil Clark farm," the "Lewis Clark farm" or simply the "Clark farm." In addition, the only name from the Hill in the Huntington grand lists for this decade is "Shubel Clark Estate." I interpreted this information to be further evidence that the house where the Langleys lived was not on their land in Huntington but

in Hinesburgh near the cemetery on Clark land — the southern dot for George Smedley on the 1857 Wallings map (figure 1.3) — and that the house is still standing today on top of the Hill in Hinesburg.

48. Hinesburgh Town Clerk, *Hinesburgh Land Records*, v. 14: 423.

49. Hinesburgh Town Clerk, *Hinesburgh Land Records*, v. 15: 43.

50. Hinesburgh Town Clerk, *Hinesburgh Land Records*, v. 16: 104.

51. Langley, Letter to the editor of the *Green Mountain Freeman*, 1854.

52. U.S. National Archives, Civil War Widow's Pension Request #222864.

53. Jane Williamson, personal communication with the author, 2005.

54. Jane Williamson, personal communication.

55. A young Hinesburgh girl also died of enteritis the same month. There was increasing contamination of wells, cisterns, and food sources as the century wore on and more animal manure got into the water.

56. Middlesex, Vermont, Vital Statistics, Microfilm # 30337. His death certificate named him "St. Clare Langley." Perhaps that or Edward was his middle name; both names have been passed down in the family for generations.

57. Thornton, "A Cultural Frontier." Thornton found that in nearby Charlotte, French-Canadian farmers were the poorest in town and their average worth was $912.50. The mean average for Yankee farmers was $8,000 (p. 56, 58). So the Clarks were better off than the new immigrants from Canada but not as well off as most Anglo farmers.

58. Jan Albers, *Hands on the Land* (Cambridge, MA: MIT Press, 2000).

59. Susan Ouelette, Personal communication with the author, April 2007.

60. Child, *The Gazetteer and Business Directory of Chittenden County*.

61. Albers, *Hands on the Land*, pp. 143–44.

62. Elise A. Guyette, *Justin Morrill: His Life and Times* (Colchester, VT: Vermont Public Television, 1999), p. 46.

63. The Robert Smalls Foundation, *Robert Smalls Official Website and Information Center*, available from www.robertsmalls.org/about.htm (accessed November 28 2008).

64. "The Steamer 'Planter' and Her Captor," *Harper's Weekly*, June 14, 1862, p. 372, available from http://www.sonofthesouth.net/leefoundation/civil-war/1862/june/robert-smalls-planter.htm.

*Chapter Five: The Civil War Years*

1. Guyette, *Justin Morrill, His Life and Times*, p. 47. By 1860, many countries had ended slavery or serfdom, including Russia, Portugal (on the mainland), Britain and the entire British Empire, Denmark, Haiti, Spain, Chili, Mexico,

South Africa, Danish West Indies, France, Venezuela, and Peru. The only counties to follow the United States in ending slavery were Portugal (in their colonies), Cuba, and Brazil. Only the United States and Haiti endured bloody civil wars to abolish slavery.

2. Child, *The Gazetteer and Business Directory of Chittenden County.*

3. In February 1862, the First South Carolina All-Black Volunteer Infantry had been unofficially formed and attached to the Union forces at Port Royal Island in South Carolina. They were officially re-formed in January 1863 immediately following the reading of the Emancipation Proclamation at Port Royal. After the federal government took over the raising of black troops (because of competition among Northern states for black recruits to ward off a draft), they became the South Carolina Thirty-third.

4. National Park Service, *History of African Americans in the Civil War*, available from www.itd.nps.gov/cwss/history/aa_history.htm (accessed November 2006).

5. Ira Berlin, Joseph P. Reidy, and Leslie S. Rowland, eds., *Freedom's Soldiers: The Black Military Experience in the Civil War* (Cambridge: Cambridge University Press, 1998), pp. vii, 16–17.

6. U.S. Congress, *An Act for Enrolling and Calling out the National Forces, and for Other Purposes* 37th Cong. 3d. Sess. Ch. 74, 75. March 3, 1863, available from www.yale.edu/glc/archive/962.htm (accessed November 2006).

7. Wickman, "Their Share of Glory."

8. Bay, *The White Image in the Black Mind*, p. 88.

9. Horton and Horton, *In Hope of Liberty*, p. 270.

10. Hinesburgh Town Clerk, *Hinesburgh Births, Deaths and Marriages*, v. 1: 48.

11. Hinesburgh Town Clerk, *Hinesburgh Births, Deaths and Marriages*, v. 1: 48.

12. Horton and Horton, *In Hope of Liberty*, p. 270.

13. Hinesburgh Town Clerk, *Hinesburgh Record of Burials*, p. 167.

14. Middlesex, Vermont, Vital Statistics, Microfilm # 30337.

15. There is also an Emory Anderson from Hinesburgh about whom I know little.

16. Langley, Letter to the Editor of the *Anglo-American*, January 30, 1864, from Park Barracks, New York, in "Vermont African Americans: Letters of Louden S. Langley."

17. The only change I made was to insert periods in order to make the letter easier to read. Aaron used no periods in the original letter.

18. Aaron Freeman, Letter to George Robinson (Middlebury, VT: Sheldon Museum, 1864), pp. 2–4.

19. Freeman, Letter to George Robinson, pp. 1–2.

20. Langley, Letter to the editor of the *Burlington Free Press*, March 22, 1864, from Jacksonville, Florida, in "Vermont African Americans: Letters of Louden S. Langley."

21. Vermont Public Television, *Noble Hearts, Civil War Vermont* (Colchester, VT).

22. We know they all lived in Charlotte because Cora Langley was born there June 25, 1864. Jeffrod A. Langley was also born in Charlotte, on July 5, 1864. Both births are found in microfilm # 30337 in the Middlesex Vital Statistics, p. 285. Lewis's and Pamelia's death certificates both say they were from Charlotte, according to microfilm # 30337, Middlesex Vital Statistics, p. 317. They may have all lived together.

23. A piece of evidence is Lewis Langley's estate inventory, with important items missing, such as a cook stove and parlor furniture. These items may have been owned by other Langley women and shared in the household. Probate Court of Chittendon County, Vermont, Estate Inventory, for Lewis Langley, *Probate Court Records*, v. 50, 1866.

24. Rachel Freeman, who already had two children, may have had a child too while Aaron was away, but I have no birth dates for her younger two children.

25. Thomas R. Fasulo, *Battle of Olustee*; available from http://extlab1.entnem .ufl.edu/Olustee/events.html (accessed November 2006).

26. Wickman, "Their Share of Glory."

27. Langley, Letter to the editor of the *Burlington Free Press*, March 22, 1864 from Jacksonville, Florida, in "Vermont African Americans: Letters of Louden S. Langley."

28. Willie Lee Rose, *Rehearsal for Reconstruction: The Port Royal Experiment* (Oxford: Oxford University Press, 1964).

29. Langley, Letter to the editor of the *Anglo-African* from Folly Island, South Carolina, August 6, 1864, in "Vermont African Americans Letters of Louden S. Langley."

30. Langley, Letter to the Editor of the *Anglo-African*.

31. U.S. National Archives, Civil War Widow's Pension Request #222864.

32. "Contraband" was any goods or arms captured from the enemy. The North included people of color escaping the plantations in this category.

33. Wickman, "Their Share of Glory," p. 26.

34. Wickman, "Their Share of Glory," p. 27.

35. Probate Court of Chittenden County Vermont, Probate File #3356 for Pamelia Langley, 1865.

36. Probate Court of Chittenden County Vermont, Probate File #3356 for Pamelia Langley, 1865.

37. The government muster roles give Newell's height. U.S. National Archives, Muster and Descriptive Roll of a Detachment of U.S. Volunteers for the 54th Reg't Mass. Inf. (Col'd) for Newell C. Langley (1864).

38. Williston Town Clerk, *Williston Land Records*, 1865–1905, vols. 13–19, v. 13: 11.

39. Williston Town Clerk, *Williston Land Records*, v. 17: 320.

40. Williston Town Clerk, *Williston Land Records*, v. 17: 322.

41. Aaron and Rachel's first born, Clark, must have died young; he disappears from the records after his birth.

42. Hinesburgh Town Clerk, *Hinesburgh Land Records*, v. 17: 181.

43. South Burlington Town Clerk, *South Burlington Land Records*, vol. 1, 1865.

44. Because of this research, there are efforts to place a historic marker at the bottom of what is now Lincoln Hill commemorating the lives of these families.

45. This term is used only for people born and raised in the state by others who were born and raised in the state, those steeped in Vermont traditions, who think and talk like Vermonters. "Real Vermonters" have always been thought of as being white; skin of another color automatically disqualified people. However, this research and other similar projects show that many people of color have lived in Vermont for generations and certainly can claim the distinction of "real Vermonter."

*Chapter Six: Post–Civil War Years*

1. Bay, *The White Image in the Black Mind*, p. 88.

2. Bay, *The White Image in the Black Mind*, p. 89.

3. Bay, *The White Image in the Black Mind*, p. 229.

4. Foner, *Who Owns History?* p. 201.

5. Foner, *Who Owns History?* p. 201.

6. Blight, *Beyond the Battlefield*, p. 95.

7. Previous to this, and into the modern era, it has been called "nigger hill." A black former state police officer told me, "When I came on the Vermont state police in the nineties the Williston state police dispatch map listed Lincoln Hill as 'nigger hill road.' This was a point of great embarrassment to them the first

time I was dispatched over the radio to that location." The first time I visited the town clerk of Huntington in 1992, she used the same name for the Hill. In 2008, I was talking to a man who used to teach in Hinesburg and told him about my research on Lincoln Hill. He said, "You mean nigger hill." The use of this name shows that negative stereotypes still exist and demonstrates how easily that painful word roles off some people's tongues.

8. Probate Court of Chittendon County, Estate, File #2403 for Josephus Peters, 1870 (Burlington, VT: Chittenden County Court).

9. Hinesburgh Town Clerk, *Hinesburgh Land Records*, v. 17: 343.

10. Hinesburgh Town Clerk, *Hinesburgh Land Records*, v. 20: 20.

11. From a typed sheet on the back of the photo (fig 6.1).

12. My thanks to Deborah Van Dyne for the family history.

13. Hinesburgh Town Clerk, *Hinesburgh Land Records*, v. 20: 20.

14. Child, *The Gazetteer and Business Directory of Chittenden County.*

15. Hinesburgh Town Clerk, *Hinesburgh Land Records*, v. 21: 80. Henry W. Edwards sold his mortgage deed to J. J. Enright for one dollar and services received. For collateral, he put up "My homestead . . . which I bought from the Josephus Peters Estate." He hired Enright to put out money on his behalf for "my case . . . on which I am confined in jail." Later census reports show a Henry W. Edwards in Benson, Vermont.

16. Hinesburgh Town Clerk, *Hinesburgh Land Records*, v. 17: 249.

17. Hinesburgh Town Clerk, *Hinesburgh Land Records*, v. 17: 189.

18. The 1870 census listed a Lewis Clark in Worcester who was born in Vermont, was sixty-five, a mulatto, and living with a group of men also identified as mulatto. Lewis had been living in Massachusetts since at least 1865 (according to the Hinesburgh land records) and died of old age in Worcester in 1876. His death record says he was a laborer, and it identified his parents as "Shubel" and "Viola" Clark, both from Connecticut.

19. On the page dated June 15, 1861, there is an added note at the bottom of the female column: "Rute [*sic*] Clark died Fe the 6th 1863." *Records of the Baptist Church of Huntington.*

20. Nina Silber, *Daughters of the Union: Northern Women Fight the Civil War* (Cambridge, MA: Harvard University Press, 2005), p. 9.

21. Whitfield, "African Americans in Burlington," p. 92. Whitfield's article also discusses the Anthony family and other black Vermonters in Burlington.

22. This music teacher was Frederick Jeremiah Loudin, who many years after being denied a space among his church's choir because of his color, became the leader of the world famous Fisk Jubilee Singers.

23. Jane Williamson, personal communication with the author, 2008.

24. Williston Town Clerk, *Williston Land Records*, v. 14: 291.

25. For other information on the Civil War and changing roles for women, see Catherine Clinton and Nina Silber, *Divided Houses: Gender and the Civil War* (New York: Oxford University Press, 1992); Melanie Lawson, *Patriot Fires: Forging a New American Nationalism in the Civil War North* (Lawrence: University of Kansas, 2002); Mary Massey, *Bonnet Brigades: American Women in the Civil War* (New York: Knopf, 1966).

26. My thanks to Don Papson of the North Country Underground Railroad Historical Association in Plattsburgh, New York, for this information.

27. Williston Town Clerk, *Williston Land Records*, v. 17: 562.

28. Probate Court of Chittendon County, Estate Probate File #7906 for Harriet Langley, 1909 (Burlington, VT: Chittenden County Court).

29. Many Langleys whose histories I have not explored remained in Rutland.

30. Manhattan Municipal Archives, Aaron Freeman Death Certificate, 1869.

31. South Burlington Town Clerk, *South Burlington Deaths*, 1877, 1: 69.

32. Her surviving daughter was Gertrude Kelly, a cook who had two children.

33. Her granddaughter was Blanche Kelly. According to the Burlington, Vermont, City Directories of 1883–93, they rented rooms at 208 Elmwood Avenue. The 1900 and 1910 census reports place them in the same home throughout that decade.

34. For more on this family, see Whitfield, "African Americans in Burlington."

35. See Gene Sessions, "'Years of Struggle': The Irish in the Village of Northfield, 1845–1900," *Vermont History* 55 (1987); Thornton, "A Cultural Frontier."

36. Thomas Holt, *Black over White, Negro Political Leadership in South Carolina during Reconstruction* (Champaign: University of Illinois Press, 1979).

37. Monica Tetzlaff, *Cultivating a New South: Abbie Holmes Christensen and the Politics of Race and Gender, 1852–1938* (Columbia: University of South Carolina Press, 2002), p. 39.

38. Tetzlaff, *Cultivating a New South*, p. 39.

39. Eric Foner, *Reconstruction: America's Unfinished Revolution, 1863–1877* (New York: Harper Collins, 2002), p. 329. My thanks to Alan Berolzheimer for pointing this out.

40. Smalls served as a customs collector in Beaufort until 1913, "when he was removed as part of a purge of blacks from the federal bureaucracy by Woodrow Wilson, the first Southern-born president since Reconstruction." Eric Foner, "Rooted in Reconstruction: The First Wave of Black Congressmen" (electronic version), *Nation*, October 15, 2008.

41. The Confederate states had to write new constitutions in order to be accepted back into the Union.

42. Our Special Correspondent, "The Reconstruction Convention — How It Is Composed — Relief Measures Adopted — Educational Reforms," *New York Times*, February 11, 1868.

43. *Proceedings of the Constitutional Convention of South Carolina* (Charleston: Denny & Perry, 1868).

44. Foner, *Reconstruction*, p. 329.

45. Douglas A. Blackmon, *Slavery by Another Name, the Re-Enslavement of Black People in America from the Civil War to World War II* (New York: Doubleday, 2008), p. 42.

46. Blackmon, *Slavery by Another Name*. The most terrifying part of the new system to control blacks, uncovered by Douglas Blackmon of the *Wall Street Journal*, was the legal system of leasing convicts to companies and farmers to perform free labor. Prior to emancipation, there had been a horrifying and efficient internal slave trade across the South for renting, leasing, and selling enslaved people wholesale to farmers and industrialists. After the end of Reconstruction, white Southerners gradually reinvented this system using convicts. With the return of all-white legislators, representatives across the South passed laws making it illegal for blacks to sell anything after dark, to walk along railroad tracks, to speak loudly in the presence of a white woman, to change jobs without the permission of the boss, and the like. When labor needs were high, sheriffs scoured towns and the countryside looking for black men to arrest on any flimsy pretext, then sold them to the highest bidder. Once bought by companies such as steel mills, coal mines, railroads, lumber camps, and quarries the government took no notice of how they were treated. Company guards brutalized the men through the use of heavy chains twenty-four hours a day, starvation, inadequate water, filthy living conditions and no medical attention. Those who resisted were whipped and otherwise tortured, some to death. This system, legally set up in every Southern state except Virginia by 1880, was the South's "primary weapon of suppression of black aspirations" (p. 7) for sixty years. Blackmon contends that the post–Civil War judicial systems across the South had as their primary purpose the control and forced labor of black men. Leading black Republicans were often arrested and sent to work in factories, mines, and on farms. There is no evidence that this happened to Loudon Langley.

47. U.S. National Archives, Civil War Widow's Pension Request #222864.

48. U.S. National Archives, Civil War Widow's Pension Request #222864.

49. St. Clair was the name of Jane and Loudon's first-born, buried as a baby

in the Hill cemetery. There was obviously significance in the name. A tantalizing bit of data is that there was a black John St. Clair, a twenty-nine-year-old farmer, from Milton, Massachusetts, who fought in the Revolutionary War. Further research could possibly uncover a relationship between that man and the Langleys, Clarks, or Peters.

50. Blight, *Beyond the Battlefield*, p. 95. Also see Blackmon, *Slavery by Another Name*, p. 41.

51. Saxon W. James was her son-in-law.

52. My thanks to Amani Whitfield for insights into the post–Civil War South.

53. The other 5 states were Alabama, Georgia, Louisiana, Mississippi, and Virginia.

*Some Conclusions: Vulnerable Spaces*

1. For other studies of rural black communities, see T. H. Breen and S. Innes, *"Myne Owne Ground": Race and Freedom on Virginia's Eastern Shore, 1640–1676* (New York: Oxford University Press, 1980); J. Deetz, *In Small Things Forgotten: The Archaeology of Early American Life* (Garden City, NY: Anchor Press, 1977); Melvin P. Ely, *Israel on the Appomattox: A Southern Experiment in Black Freedom from the 1790s through the Civil War* (New York: Alfred A. Knopf, 2004); Graham R. Hodges, *Slavery and Freedom in the Rural North: African Americans in Monmouth County, New Jersey, 1665-1865* (Madison, WI: Madison House, 1997); M. S. LoRusso, "The Betsey Prince Site: An Early Free Black Domestic Site on Long Island," in *Nineteenth- and Early-Twentieth-Century Domestic Site Archaeology in New York State*, ed. John P. Hart and C. L. Fischer (Albany: New York State Museum Bulletin, 2000); S. A. Vincent, *Southern Seed, Northern Soil: African American Farm Communities in the Midwest, 1765-1900* (Bloomington: Indiana University Press, 1999).

2. This is similar to Paynter's findings in western Massachusetts. See Robert Paynter, "The Cult of Whiteness in Western New England," in *Race and the Archaeology of Identity*, ed. Charles E. Orser Jr. (Salt Lake City: University of Utah Press, 2001), p. 130.

3. Elizabeth R. Bethel, *The Roots of African American Identity: Memory and History in Antebellum Free Communities* (New York: St Martin's Press, 1997), p. 77.

4. Bethel, *The Roots of African American Identity*, p. vii.

5. Paynter, "The Cult of Whiteness in Western New England," p. 136.

6. Paynter, "The Cult of Whiteness in Western New England," p. 138.

7. David Roediger, *History against Misery* (Chicago: Charles H. Kerr, 2006), p. 170.

8. Paynter, "The Cult of Whiteness in Western New England," p. 133.

9. Roediger, *History against Misery*, p. 170.

10. Bethel, *The Roots of African American Identity*, p. 86.

11. "For wee must Consider that wee shall be as a Citty upon a Hill, the eies of all people are uppon us." John Winthrop, "Sermon" (aboard the *Arbella* off the coast of the Massachusetts Bay Colony, 1630), available from http://www.mtholyoke.edu/acad/intrel/winthrop.htm.

12. Roediger, *History against Misery*, p. 175.

# Bibliography

Adby, Edward Strutt. Journal of Residence and Tour in the United States of North America, from April, 1833 to October, 1834. London: 1835.

Albers, Jan. *Hands on the Land.* Cambridge, MA: MIT Press, 2000.

Anderson, Benedict. *Imagined Communities.* London: Verso, 1991.

Baldwin, Edmund. *Moses Lash v. Samuel Peters.* Vol. 6: 80, Town Clerk's Office, Hinesburg, VT, June 30, 1821.

Bassett, T. D. S. *Outsiders inside Vermont.* Canaan, NH: Phoenix Publishing, 1967.

Bay, Mia. *The White Image in the Black Mind: African American Ideas about White People, 1830–1925.* New York: Oxford University Press, 2000.

Berlin, Ira. *Generations of Captivity.* Cambridge, MA: Belknap Press of Harvard University Press, 2003.

Berlin, Ira, Joseph P. Reidy, and Leslie S. Rowland, eds. *Freedom's Soldiers: The Black Military Experience in the Civil War.* Cambridge: Cambridge University Press, 1998.

Bethel, Elizabeth R. *The Roots of African American Identity: Memory and History in Antebellum Free Communities.* New York: St Martin's Press, 1997.

Blackmon, Douglas A. *Slavery by Another Name: The Re-Enslavement of Black People in America from the Civil War to World War II.* New York: Doubleday, 2008.

Blight, David W. *Beyond the Battlefield: Race, Memory and the American Civil War.* Amherst: University of Massachusetts Press, 2002.

Bowen, J. "Seasonality: An Agricultural Construct." In *Documentary Archaeology in the New World*, ed. Mark C. Beaudry, 161–71. Cambridge: Cambridge University Press, 1993.

Brace, Jeffrey. *The Blind African Slave, or Memoirs of Boyrereau Brinch, Nick-Named Jeffrey Brace.* Chapel Hill: The University of North Carolina, 1810. Available from http://docsouth.unc.edu/neh/brinch/brinch.html (accessed 2001).

Breen, T. H., and S. Innes. *"Myne Owne Ground": Race and Freedom on Virginia's Eastern Shore, 1640–1676*. New York: Oxford University Press, 1980.

Bryant, Louella. *The Black Bonnet*. Shelburne, VT: The New England Press, 1996.

Carvalho, Joseph, III. *Black Families in Hampden County, Massachusetts, 1650–1855*. Boston: New England Historic Genealogical Society, 1984.

Castiglioni, Luigi. *Viaggoneglistati uniti dell' America settentrionale, fatto negli 1785, 1786, e 1787*. Translated by Armand Citarella. Milan: Giuseppe Marelli, 1790.

Catterall, Helen T. *Judicial Cases Concerning American Slavery and the Negro*. Washington, DC: Carnegie Institute, 1936.

Child, Hamilton. *The Gazetteer and Business Directory of Chittenden County, Vt., 1882–83* (electronic version). Syracuse, NY: The Journal Office.

Chipman, Daniel. *A Memoir of Thomas Chittenden*. Middlebury, VT: Author, 1849.

Clark, Byron N. *A List of Pensioners of the War of 1812* (Vermont Claimants). Baltimore: Genealogical Publishing Company, 1969.

Clinton, Catherine, and Nina Silber. *Divided Houses: Gender and the Civil War*. New York: Oxford University Press, 1992.

Conlin, Katherine E. "Dinah and the Slave Question in Vermont." *Vermont History* 21, no. 4 (1953): 289–92.

Converse, J. K. "The History of Slavery, and the Means of Evaluating the African Race: A Speech before the Vermont Colonization Society," 15 October 1840. Montpelier, VT: Chauncey Goodrich.

Crafts, Hannah. *The Bondwoman's Narrative*, ed. Henry Louis Gates Jr. New York: Warner Books, 2002.

Crocker, Henry. *History of the Baptists in Vermont*. Bellows Falls, VT: P. H. Gobie Press, 1913.

Dain, Bruce R. *A Hideous Monster of the Mind: American Race Theory in the Early Republic*. Cambridge, MA: Harvard University Press, 2002.

Danbom, David B. *Born in the Country: A History of Rural America*. Baltimore, MD: Johns Hopkins University Press, 2006.

Davis, David B. *Inhuman Bondage: The Rise and Fall of Slavery in the New World*. New York: Oxford University Press, 2006.

Davis, Sharon Carbonti. "Vermont's Adopted Sons and Daughters." *Vermont History* 31 (1963): 122–27.

de Beaumont, Gustave. *Marie, or Slavery in the United States: A Novel of Jacksonian America*. France: 1835.

Deetz, J. *In Small Things Forgotten: The Archaeology of Early American Life*. Garden City, NY: Anchor Press, 1977.

Delany, Martin R. *The Condition, Elevation, Emigration, and Destiny of the Colored People of the United States*. 1852. Reprint New York: Arno Press, 1968.

Demos, John. *Past, Present, and Personal: The Family and the Life Course in American History*. New York: Oxford University Press, 1986.

de Tocqueville, Alexis. *Democracy in America*. 1835. Reprint Garden City, NY: Doubleday & Company, 1969.

Digital Library Program. *Canada, the Promised Land*. New York: New York Public Library. Available from http://www.inmotionaame.org/migrations/topic.cfm?migration=2&topic=9 (accessed April 29, 2009).

———. *Migration to Haiti*. New York: New York Public Library. Available from http://www.inmotionaame.org/migrations/topic.cfm?migration=4&topic =5 (accessed April 29, 2009).

"Dred Scott Decision, 1850." Available from http://www.tourolaw.edu/patch/Scott/ (accessed September 25 2006).

Dunham, Nathaniel. *Hinesburg, Vermont, General Store Day Book*, 1827–1830 Burlington: University of Vermont Special Collections.

Easton, H. "A Treatise on the Intellectual Character, and Civil and Political Condition of the Colored People of the United States; and the Prejudice Exercised Towards Them: With a Sermon on the Duty of the Church to Them." In *Negro Protest Pamphlets: A Compendium*. Boston: Isaac Knapp, 1837.

Ely, Melvin P. *Israel on the Appomattox: A Southern Experiment in Black Freedom from the 1790s through the Civil War*. New York: Alfred A. Knopf, 2004.

Fairbanks, Henry G. "Slavery and the Vermont Clergy." *Vermont History* 27, no. 4 (1959): 305–12.

Fasulo, Thomas R. "Battle of Olustee." Available from http://extlab1.entnem .ufl.edu/Olustee/events.html (accessed November 2006).

Ficara, John F. *Black Farmers in America*. Lexington: University Press of Kentucky, 2006.

Fisher, Carlton E., and Sue G. Fisher. *Soldiers, Sailors, and Patriots of the Revolutionary War, Vermont*. Rockland, ME: Picton Press, 1992.

Fitzgerald, Deborah. *Every Farm a Factory: The Industrial Ideal in American Agriculture*. Yale Agrarian Studies. New Haven, CT: Yale University Press, 2003.

Foner, Eric. *Reconstruction: America's Unfinished Revolution, 1863-1877*. New York: Harper Collins, 1988.

———. *Reconstruction: America's Unfinished Revolution, 1863-1877*. New York: Harper Collins, 2002.

———. *Who Owns History? Rethinking the Past in a Changing World*. New York: Hill & Wang, 2002.

———. "Rooted in Reconstruction: The First Wave of Black Congressmen" (electronic version). *Nation*, October 15, 2008.

Foner, P. S., and Robert James Branham, eds. *Lift Every Voice: African American Oratory 1787–1900*. Tuscaloosa: University of Alabama Press, 1998.

Freeman, Aaron. Letter to George Robinson. Middlebury, VT: Sheldon Museum, 1864.

Fuller, J. *Men of Color, to Arms! Vermont African Americans in the Civil War*. San Jose, CA: iUniversity Press, 2001.

Gerzina, Gretchen Holbrook. *Mr. and Mrs. Prince*. New York: Harper Collins, 2008.

Graffagnino, J. Kevin, Samuel B. Hand, and Gene Sessions, eds. *Vermont Voices, 1609 through the 1990s*. Montpelier: Vermont Historical Society, 1999.

Greeley, Horace. *Recollections of a Busy Life*. New York: J. B. Ford & Company, 1868.

Greene, L. *The Negro in Colonial New England, 1620–1776*. New York: Columbia University Press, 1942.

Grover, Kathryn. *Make a Way Somehow, African-American Life in a Northern Community, 1790–1965*. Syracuse, NY: Syracuse University Press, 1994.

Gutman, Herbert G. *The Black Family in Slavery and Freedom, 1750–1925*. New York: Vintage Books, 1976.

Guyette, Elise A. *Vermont: A Cultural Patchwork*. Peterborough, NH: Cobblestone, 1986.

———. "Behind the White Veil: A History of Vermont's Ethnic Groups." In *Many Cultures, One People: A Multicultural Handbook about Vermont for Teachers*, ed Gregory Sharrow, 17–27. Middlebury: Vermont Folklife Center, 1992.

———. "Black Lives and White Racism in Vermont 1760–1870." MA thesis, University of Vermont, 1992.

———. "The Working Lives of African Vermonters in Census and Literature, 1790–1870." *Vermont History* 61, no. 2 (1993): 69–84.

———. *Justin Morrill, His Life and Times*. Colchester: Vermont Public Television, 1999.

Hahn, Michael T. *Alexander Twilight: Vermont's African American Pioneer*. Shelburne, VT: The New England Press, 1998.

Hannon, Matthew E. "From Vermont to Liberia: An Examination of the Vermont Colonization Society." MA thesis, University of Vermont, 2008.

Harris, Christopher. "Counting Sheep and Other Critters: Land Use, Soil Fertility and Population in Post-Civil War Vermont." In *Center for Research on*

*Vermont: Research in Progress Seminar* #202. University of Vermont, October 2, 2006.

Hatch, Kathlyn, and Nancy Engels. *Architectural Heritage Education: A Summary Report*. Washington, DC: NEH, 1982.

Hemenway, A. M., ed. *The Vermont Historical Gazetteer: A Magazine Embracing a History of Each Town, Civil, Ecclesiastical, Biographical, and Military*. Vol. 1. Burlington, VT: Author, 1868.

Hinesburgh Town Clerk. *Check Stubs for Town of Hinesburgh*, 1859–1867.

——. *Grand Lists for the Town of Hinesburgh*, 1799–1865.

——. *Hinesburgh Births, Deaths and Marriages*, 1795–1906.

——. *Hinesburgh Land Records*.

——. *Hinesburgh Record of Burials*.

——. *Hinesburgh Town Records*. Vol. 2 (1813–1830).

——. *Record of Writs and Executions for Hinesburgh*, 1829–1853.

Hodges, Graham R. *Root and Branch, African Americans in New York and New Jersey, 1613-1863*. Chapel Hill: University of North Carolina Press, 1999.

——. *Slavery and Freedom in the Rural North, African Americans in Monmouth County, New Jersey, 1665-1865*. Madison, WI: Madison House, 1997.

Holt, Thomas. *Black over White, Negro Political Leadership in South Carolina during Reconstruction*. Champaign: University of Illinois Press, 1979.

Horton, J. O., and L. E. Horton. *In Hope of Liberty: Culture, Community and Protest among Northern Free Blacks, 1700-1860*. New York: Oxford University Press, 1997.

Hubbell, Seth. *A Narrative of the Sufferings of Seth Hubbell and Family*. Bennington: Vermont Heritage Press, 1824. Available from http://www.rootsweb .com/~vermont/LamoilleWolcott.html (accessed 2006).

Huntington Town Clerk. *Huntington Land Records*.

——. *Huntington Ordinations & Public Notices*. 1817.

——. *Huntington School Records*, 1816–1858.

Hyde, A. L., and F. P. Hyde. *Burial Grounds of Vermont*. Bradford: Vermont Old Cemetery Association, 1992.

Irvine, Russell W. "Martin H. Freeman of Rutland: America's First Black College Professor and Pioneering Black Social Activist." *Rutland Historical Society Quarterly* 26, no. 3 (1996): 71–98.

Jacobson, Matthew Frye. *Whiteness of a Different Color: European Immigrants and the Alchemy of Race*. Cambridge, MA: Harvard University Press, 1998.

Kaplan, Sidney, and Emma Nogrady Kaplan. *The Black Presence in the Era of the American Revolution*. Amherst: University of Massachusetts Press, 1989.

Katz, B, and J. Katz. *Black Woman*. Toronto: Pantheon Press, 1973.

Kaufman, K. C. *Dred Scott's Advocate: A Biography of Roswell M. Field*. Missouri Biography Series. Columbia: University of Missouri Press, 1996.

Kenny, Kate. "Burlington's War of 1812 Soldiers' Burial Ground." In *The Center for Research on Vermont Research-In-Progress Seminar #190*. University of Vermont, 2005.

Kessler-Harris, A. *Out to Work: A History of Wage Earning Women in the United States*. New York: Oxford University Press, 2003.

Langley, L. S. Letter to the Editor of the *Green Mountain Freeman*, April 27, 1854. Available from Vermont Civil War Database: http://vermontcivilwar .org/units/afam/ll.php (accessed 2006).

——. Letter to the Editor of the *Green Mountain Freeman*, February 8, 1855. Available from Vermont Civil War Database: http://vermontcivilwar.org/ units/afam/ll.php (accessed 2006).

——. Letter to the Editor of the *Burlington Free Press* from Jacksonville, Florida, March 22, 1864. Available from Vermont Civil War Database: http:// vermontcivilwar.org/units/afam/ll.php (accessed 2006).

——. Letter to the Editor of the *Anglo-African* from Folly Island, South Carolina, August 6, 1864. Available from Vermont Civil War Database: http:// vermontcivilwar.org/units/afam/ll.php (accessed 2006).

——. Letter to the Editor of the *Anglo-African* from Park Barracks, New York, January 30, 1864. Available from Vermont Civil War Database: http:// vermontcivilwar.org/units/afam/ll.php (accessed 2006).

Laroe, Dawn. "The Prince Family: A Community History of Life in Franklin County Vermont." BA thesis, Burlington College, 2008.

Lawson, Melanie. *Patriot Fires: Forging a New American Nationalism in the Civil War North*. Lawrence: University of Kansas, 2002.

Lee, Maureen E. *Black Bangor: African Americans in a Maine Community, 1880–1950*. Hanover, NH: University Press of New England, 2005.

Lewis, John W. *The Life, Labors and Travels of Elder Charles Bowles of the Free Will Baptist Denomination*. Watertown, NY: Ingalls and Stowell's Steam Press, 1852.

Lexington, Town of. *Proceedings at the Centennial Celebration of the Battle of Lexington, April 19, 1875*. Boston: Lockwood, Brooks, and Co., 1875.

Library of Congress Exhibition. *The African Mosaic: Colonization*. Washington, DC: 2005. Available from http://www.loc.gov/exhibits/african/afam002 .html (accessed 2009).

Litwak, L. F. *The Negro in the Free States, 1790–1860*. Chicago: University of Chicago Press, 1961.

LoRusso, M. S. "The Betsey Prince Site: An Early Free Black Domestic Site on Long Island." In *Nineteenth- and Early-Twentieth-Century Domestic Site Archaeology in New York State*, ed. John P. Hart and C. L. Fischer, 495, 195–224. Albany: New York State Museum Bulletin, 2000.

Magnusson, Sigurdur G. "Social History as 'Sites of Memory'? The Institutionalization of History: Microhistory and the Grand Narrative." *Journal of Social History*, Spring (2006): 891–913.

Manhattan Municipal Archives. Aaron Freeman Death Certificate, 1869. Microfilm #43884.

Massachusetts, Commonwealth of. *Massachusetts Soldiers and Sailors in the War of Revolution*. Vol. 12. Boston: Wright and Potter Printing Company, 1896.

Massachusetts Historical Society. *The Legal End of Slavery in Massachusetts*. Available from http://www.masshist.org/endofslavery/?queryID=54 (accessed April 10, 2009).

Massey, Mary. *Bonnet Brigades: American Women in the Civil War*. New York: Knopf, 1966.

McManus, E. J. *Black Bondage in the North*. Syracuse, NY: Syracuse University Press, 1973.

McMurry, S. *Families and Farmhouses in Nineteenth-Century America*. New York: Oxford University Press, 1988.

Medearis, Michael, and Angela S. Medearis. *Daisy and the Doll*. Middlebury: Vermont Folklife Center, 2000.

Melish, Joanne Pope. *Disowning Slavery: Gradual Emancipation and "Race" in New England, 1780–1860*. Ithaca, NY: Cornell University Press, 1998.

Middlesex, Vermont, Vital Statistics, Microfilm # 30293.

Middlesex, Vermont, Vital Statistics, Microfilm # 30337.

Monkton Town Clerk. *Monkton Land Records*. January 13, 1791. Vol. 2: 103.

Moore, Francis, Bartholomew Stibbs, and Leo Africanus. *Travels into the Inland Parts of Africa: Containing a Description of the Several Nations for the Space of Six Hundred Miles up the River Gambia; Their Trade, Habits, Customs, Language, Manners, Religion and Government; the Power, Disposition and Characters of Some Negro Princes*. London: E. Cave, 1738.

Morrison, Toni. *Sula*. New York: Alfred A. Knopf, 1974.

———. *Playing in the Dark: Whiteness and the Literary Imagination*. Cambridge, MA: Harvard University Press, 1992.

*Moses Sash v. Samuel Peters*. Vermont State Archives, Box PRA-00993, September 1820–September 1824. Vol. 2: 65–66. Chittenden County Court, June 30, 1821.

Mullane, D., ed. *Crossing the Danger Water: Three Hundred Years of African-American Writing.* New York: Anchor Books, 1993.

Muller, H. Nicholas III. "Freedom and Unity: Vermont's Search for Security of Property, Liberty and Popular Government." In *The Bill of Rights and the States: The Colonial and Revolutionary Origins of American Liberty,* ed. Patrick T. Conley and John P. Kaminski. Lanham, MD: Rowman & Littlefield, 1992.

Nash, Gary B., and Graham R. G. Hodges. *Friends of Liberty: Thomas Jefferson, Tadeusz Kosciuszko, and Agrippa Hull.* Philadelphia: Basic Books, 2008.

National Park Service. *History of African Americans in the Civil War.* Available from http://www.itd.nps.gov/cwss/history/aa_history.htm (accessed November 2006).

Nell, William Cooper. *The Colored Patriots of the American Revolution: With Sketches of Several Distinguished Colored Persons: To Which Is Added a Brief Survey of the Condition and Prospects of Colored Americans* (electronic edition). Boston: Robert F. Wallcut, 1855.

Newman, Richard S. "Faith in the Ballot: Black Shadow Politics in the Antebellum North" *Commonplace,* October 2008. Available from http://www.common-place.org (accessed April 14, 2009).

Ogot, Bethwell A., and Kieran, J. A., eds. *Zamani: A Survey of East African History.* New York: Humanities Press, 1968.

Parks, Roger N. *Roads and Travel in New England, 1790–1840.* Sturbridge, MA: Old Sturbridge Village, 1967. Available from http://www.teachushistory.org/detocqueville-visit-united-states/articles/roads-travel-new-england-1790-1840 (accessed September 15, 2008).

Paterson, Katherine. *Jip: His Story.* New York: Lodestar Books, 1996.

Paynter, Robert. "The Cult of Whiteness in Western New England." In *Race and the Archaeology of Identity,* ed. Charles E. Orser Jr. Salt Lake City: University of Utah Press, 2001.

Pennington, James W. C. *A Textbook of the Origin and History, Etc., Etc., of the Colored People of the United States.* Hartford, CT: L. Skinner, 1841.

Perkins, Nathan. *A Narrative of a Tour through the State of Vermont from April 27 to June 12, 1789.* In T. D. S. Bassett, *Outsiders inside Vermont.* Canaan, NH: Phoenix Publishing, 1967, 42–45.

"Petition of 1788 by Slaves of New Haven for the Abolition of Slavery in Connecticut." Available from http://www.hartford-hwp.com/archives/45a/023.html (accessed 2007).

Piersen, W. D. *Black Yankees: The Development of an Afro-American Subculture in Eighteenth-Century New England.* Amherst: University of Massachusetts Press, 1988.

Pierson, George W. *Tocqueville and Beaumont in America*. New York: Oxford University Press, 1938.

Potash, P. Jeffrey. *Vermont's Burned-Over District*. Brooklyn, NY: Carlson Publishing, 1991.

Probate Court of Chittenden County, Vermont. Probate File #3356, for Pamelia Langley, 1865. Burlington, VT: Chittenden County Court.

———. Estate Probate File #844, for Prince Peters, 1832. Burlington, VT: Chittenden County Court.

———. Estate Probate File #1093, for Shubael Clark, 1842. Burlington, VT: Chittenden County Court.

———. Estate Probate Inventory for Lewis Langley. *Probate Court Records*. Vol. 50, 1866. Burlington, VT: Chittenden County Court.

———. Estate Probate, File #2403, for Josephus Peters, 1870. Burlington, VT: Chittenden County Court.

———. Estate Probate File #7906, for Harriet E. Langley, 1909. Burlington, VT: Chittenden County Court.

*Proceedings of the Constitutional Convention of South Carolina*. Charleston, SC: Denny & Perry, 1868.

Proper, David. *Lucy Terry Prince: Singer of History*. Deerfield, MA: Historic Deerfield, Inc., 1997.

Quarles, Benjamin. *Black Mosaic: Essays in Afro-American History and Historiography*. Amherst: University of Massachusetts Press, 1988.

Raemsch, Carol A., and J. W. Bouchard. "The Henry Lehman Family Cemetery: A Unique Contribution to Nineteenth-Century Domestic Archaeology." In *Nineteenth- and Early Twentieth-Century Domestic Site Archaeology in New York State*, ed. John P. Hart and C. L. Fischer, 495, 95–124. Albany: New York State Museum Bulletin, 2000.

Ratner, L. *Powder Keg: Northern Opposition to the Antislavery Movement, 1831–1840*. New York: Basic Books, 1968.

*Records for the Baptist Church in Christ of Hinesburgh*, 1810–1840. Hinesburg, VT: Carpenter-Carse Library.

*Records of the Baptist Church of Huntington*, 1828–1872. Burlington: University of Vermont Special Collections.

"The Reconstruction Convention—How It Is Composed—Relief Measures Adopted—Educational Reforms." *New York Times*, February 11, 1868.

Robert Smalls Foundation. *Robert Smalls Official Website and Information Center*. Available from http://www.robertsmalls.org/about.htm (accessed November 28, 2008).

Robinson, George. Letter to his family, 1847. Middlebury, VT: Sheldon Museum.

Roediger, David R. *History against Misery*. Chicago: Charles H. Kerr, 2006.

———. *Black on White: Black Writers on What It Means to Be White*. New York: Schocken Books, 1998.

———. *Colored White: Transcending the Racial Past*. Berkeley: University of California Press, 2002.

———. *How Race Survived U.S. History*. Berkley: University of California Press, 2002.

Rose, Willie Lee. *Rehearsal for Reconstruction: The Port Royal Experiment*. Oxford: Oxford University Press, 1964.

Roth, Randolph. *The Democratic Dilemma: Religion, Reform and the Social Order in the Connecticut River Valley of Vermont, 1791-1850*. New York: Cambridge University Press, 1987.

Rutland Town Clerk. *Rutland, Vermont, Land Records*. 8:182, 9:237, 10:74 and 95.

Saillant, J. *Black Puritan, Black Republican: The Life and Thought of Lemuel Haynes, 1753-1833*. New York: Oxford University Press, 2003.

Sammons, Mark J., and Valerie Cunningham. *Black Portsmouth: Three Centuries of African-American Heritage*. Durham, NH: University of New Hampshire Press, 2004.

Saunders, Prince. *Documents Relative to the Kingdom of Hayti with a Preface*. London: 1816.

Searls, Paul. "America and the State That 'Stayed Behind': An Argument for the National Relevance of Vermont History." *Vermont History* 71 (2003): 75–87.

Sessions, Gene. "'Years of Struggle': The Irish in the Village of Northfield, 1845–1900." *Vermont History* 55 (1987): 69–95.

Shaeffer, John N. "A Comparison of the First Constitutions of Vermont and Pennsylvania." In *In a State of Nature*, ed. H. Nicholas Muller and Samuel B. Hand. Montpelier: Vermont Historical Society, 1982.

Sherman, Michael, Gene Sessions, and P. Jeffrey Potash. *Freedom and Unity: A History of Vermont*. Barre: Vermont Historical Society, 2004.

Silber, Nina. *Daughters of the Union: Northern Women Fight the Civil War*. Cambridge, MA: Harvard University Press, 2005.

Smith, Elias. *The Life, Conversion, Preaching, Travels, and Sufferings of Elias Smith*. Portsmouth, NH: Beck and Foster, 1816.

Smith, Elsie B. "William J. Anderson: Shoreham's Negro Legislator in the Vermont House of Representatives." *Vermont History* 44, no. 4 (1976): 203–11.

J. V. C. Smith, M.D., ed, *The Boston Medical and Surgical Journal* 14 (1836) (electronic version), pp. 217–20.

South Burlington Town Clerk. *South Burlington Deaths*, 1877. Book 1: 69.

———. *South Burlington Land Records*. Vol. 1, 1865.

Stark, Bruce. "Slavery in Connecticut: A Re-Examination." *Connecticut Review* 9 (November 1975): 75–81.

"The Steamer 'Planter' and Her Captor." *Harper's Weekly* (electronic version), June 14, 1862, 372–73.

Stewart, James Brewer. *Abolitionist Politics and the Coming of the Civil War.* Amherst: University of Massachusetts Press, 2008.

Stillwell, Lewis D. *Migration from Vermont.* Montpelier and Rutland: Vermont Historical Society and Academy Books, 1948.

Superior Court of Vermont. *William Langley v. Amanda Norton & Joseph Marsh.* (May 18, 1846): 471–75.

Takaki, Ronald T. *Iron Cages: Race and Culture in 19th-Century America.* New York: Oxford University Press, 1990.

Tetzlaff, Monica. *Cultivating a New South: Abbie Holmes Christensen and the Politics of Race and Gender, 1852–1938.* Columbia: University of South Carolina Press, 2002.

Thornton, Kevin. "A Cultural Frontier: Ethnicity and the Marketplace in Charlotte, Vermont, 1845–1860." In *Cultural Change and the Market Revolution in America, 1789–1860*, ed. Scott C. Martin, 47–69. Lanham, MD: Rowan & Littlefield, 2005.

Trask, Hunani-Kay. "From a Native Daughter." In *The American Indian and the Problem of History*, ed. C. Martin, 171–79. New York: Oxford University Press, 1987.

True, Marshall. " Slavery in Burlington? An Historical Note." *Vermont History* 50, no. 4 (1982): 227.

U.S. Congress. *An Act for Enrolling and Calling Out the National Forces, and for Other Purposes*, 37th Cong., 1863. Available from www.yale.edu/glc/archive/962.htm (accessed November 2006).

U.S. National Archives and Records Administration. Civil War Widow's Pension #222864 for Jane M. Langley, 1881.

———. Muster and Descriptive Roll of a Detachment of U.S. Volunteers for the 54th Reg't Mass. Inf. (Col'd) for Loudon S. Langley. # MIUSAI861M_088389, 1864.

———. Muster and Descriptive Roll of a Detachment of U.S. Volunteers for the 54th Reg't Mass. Inf. (Col'd) for Newell C. Langley. # MIUSAI861M_088389, 1864.

———. Revolutionary Pension #S41943, 1818, for Prince Peters.

———. Revolutionary Pension #S36291, 1818–1820, for Moses Sash.

Vermont Historical Society. *Yours in the Cause of a Slave*. Montpelier, VT: Vermont Historical Society, n.d.

Vermont Public Television. *Noble Hearts: Civil War Vermont*. Colchester, VT, 2005.

Vermont, State of. "An Act Pertaining to Negroes and Mollatoes" (1791). In *Journals and Proceedings of the General Assembly of Vermont*, ed. W. H. Crockett. Vol. 3: 80. Bellows Falls, VT, 1932.

———. *Roster of Soldiers in the War of 1812-14*. St. Albans, VT: The Messenger Press, 1933.

Vincent, S. A. *Southern Seed, Northern Soil: African American Farm Communities in the Midwest, 1765-1900*. Bloomington: Indiana University Press, 1999.

Walter, Mildred P. *Alec's Primer*. Middlebury: Vermont Folklife Center, 2005.

White, A. O. "Prince Saunders: An Instance of Social Mobility among Antebellum New England Blacks." *Journal of Negro History* 60, no. 4 (1975): 526–35.

Whitfield, Harvey Amani. "African Americans in Burlington, 1880–1900." *Vermont History* 75, no. 2 (2007): 101–123.

Whitman, Zachariah. *The History of Ancient and Honorable Artillery Company*. Boston: John H. Eastman, Printer, 1842.

Wickman, D. "Their Share of Glory: Rutland Blacks in the Civil War." *Rutland Historical Society Quarterly* 22, no. 2 (1992): 18–39.

Williams, Samuel. *The Natural and Civil History of Vermont*. Walpole, NH: Author, 1794.

Williamson, Jane. "Telling It Like It Was at Rokeby." In *Passages to Freedom*, ed. David W. Blight, 248–59. Washington, DC: Smithsonian Books, 2004.

———. "'I Don't Get Fair Play Here': A Black Vermonter Writes Home." *Vermont History* 75, no. 1 (2007): 35–38.

Williston Town Clerk. *Williston Land Records*. Vols. 13–19, 1865–1905.

———. *Williston Marriages, Births and Deaths*, 1863–1883 and 1883–1947.

Wilson, Harriet. E. *Our Nig; or Sketches from the Life of a Free Black, in a Two-Story White House, North. Showing That Slavery's Shadows Fall Even There. By "Our Nig."* 1859. Boston: Author. Reprint, New York: Vintage, 1983.

Winter, Kari J., ed. *The Blind African Slave, or Memoirs of Boyrereau Brinch, Nicknamed Jeffrey Brace*. Madison: University of Wisconsin Press, 2004.

Winthrop, John. Sermon. Aboard the *Arbella* off the coast of the Massachusetts Bay Colony, 1630. Available from http://www.mtholyoke.edu/acad/intrel/winthrop.htm.

Woodson, Carter G. *The Mind of the Negro as Reflected in Letters*. New York: Negro Universities Press, 1969.

Yentsch, Anne Elizabeth. "Legends, Houses, Families and Myths: Relationships between Material Culture and American Ideology." In *Documentary Archaeology in the New World*, ed. Mark C. Beaudry, 5–19. Cambridge: Cambridge University Press, 1993.

Zirblis, Ray. *Friends of Freedom: The Vermont Underground Railroad Survey Report*. Montpelier, VT: Division for Historic Preservation, 1996.

# Index